Forced Ranking

Forced Ranking

Making Performance
Management Work

Dick Grote

Harvard Business School Press
Boston, Massachusetts

Library of Congress Cataloging-in-Publication Data

Grote, Richard C.
  Forced ranking : making performance management work / Dick Grote.
      p. cm.
  Includes bibliographical references and index.
  ISBN 1-59139-748-0
  1. Employees—Rating of. 2. Performance standards. I. Title.
  HF5549.5.R3G6414 2005
  658.3'125—dc22

                                        2005012941

To

Jacqueline

My best friend

My business partner

My wife

Contents

Preface

FOR MORE THAN thirty years I have helped organizations successfully create and implement forced ranking systems. My experience began when I was the director of training and development for Frito-Lay, the largest and most profitable division of PepsiCo. There I was involved with the system in two ways: first, in administering it; second, as one of the large pool of PepsiCo managers whose performance and potential was annually ranked in the quartiling system we used at that time. Since leaving PepsiCo in 1977 to begin a consulting career in which I have specialized exclusively in performance management, I have helped many organizations develop and enhance their forced ranking processes.

Over the past few years, the procedure called forced ranking has gained a great deal of attention from the media and consultants and academics. Curiously, almost all of that attention has concentrated on the shortcomings and failings of the procedure.

The debate over forced ranking began in 2000 with the publication of General Electric's "Annual Report to GE Share Owners." CEO Jack Welch both explained and extolled the forced ranking procedure that the company had used for many years. In his report Welch said, "We break our population down into three categories: the top 20 percent, the high-performance middle 70 percent, and the bottom 10 percent." He went on to argue that the top 20 percent must be loved and nurtured in the soul and wallet, while the bottom 10 percent must be removed.

Welch continued by arguing that this removal process must happen every year. Not doing so, he said, "is not only a management failure but a false kindness as well," since eventually a new leader would take out that 10 percent, leaving them stranded and having to start over somewhere else. GE leaders, Welch said, "must develop the determination to change out, always humanely, that bottom 10 percent, and do it every year. That is how real meritocracies are created and thrive."[1]

Welch's endorsement of a procedure that seemed to pit people against each other rather than against how well they did at meeting predetermined standards and objectives ignited a national argument on the merits of this approach to performance management. The reaction to forced ranking was almost universally negative. Critics argued that identifying and eliminating the bottom 10 percent of an organization every year was not only impractical, it was unethical to "rank and yank" people who had always been told they were performing at an acceptable level. The press reported stories of class action lawsuits brought by terminated employees against companies that had used a forced ranking process. The implosion of Enron, a company that notoriously celebrated its culture of talent and trumpeted its forced ranking process, seemed to offer another argument against the use of the technique.

But while the critics of the procedure were vocal and got a great deal of media attention, the advocates of forced ranking were largely silent. Part of the reason for the negative press is that there certainly have been examples—like Enron—where forced ranking systems were poorly designed and badly executed. In addition, there is no subject about which companies are more reluctant to speak. The publicity given to the high-profile lawsuits, and the amorphous feeling that, somehow, forced ranking isn't "fair," made those organizations that use the process hesitant to go on record about their practices.

The result is that information about this talent management process, this powerful tool with the potential to offer a great deal of benefit to organizations if it is well designed and well executed, is not widely available. When the only reports are downbeat and pessimistic, good information about how to create and make the most of a forced ranking system is hard to come by. Companies find themselves in the position of having to reinvent the wheel.

My objective for this book is to demonstrate that forced ranking can be a valuable component of a company's total talent management palette, and to describe how to do it right. Forced ranking is a supplement to, and not a replacement for, the familiar performance appraisal system used by virtually every organization. It is a rigorous process for distinguishing the relative talent in your organization and eliminating the problems of inflated ratings and ratings variability that are so often complained about. It can serve as a good check and balance for the results produced by conventional performance assessments.

I will make the case that the payoff for developing a rigorous forced ranking process to identify the best talent in your organization is enormous and well worth the effort to do so. I will examine all of the criticisms and disparagements that have been made of forced ranking, acknowledge those that are legitimate and well founded, and review the under-described benefits of the procedures.

In this book I will address some of the common misunderstandings about forced ranking. One of the most common, and the cause of a significant amount of resistance to the procedure, is the belief that the people who are ranked in the bottom category of a forced ranking process are "poor performers" or some other term that indicates that their performance is unsatisfactory, or that they are failing to meet the expectations that have been set out for them.

Of course, managers will resist when they are told to identify a certain percentage of their team as "duds" or those who "aren't cutting it." The truth is that what they are actually being asked to do is to identify, among their group of at least satisfactory and acceptable performers, who is doing the best and who is doing the worst. They're not being asked to finger those whose performance is substandard, since it may be that none of the people being reviewed is performing at an unsatisfactory level.

That people who end up in the bottom ranking category are necessarily poor performers is a common belief, but as we'll see later, it is simply not true. They may be duds, but they also may well be good, solid performers who are working on a team of all-stars.

This book will clear the air. Frankly, I don't believe that forced ranking is a panacea, a system that every company should use. It's not. I will explain the conditions under which forced ranking works and make clear the circumstances in which other approaches to talent management would be better bets.

This book is about helping you to be better able to identify and understand your talent pool. It's about jump starting a leadership development process for those organizations that have gone stale or have lost sight of who their best performers really are. It's about under-standing the depth of your talent pool and seeing where the true leadership potential lies in your company. It's about talent manage-ment and how to be more strategic about it; it's about grooming great leaders. This book will help you raise the bar and lift the boat.

My primary audience for this book is the executives responsible for human resources in an organization that takes performance and talent management seriously. There is another audience I have in mind, too. I also want to speak to senior executives and line managers in organi-zations that use forced ranking or are considering implementing such a system. Just as it's essential that the company's system be designed well, it's also critical that it be fully understood and used well by every-one involved in its operation.

A Note on References

In this book I will refer to companies and their practices. Wherever I identify a company by name in this book, everything in the example or illustration is taken from published and universally accessible sources, whether the company's own statements and reports or reports on it in the public press. The interpretation in every case is, of course, mine; but the facts are in the public domain. Wherever a company is not specifically identified by name, I have used information obtained in the course of consulting work or through personal acquaintance, discussions in management meetings and seminars, or private corre-spondence. In every such case, the company has been so carefully camouflaged that even people in the company itself will probably not recognize it. As Peter Drucker explained in the introduction to *Management: Tasks, Responsibilities, Practices*, his still-influential book of three decades ago, "The one thing the reader can be sure if he reads of a 'hardware manufacturer in the American Midwest' is that the company is not a hardware manufacturer and is not located in the Midwest. The facts given in the illustration are reported faithfully and accurately; the specific company where they occurred is carefully concealed."[2]

A Debt of Thanks

While this book was informed and enhanced by the knowledge of executives from many different companies who shared with me their experience with using forced ranking systems, and academics who have studied and published their research on best practices in performance management, there is one person in particular to whom I owe a great deal of thanks: my editor at the Harvard Business School Press, Melinda Merino. Throughout the process of writing this book, she was intelligent, funny, concerned, and demanding. This book has benefited enormously from her high standards and wise suggestions.

1

The Differentiation of Talent

ON MARCH 27, 1967, I was a young industrial engineer on General Electric's management training program. On that day my boss, Ray Moeller, called me into his office and handed me a document to review. It was my first performance appraisal.

I read it. It was bad.

At that time GE had four performance ratings: Outstanding, Above Standard, Standard, and Below Standard. Not one check mark was in any of the Outstanding or Above Standard categories. For all of the attributes assessed—leadership, working with others, personal traits—Ray had scored me as either Standard or Below Standard.

It got worse. The last question on GE's four-page performance evaluation form asked bluntly, "Is he the kind of man you would hire in your organization, opportunity permitting?" The form provided two boxes, Yes and No. Ray had checked No.

I was more than embarrassed. I was humiliated. And the only saving grace was in one comment in the final narrative section, where Ray had summed up all of my failures in my work but then added, "Until he came with us I am certain he knew of no problems, since no one appeared to have discussed any with him."

That statement was true. No one had told this young GE trainee that he wasn't as good as he thought he was. Ray had the courage to

tell me that my work wasn't very good, and he was right. I was imma-
ture. I hadn't yet made the emotional transition from the world of
school to the world of work.

That damning performance appraisal Ray wrote was the blunt slap
in the face I needed to wake up and take my adult responsibilities seriously. I got to work, buckled down, and made the necessary changes. I
ended up spending five years at GE before being recruited away by
United Airlines. After five years at United, I was recruited away again,
this time by PepsiCo, to move to Dallas and head up all corporate
training and management development efforts at Frito-Lay. After five
years at Frito-Lay, I left to begin a consulting career that has now
spanned more than a quarter century. I have had a wonderful career.

But when I ran across that old performance appraisal a few years
ago, I wondered what would have happened if Ray Moeller had been
like so many managers and had fudged on the truth.

Ray had the courage to tell it like it was, and it wasn't pretty. Not
many managers would have been as blunt, as candid as Ray had been.
They could easily have rationalized away my poor performance and
found plenty of excuses for not laying it on the line with me: "This is
just his first assignment . . . I'm sure he'll improve as time goes by . . .
He's just a young guy and I don't want to hurt his career by putting a
black mark in his file . . . Dick's a little hotheaded—I don't want a confrontation . . . If I rate him low, I may look bad and not get any more
trainees assigned . . ." And the result of my thus getting a less-than-
truthful appraisal would have been that I never would have known
that I wasn't as good as I thought I was, and I would have ended up
with a far less successful career than I have enjoyed.

But that's not the way performance appraisal usually works. Let me
give you an example of the opposite case—an example of what happens
too often when boss and subordinate sit down for a performance
review. About two years ago, my wife and I were having dinner in a
Mexican restaurant with our Web site designer and his wife, Esther. As
we talked she told us that earlier that day her boss had met with her to
go over the performance appraisal he had written, evaluating her first
six months of employment at one of America's largest humanitarian
service organizations. She was upset about his evaluation.

But as she talked about the appraisal she had received, it seemed as
if she had little to be upset about. He had rated her performance as
outstanding on every factor he had evaluated.

"But I know I'm not that good," she said. "I've only been there six months. I've still got a lot to learn. I think basically I'm doing a good job, but I know I dropped the ball on at least one project—and he never even mentioned it. He didn't tell me anything I can use to get better. Why didn't he tell me the truth?"

Maybe Esther's case was an unusual one—a complaint that her performance appraisal was unfair because it wasn't tough enough. She wanted straightforward feedback that tempered honest praise with a truthful discussion of exactly what her shortcomings were and where she needed to do better. She wanted the truth, but instead she got an inflated performance evaluation that gave her no real information on where she genuinely was doing a good job and where she still needed to do better.

If managers met their responsibilities to appraise the performance of subordinates honestly and communicate those assessments straightforwardly, complaints like Esther's would never arise. If all managers showed the courage that Ray Moeller had shown in recognizing and discussing my deficiencies, the standard performance appraisal procedure of almost any organization would probably be sufficient for delivering feedback and managing organizational talent.

But too many managers flinch at the prospect of having to sit down, face-to-face, and deliver an honest appraisal of a subordinate's performance. They prefer to avoid any situation that presents the possibility of conflict, preferring to live in a fictitious Lake Wobegon world where all the children—and all the workers—are above average.

But there is a genuine need to communicate exactly what is expected, to assess accurately just how well people are doing, and to let them know honestly and straightforwardly exactly where they stand. Truthfully evaluating the quality of people's performance—and their potential—allows organizations to make critically important decisions correctly. Decisions like:

- How should rewards be allocated? Who should get a big raise; who should be denied any increase at all?

- When a vacancy arises, who should be tapped for promotion? Do we already have excellent candidates ready and waiting inside the organization, or do we have to go outside to get the talent we need?

- What is the depth of our talent pool? Do we have the people we need to meet the demands of the future?

- What is the relative strength of talent across our organization? Are there pockets of excellence and pockets of mediocrity within the company?

- Do we have a level playing field in our talent assessment and performance evaluation practices? Are the criteria and standards used by different managers and different departments reasonably consistent across the company, or are some parts of our organization much tougher (or more indulgent) than others?

- What kind of training and development efforts should we invest in? Who should they be directed toward? Where will we get the biggest bang for the training buck?

- Who are our best performers, the people who are outstanding performers in their present positions with the potential to take on more demanding roles? Do we have retention strategies in place to make sure that they don't leave us?

- Who are our worst performers and what do we need to do about them? Which ones can we salvage? Which ones should we cut loose?

Without a sophisticated performance management system that is intelligently designed and skillfully executed, the answers to the critical questions I just raised will be wrong. Worse, the questions won't even be asked, and the organization will stumble toward achieving its strategic goals without knowing whether it has the talent it needs to ensure their achievement.

The Challenges of Conventional Performance Management

One of the most common complaints in organizations today is about the ineffectiveness of conventional performance appraisal systems and practices. These loud complaints arise from all quarters. They come from employees at all levels who see themselves as the victims of appraisal systems that are failure-focused and aimed at highlighting faults and flaws. They come from managers who are required to make the assessments and feel unskilled and ill prepared. Complaints about performance appraisal come from corporate executives who need solid data on the quality of talent and performance of members of the organization and find that their performance management systems just don't deliver the goods. And complaints regularly arise among human resource specialists and executives who are charged with making sure that these systems are designed correctly and executed effectively, and blamed when things don't go as they should. As important as performance management is, no one seems to like the current state of affairs.

Why is a management tool that seems to offer the potential of such enormous benefit used so poorly? While it is always difficult to evaluate the quality of a person's performance, and providing honest and usable feedback takes patience and skill, one significant reason that managers are reluctant to use their performance management system properly is that the system requires them to differentiate: to go on record that one employee performs better than another.

Why don't conventional appraisal systems work right? For the most part, except in cases of blatant failure or triumphant achievement, it's because managers hesitate to say that an individual's performance is anything other than fully satisfactory. To avoid conflict and confrontation, managers fiddle with their expectations, demanding more of some than of others so that at the end everyone comes out with a satisfactory appraisal rating. Many organizations compound the problem by building disincentives to honest assessment directly into the system itself. For example, if the performance management system tightly links the amount of the individual's salary increase with her rating on the performance appraisal form, managers will be tugged between honesty and generosity. Managers understandably want to be generous with their team, and may decide to artificially inflate a rating in order to bump up a merit increase.

Another disincentive to accurate performance differentiation that many systems build into the appraisal process is a requirement that managers must get special permission in order to assign an appraisal rating at one of the extremes. For example, a large petrochemical company's performance appraisal form provides a familiar five-level rating scheme. But in the closing section where the appraiser must check the box that represents his or her final evaluation of the employee's performance, there's a note: "Please contact the Human Resources Department if either an Unsatisfactory or Needs Improvement rating is assigned." This requirement alone will guarantee that all ratings scores will cluster in the middle, since managers will escalate the ratings of any marginal performers in order to avoid having to explain to the personnel cops why they're retaining these laggards on their payroll. While the rationale for these requirements is easy to see and understandable, the effect is to reduce the amount of differentiation in appraisal ratings.

But true professionals like to be evaluated, to compete, and to know that they have excelled against their peers, James Brian Quinn and his coauthors argue in their *Harvard Business Review* article "Managing Professional Intellect: Making the Most of the Best." They want to be evaluated objectively and by people at the top of their field.

> Hence, heavy internal competition and frequent performance appraisal and feedback are common in outstanding organizations. As a result, there is a progressive winnowing of talent. For example, at Andersen Consulting [now Accenture], only 10 percent of the carefully selected professional recruits move on to partnerships—a process that takes 9 to 12 years. Microsoft tries to force out the lowest-performing 5 percent of its high screened talent each year. Great organizations are unabashed meritocracies; great organizations that fail are often those that forget the importance of objective praise and selective weeding.[1]

The problems I just described with the familiar performance appraisal process are, for the most part, intrinsic to the process itself. Managers will always be uncomfortable standing in judgment of other individuals, particularly when the judgment they make affects such critical areas as pay and promotions. But the answer is not to abolish the performance appraisal system. The answer is to do two things. First, make sure that the performance appraisal system is up-to-date, reflects best practices, and is used effectively by everyone in the organization. Make it as good as it possibly can be. Second, realize that no matter how well the performance appraisal system may be designed and how well it operates, there are inherent limitations to the results it can produce. Even the best performance appraisal system simply can't do everything that we want it to do. And one thing that most conventional performance appraisal systems have difficulty doing is ensuring the rigorous differentiation of talent.

That's where forced ranking comes in. Unlike conventional performance appraisal, forced ranking is a management process that requires managers to assess how well people performed compared with how well other people performed. The familiar performance appraisal system asks managers how well George did in meeting his goals. A forced ranking process asks a different question: How well did George meet his goals compared with how well Bob and Sally and Joe met theirs? In addition, performance appraisal focuses on how well the person performed in the previous twelve months. Most forced ranking procedures ask about how much stretch the person has for the future. Forced ranking requires that managers differentiate their talent into predetermined buckets—top 20 percent, middle 70 percent, bottom 10 percent, or some other ranking scheme. It both demands and guarantees differentiation.

The Demand for Differentiation

"Differentiation is the mother's milk of building a performance culture," Larry Bossidy, chairman of Honeywell and former chief operating officer of GE, argues.[2] The critical flaw with lumping everyone in the middle and failing to differentiate among the small number of top performers, the great majority of good solid citizens, and the few whose contribution is marginal at best, is that it generates a culture of mediocrity. The best performers quickly discover that their immediate supervisor or the organization as a whole is unwilling to do any more for them than he is for those whose performance is not nearly as good. As a result, they either leave for employment with a company that truly values and rewards excellence, or they slide down the performance curve to a spot just comfortably above the middle where they can contentedly coast along. And the weakest performers discover that they are in a culture that is greatly to their liking, where nothing more is asked of them than they are willing to deliver.

Changing the culture from one of mediocrity to one of accountability and differentiation is a task that an effective performance management system, if well designed and well executed, might be able to accomplish. It doesn't require forced ranking. In fact, the better the organization's standard performance appraisal system is designed and used, the less need there may be for a formal and separate forced ranking process. An effective appraisal system has the capability of differentiating the contributions made by the members of the enterprise so that those who contribute the most are retained and rewarded, while those who contribute the least are confronted with the demand that they change or leave. But effectively using the organization's performance management system requires managers to confront unpleasant truths and hold conversations that many would prefer to avoid. Moreover, conventional performance appraisal systems don't solve the problems of different managers having different expectations. They don't allow for valid cross-department comparisons. They provide no information about how well people perform relative to their peers. A different process is needed to bring these outcomes about.

Let me tell you bluntly—I believe in performance appraisal. I am convinced that performance appraisal may be the most powerful tool in the organization's arsenal to influence and guide and improve human performance. Performance appraisal is the core process that influences so many other critical areas: compensation, promotion, development, termination, career development, and many more. As a result, we have an ethical responsibility to do performance appraisal well. Every member of every organization wants the answers to two questions, and as organizational leaders, we have a moral obligation to answer them honestly. The two questions are, What do you expect of me? and, How am I doing at meeting your expectations?

So in addition to the organizational reasons why we do performance appraisal, we also are meeting an ethical responsibility when we sit down and discuss the answers to those two questions through the organization's conventional performance appraisal procedure. Whether or not the performance appraisal process is linked to the compensation system, the most basic reason we evaluate performance and discuss our evaluation with staff members is that we have a moral obligation to do so. And the better each manager discharges this moral obligation, the better the performance of the entire organization will be. People will know what's expected, and they'll know how they're doing. But no matter how honest we are, they still won't have the full story.

Absolute and Relative Comparisons

We answer the first question, What do you expect of me? by setting goals, clarifying job responsibilities, and communicating clear expectations about the behaviors we expect of organization members. There are two ways to answer the second question, How am I doing? One way is to respond in terms of *absolute* performance. The other way is to focus on *relative* performance. Conventional performance appraisal uses an absolute comparison method; forced ranking uses a relative comparison approach.

Absolute Comparison

When a person's performance is appraised using an *absolute comparison* approach, he is evaluated in terms of what he achieved and how he went about achieving it—his results and his behaviors. It's a person-to-standard comparison. This is the familiar approach employed by conventional performance appraisal processes. At its best, here's how it works: At the beginning of the year, Sam and his boss sit down and review the key job responsibilities in Sam's position. They come to agreement on the goals that Sam will achieve in the upcoming twelve months. They discuss the competencies or expected behaviors that Sam needs to exhibit as he goes about meeting his responsibilities (typically including such attributes as communication skills, interpersonal skills, decision making, leadership, and similar behavioral elements of effective organizational performance). They talk about what development plans Sam has in mind and discuss how Sam's performance will be measured.

During the year, Sam and his boss meet for updates and feedback and informal reviews. At the end of the appraisal period, the manager formally evaluates how well Sam performed. How good a job did he do in achieving the goals he was expected to achieve, the key job responsibilities that they identified, and the competencies or behaviors they discussed? With this *absolute comparison* approach, the question the manager answers is, "How well did Sam do against the goals and objectives that were set at the beginning of the year?"

Conventional performance appraisal procedures, the kind used by almost every organization, evaluate performance in this way. They operate on the basis of an *absolute* comparison by asking how well the employee performed compared with the goals she set and the expectations of her boss. The year-end performance appraisal rating depends then on two factors: how tough the goals were and how high or low the boss's expectations are. And if the goals are easy and the boss's expectations are low, it's possible for everyone to get a Superior rating.

Relative Comparison

When employee performance is appraised using a *relative comparison* approach, employees are evaluated in terms of how well they did compared to how well other people did. The question the manager is asking is no longer, "How well did Sam do in meeting his goals?" Instead, he's now asking, "How good a job did Sam do compared with how well Betty and George and Tom did?"

A relative comparison process requires the manager to evaluate the employee's performance compared with that of others in the organization. An employee who is rated Superior in a conventional performance appraisal procedure may well be ranked toward the bottom in a forced ranking, relative comparison process when his performance is compared with that of others who happen to be more talented. It could be very accurate for a manager to rate an employee high in terms of how well she did in meeting her objectives, and at the same time rank her low in terms of how well she performed compared with how well others performed. It may be that Sam met all of his objectives but performed far below the performance of his peers. And it may also be that, in spite of missing every one of his targets, Sam's performance was superior to the even more dismal performance turned in by others in his unit.

The Problems with Absolute Comparisons

The primary pitfall in using an absolute comparison method for performance evaluation is obvious: if the expectations are set low enough, almost anyone can exceed them. Likewise, set the standards too high and everyone will fail.

Another problem with using absolute comparisons—How well did the person perform against expectations?—is that the level of expectations may vary greatly across the organization. One manager will develop a reputation as a tough grader where no one is likely to perform at a level that earns a top rating. In other parts of the organization, there will be supervisors who award Superior performance appraisal ratings to everyone who does nothing more than show up.

Another subtle difficulty with the absolute comparison approach is that managers tend to set performance standards at a level that they are reasonably sure their subordinates can meet. As a result, the situation can easily arise where every person, from the least talented member of the crew to the star, ends up exceeding expectations and there is no differentiation in terms of their performance. Worse, a manager who either deliberately or unconsciously sets expectations at the level of his subordinates' capability may end up with the following difficult but not improbable scenario:

George, the manager, has three people on his team: Peter, Paul, and Mary. Peter is highly talented and is invariably a top producer. Paul is a good solid citizen. Mary, the least of the lot, is talent-free and work-averse.

In their annual planning and goal-setting sessions, George—believing that he is following good managerial practice—takes into consideration his subordinates' strengths and weaknesses, talents and capabilities. As a result, he ends up assigning a goal of 65 to Peter, 45 to Paul, and 25 to Mary.

At the end of the year, George evaluates their performance. He discovers that Paul has met the goal of 45. Mary has exceeded expectations by achieving 28. Peter, however, has failed to meet expectations—he produced only 63.

If absolute performance against goals is the only consideration in George's appraisal of his staff's performance, then Mary, the worst performer, will get the Superior rating, big bonus, and promotion, while Peter—who produced more than twice as much—will be assigned to the layoff list. It's not fair.

The alternative, of course, is to assert that since they are all in the same job category and are all being paid similarly, the goals should be the same for each of them. But this contradicts some firmly established managerial principles that argue that managers should take their subordinates' capabilities into account in goal setting. They should not assign goals that they know are impossible for an individual to achieve (like assigning a goal of 45 to Mary, who will argue, "He set me up for failure!") or are like shooting fish in a barrel (like assigning a goal of 45 to Peter, who can do it in his sleep).

Making use of relative comparisons solves George's problem. Compared against each other, Peter is the top dog and Mary is at the bottom. And while few people would argue with the inherent justice of using relative comparison in this simple example, concerns mount when the procedure is used on a broad basis in organizations and employees are compared not against what was expected of them in their jobs but against each other.

Conventional performance appraisal uses an absolute comparison methodology and asks the appraiser to evaluate the individual's performance and assign it a value: for example, was Gloria's performance Marginal, Fair, Competent, Superior, or Distinguished? Did Bill exceed expectations, Meet expectations, or Fail to meet expectations? Is Charlie's overall performance a 1, 2, 3, 4, or 5?

In a relative comparison process, however, the comparison is not to numbers on a scale. Instead, the comparison is person to person. When people are evaluated in isolation, against numbers on a scale, it's easy to rate everyone about the same. When people are compared side by side, person to person, the relative differences in their performance become much more apparent. Both approaches—relative and absolute comparisons—are appropriate, and both are needed to get a well-rounded and fully accurate picture of just how well someone has performed.

Two professors at the UCLA law school argue in a *New York Times* op-ed article that the use of relative comparisons of performance will even lead to better selection of CEOs for organizations. In observing how corporate boards frequently turn to outsiders in a CEO succession search, they raise the caution that "many shareholders may prefer an outsider, especially if the corporation has been tainted by scandal or received bad publicity. Often, however, an insider is the better choice."

"Think of the chief executive position as a prize awarded to the executive who wins the modern-day equivalent of gladiatorial combat in Rome," they argue. Executives compete with each other to win promotion, and those chances of winning the CEO tournament are neither random nor based entirely "on how well he performs in an absolute sense. Instead, a manager's odds of being promoted depend on how well he performs relative to his peers." Relative comparisons, they note, are "much easier to measure and judge than absolute performance."[3]

So the answer to the How am I doing? question can never be complete if the only thing the manager evaluates is how well the individual did in meeting the goals and expectations that were assigned. Only when we assess both the individual's *absolute* performance against the goals and job expectations, and the individual's *relative* performance compared with others in the department or work unit or company, do we have all the information we need to answer the How am I doing? question.

Companies that use forced ranking require their managers to use a relative comparison process to assign employees into different categories based on both their past performance and leadership potential. But the use of relative comparisons—comparing one person against another—can cause cultural dislocations. In analyzing Ford's forced ranking system when it was under attack, *Fortune* magazine writer Geoffrey Colvin got to the heart of the dilemma managers confront in having to differentiate performance:

> The reason that all this is so traumatic for Ford and many other companies is that it's about changing a deeply rooted corporate culture. At Ford and at a whole lot of other firms, especially big ones, managers were almost always good enough. How am I doing? You're doing fine. Everybody's doing fine. To say out loud that not everybody is doing fine—and name names—turns that world upside down. I'm guessing that many of those plaintiffs at Ford were told for 20 or 30 years that they were doing fine. To be told now, in their 50s, with kids in college, that they aren't—well, who can blame them for getting mad. It isn't their fault that they were in the wrong place when the culture was changed. But it still has to be changed.[4]

Seven months later, after Ford scuttled its system, Colvin analyzed the cause of the well-publicized collapse:

> Maybe you remember when Jacques Nasser, as Ford's CEO, tried to install a performance ranking system for executives. Every manager would have to be rated A, B, or C, with at least 5 percent required in the C category. Not exactly radical, you might think, but it was radical at Ford where the organization rose up and smote Nasser for his cruel, arbitrary, cold, heartless proposal. What's amazing is how people who are outraged by Nasser-like suggestions respond quite differently to the performance of ballplayers. If an outfielder can't catch a cold and is

batting .125, the fans want him out—now. He's a really good guy who had a great season in '91? Wonderful, but any manager who kept playing him on that basis would need police protection.[5]

Colvin's colorful description is echoed by Scott Cohen, the Watson Wyatt Worldwide researcher who conducted the consulting firm's survey that revealed that less than 40 percent of managers in the organizations he studied felt that their performance management system established clear performance goals or generated honest feedback. The cause of the failure? According to Cohen, "There's no accountability. Senior leaders aren't holding junior managers accountable. Everybody's a 4 or a 5."[6]

The Rationale for Forced Ranking

In his analysis of the controversy surrounding the use of forced ranking systems, consultant Byron Woollen explains the rationale for the increased interest in relative-assessment schemes:

> The leadership of many businesses found that as they initiated significant workforce reductions in 2001 and 2002, they were not armed with the appropriate data by which to make decisions about layoffs. Specifically, their performance review systems had not been appropriately practiced and inflated scores left little means by which to systematically identify the lowest performers. These inflated scores were a byproduct of (a) cultures that were overly polite and avoidant of the potential conflict incurred from a manager giving a low score; (b) managers and supervisors who were inadequately trained on delivering performance management feedback and scoring systems; and c) managers and supervisors who discounted the performance management systems because of their belief that the systems were overly abstract and too distant from the business goals.[7]

In addition to the issues that Woollen described, the impetus for developing relative comparison ranking systems came out of a frustration with organizations' seeming to tolerate a cadre of marginal performers. In their *Harvard Business Review* article "A New Game Plan for C Players," the authors reported that of the thousands of senior managers they polled, "96 percent of them said they would be delighted if their companies moved more aggressively on low performers."[8]

Other employee satisfaction surveys revealed that top performers felt unrecognized and inadequately distinguished from peers who were not performing at similarly high levels. The authors of a Society for Human Resource Management (SHRM) study reported that "a Hay Employee Attitude survey conducted at 335 companies worldwide found that 32 percent of employees agreed that poor performance is tolerated in their companies."[9] At Hewlett-Packard, one of the companies that openly acknowledge using a forced ranking system to identify and either improve or remove poor performers, former CEO Carly Fiorina reported that in employee surveys at HP during the last eight years, more than 80 percent of employees said the company did not deal well with poor performers.[10]

The *Wall Street Journal* editorialized about the impact that a forced ranking process can have in identifying and removing marginal performers:

> Microsoft, Lucent, Conoco and EDS all have used forced ranking to maintain or improve the quality of their work force. While many find the idea distasteful or complain that it substitutes a yearly spasm for what should be a continuous process, at least it solves a real problem. Survey after survey finds that even the happiest worker-bees gripe about their employer's reluctance to get strict with poor performers. A recent McKinsey poll of managers at big companies found that only 16 percent said their employer could even recognize the difference between stars and slackers.[11]

The Business Case for Forced Ranking

Forced ranking is the antidote to the problems of inflated rating and the failure to differentiate that many organizations have installed to help bring the truth into the performance management process.

By implementing a forced ranking procedure, organizations guarantee that managers will differentiate talent. While conventional performance appraisal systems may allow managers to inflate ratings and award Superior ratings to all, a forced ranking system ensures that distribution requirements will be met. Assuming that the system is wisely constructed and effectively executed, a forced ranking system can provide information that conventional performance appraisal systems can't.

But just ensuring differentiation, while valuable in itself, isn't the whole reason companies have gone to using forced ranking systems. Creating a forced ranking system forces a company to articulate the criteria that are required for success in the organization. GE, for example, has identified its four Es: the set of criteria it uses to rank its managers and executives: high *energy* level, the ability to *energize* others around common goals, the *edge* to make tough yes/no decisions, and the ability to consistently *execute* and deliver on promises. These criteria were determined over a period of several years and were the result of serious deliberation. Other companies have settled on different criteria. Some have used nothing more than "Good results, good behavior." Whatever the criteria the organization decides on, the deliberations that senior managers engage in in determining these criteria help them to define and understand what they believe genuinely is important for success in the organization. The discussion of criteria often sparks significant, even boisterous, arguments about exactly what the measures and factors should be. There is value in this process even if no further action is taken. And simply knowing the criteria that senior executives use to assess talent increases the probability that organization members will alter their behavior in order to demonstrate more of the attributes that they now know will lead to success.

Another important business outcome that is often unrecognized is forced ranking's ability to provide the organization with useful data on the ability of managers to spot and champion talent. In one company I worked with, one of its criteria for its forced ranking system was the ability to make tough decisions. In the course of briefing the senior executive team, I pointed out that one of the best sources of data would be the way that the vice presidents, their direct reports, went about making the forced ranking decisions during the sessions where they would all be together. Who is able to come up with telling examples of a subordinate's strengths and weaknesses? How well do various managers really understand the major strengths and development needs of their subordinates? A forced ranking procedure forces managers to think in far greater depth about the quality of talent in their unit than conventional performance appraisal systems typically require, and their ability to describe and verbalize their assessments provides a good indicator of a critical aspect of their leadership ability.

Another important reason for proceeding with a forced ranking procedure flows from the frustrations surrounding the conventional performance appraisal systems in many organizations, since forced ranking can provide an independent verification of performance appraisal data. If there are significant variations in the talent data provided by the performance appraisal system and the data provided by the forced ranking process, that conflict is worth delving in to. In addition, forced ranking can provide something of great value that even the best performance appraisal systems can't—accurate cross-department comparisons. As larger groups are evaluated, and with criteria that can be applied equally across a variety of jobs, a forced ranking process may permit more accurate cross-department comparisons.

The business environment today is making the rationale for developing forced ranking procedures more important than it has been for the past few years. After a several-year period of slower growth marked by major layoffs in several sectors of the economy, the "war for talent" seems to be heating up again. The impetus for identifying and actively acting to retain top talent is more important in an economy that now allows that top talent greater employment options than it has had for several years.

Can Forced Ranking Actually Improve the Quality of the Workforce?

Finally, the results of a major research project published in the First Quarter 2005 issue of the academic journal *Personnel Psychology* appear to answer in the affirmative the question of whether a forced ranking process will actually improve the overall quality of a workforce. An objection that has always been raised to forced ranking is that one of its fundamental principles is flawed—it is simply not possible to continually improve the overall potential of a workforce by systematically removing the bottom 10 percent every year and replacing them with better employees from the available applicant pool.

Professor Steven E. Scullen and his colleagues constructed a complex and sophisticated mathematical simulation of a multicompany, multiyear forced ranking process that they labeled "FDRS." FDRS is their acronym for a forced ranking system that they referred to as a "forced distribution rating system." For clarity's sake, I will use the term *forced ranking* for their FDRS acronym in quoting from their study.

In their model, one hundred companies of one hundred employees each over a thirty-year period identified the bottom 10 percent of their workforce every year, fired them, and then replaced them with the best available candidates from the applicant pool. In their simulation they controlled for the impact of voluntary turnover, the quality of the applicant pool, and the validity and reliability of the ranking assessments that were made. The basic question they asked was this: "Is it reasonable to expect that an organization would be able to improve the performance potential of its workforce by firing the workers judged to be performing most poorly and replacing them with its most promising applicants? If so, how much gain might be expected, and how quickly might that gain be achieved?"[12]

Their answer: "Results suggest that a forced ranking system could lead to noticeable improvement in workforce potential, that most of the improvement should be expected to occur over the first several years, and that improvement is largely a function of the percentage of workers to be fired and the level of voluntary turnover."[13] They did not mince words in stating that the basic hypothesis underlying the forced ranking, rank-and-yank methodology is solid: "Results showed that a forced ranking system can improve workforce potential, in the sense that, on average, lower-potential workers can be identified and replaced by workers with higher potential."[14]

They discovered that firing more poor performers provided greater benefit to the organization than releasing a smaller number: "In each case, however, results for 10 percent fired were superior to those for 5 percent fired."[15] While they examined the relative importance of improving selection procedures and enhancing the quality of applicant pools in increasing the overall effectiveness of the workforce, they discovered that the best results were produced by getting rid of poorer performers: "It is interesting, however, that firing poor (i.e., low-ranked) performers was the quickest route to improvement, and that reducing voluntary turnover soon became important as well."[16]

Many critics of forced ranking have acknowledged that while the procedure may in fact improve the overall quality of a company's workforce, it may do so at a steep price, producing adverse consequences in such areas as employee morale, teamwork and collaboration, the unwillingness of applicants to sign on with an employer who uses a forced ranking process, and shareholder perceptions. In their discussion of their findings, the researchers examined the possible effects of implementing a forced ranking procedure on all of these areas. They found that the potential problems were in every case balanced by equally compelling benefits. For example, while they acknowledged that there could be a detrimental effect on morale if retained employees saw no compelling differences between employees who were terminated and those who were not, or if unjust treatment of coworkers was observed, they also noted, "It is not clear, however, that employees in general would see a forced ranking system in that negative light. In fact, many employees might applaud the organization's decision to eliminate underperformers."[17] Concerning teamwork, they commented, "As with employee morale, however, it could be argued that the effects on teamwork and collaboration might actually be positive."[18]

Discussing the effects of installing a forced ranking system on the perceptions of the labor market, they noted that job seekers develop beliefs about an organization's culture while they are seeking employment. If an employment candidate becomes aware that an employer uses a forced ranking system and feels that the culture might therefore be too stressful or risky, the applicant might eliminate that company from consideration, causing the possible loss of some high-potential applicants. "It is certainly possible, however, that other high-quality applicants would see such a system as one where their contributions would be recognized and rewarded. These people would be eager to work in this type of environment. Thus, it is possible that a forced ranking system would improve the overall quality of an organization's applicant pools."[19]

Finally, they considered the impact on shareholder perceptions. While acknowledging that shareholders might have reservations about the company's use of a forced ranking system, because of potential lawsuits or other negative consequences, "investors might see the implementation of a forced ranking system as a clear signal that management is committed to accountability and to operating at an efficient staffing level. Perceptions of this sort should have a positive effect on stock prices."[20]

Finally, for many years I have argued that for most companies, forced ranking systems should be used for only a few years and then, once the obvious and immediate benefits have been achieved, replaced with other talent management initiatives. While some companies have been successful in using their forced ranking system for decades, I find that most organizations are better served by implementing a forced ranking system as short-term initiative. Scullen and his fellow researchers confirm that advice. Early in their article they lay out clearly the basic problem of using forced ranking on an ongoing basis: "Despite the allure of having a continually improving workforce, we argue that each time a company improves its workforce by replacing an employee with a new hire, it becomes more difficult to do so again. That is, the better the workforce is, the more difficult it must be to hire applicants who are superior to the current employees who would be fired."[21] Their mathematical simulation demonstrated that the greatest benefits came in the first 3.5 to 4.5 years after initiating a forced ranking system. They discovered that organizations got their best results immediately, in the first few years after implementing a forced ranking system: "The other outcome variable of interest is the rate at which workforce potential improved after the implementation of the forced ranking system. It is clear . . . that the bulk of the improvement in all scenarios was achieved during the first several years."[22] Their summary: "Results suggest that a forced ranking system of the type we simulated could improve the performance potential of the typical organization's workforce and that the great majority of improvement should be expected to occur during the first several years."[23]

Forced Ranking in Context

To what extent is the forced ranking procedure used by organizations? It's difficult to provide accurate numbers, for two reasons. First, because of the confusion that frequently arises when organizations and managers use the term *forced ranking* to describe many quite different performance management techniques and procedures. Depending on who you're talking to, forced ranking may mean three different things:

- The complex and rigorous talent assessment system used at GE, Sun Microsystems, Hewlett-Packard, and a great many other organizations where, in addition to the company's regular performance appraisal procedure, employees are evaluated and assigned into a small number of groups based on their performance and potential. This is what this book concentrates on; this is the system that the mathematical simulation published in *Personnel Psychology* focused on.

- A requirement that's part of a company's regular performance appraisal procedures requiring a specified distribution of appraisal ratings. This procedure is more appropriately called *forced distribution*. Later in the book I'll devote a whole chapter to whether forced distribution should be part of your performance appraisal process and, if so, how to get it right.

- Any relative comparison process at all, formal or informal, in which employees are compared against each other as a way to accomplish an organizational objective, like selecting the least productive members of the enterprise when a layoff is necessary or the most valuable when bonus awards are to be made.

Whenever I talk about forced ranking in this book, I will be using the term exclusively in the first meaning—the process that a large number of companies have successfully used to identify top talent and deal with low performers.

There is probably no subject that companies are more loath to talk about than their use of forced ranking. That's the second reason that accurate numbers on the extent of the use of forced ranking are hard to come by—companies keep mum. Writer Andy Meisler, in "Dead Man's Curve," his article on the subject of forced ranking for *Workforce Management* magazine, ran into an absolute stone wall when he tried to get companies to go on record about their use of the procedure. He reported:

> It's a rough-and-tumble evaluation technique practiced to at least some extent by such corporate heavyweights as GE (which didn't respond to our requests for an interview on the subject), 3M ("We're going to take a pass on this subject."), Texas Instruments ("No comment."), EDS ("The person you need to talk to is traveling and won't be available."), Microsoft ("We don't use forced ranking."), and Hewlett-Packard ("HP's performance rating is not designed to drive out a certain percentage of the company. HP has been evaluating and measuring results for a long time. It's motivational and the employee, the team, and the company all benefit.").[24]

In spite of perhaps-understandable reluctance to discuss publicly a highly controversial procedure, we can find some good estimates of how much use companies are making of the process. The estimates of the use of forced ranking vary, but the most frequent reports indicate that about a fifth to a third of large organizations—America's household name companies—are using the technique:

> "According to a June [2003] study by Pittsburgh-based HR consulting firm Development Dimensions International, about 34 percent of firms frequently use forced-ranking systems."[25]

> "Bell curve-like rating systems have spread in recent years to some 20 percent of U.S. companies and the trend is growing."[26]

> "Some form of relative performance ranking is currently practiced in about 20 percent of businesses, including some of America's most respected corporations."[27]

> "Forced ranking systems have been around for decades. Adherents include several firms on *Fortune*'s "Most Admired Companies" list, like Cisco Systems, Intel, and GE. But thanks to the slowing economy and an increased focus on pay for performance, more companies—a quarter of the *Fortune* 500 by one estimate—have instituted such forced rankings or gotten tougher with their existing systems."[28]

Finally, *Workforce Management* magazine offered its online subscribers the chance to respond to a survey about the use of forced ranking in their organizations. The survey results seem high, but again, many respondents may have been describing something other than the exact approach we're considering (even though the question *Workforce* posed was quite specific):[29]

Is there a forced ranking or "rank and yank" system of performance management in your organization?

Yes	46 percent
No	43 percent
Not sure/It depends	11 percent

Here's my best estimate: based on a quarter century of consulting with many of America's best-managed and most sophisticated organizations, together with the research I've done both academically and as a subject matter expert in sponsored best-practices benchmarking studies, it seems to me that about a quarter of all organizations of *Fortune* 500 size are using a forced ranking of their talent management systems. In addition, the number appears to be growing as more organizations are taking into account the importance of looking at both absolute and relative comparisons in the way they go about talent assessment.

The only place where forced ranking is being used, however, is in the private sector. While both my consulting practice and my research projects include a large number of organizations in the public sector— well-managed state agencies, some sophisticated municipalities, and a few large federal agencies—I have not found one that is using a forced ranking system for talent assessment. In fact, while most state agencies and municipalities make use of once-a-year formal performance appraisal systems, almost none of them provide any guidelines to managers regarding ratings distribution, and almost never is a real forced distribution of appraisal scores insisted upon in government. As a result, complaints about ratings inflation and the lack of accountability and differentiation are even louder from top-level public sector managers than they are from their private sector colleagues.

The type of organization makes little difference in the decision to use a forced ranking process, or in the success of the system once it's installed. I have created systems for companies in the heavy-industrial/manufacturing sector, in finance, in entertainment, consumer goods, and technology. I haven't found the type of business to make any significant difference.

Size does make a difference, though. Scullen and his coauthors formulated their simulation around one hundred companies of one hundred employees each, divided into ten work units of ten employees each. My experience is that one hundred employees is about the minimum-size organization that should consider implementing a forced ranking process, for several reasons. First, in a company of a hundred employees or fewer, everybody knows everybody. If senior managers have a somewhat sensitive finger on the pulse of the organization, they know who the stars are and who the duds are. They know who runs a tight ship and who lets things slide. They don't need to go to the trouble of creating a formal and mechanistic system to tell them what they already know.

As far as a maximum size, there's really no limit, as long as the company has a well-designed process for comparing talent across organizational units. In a later chapter I'll explain how to use roll-ups to manage the accuracy of forced ranking in large organizations.

Regarding the cultural conditions that support or militate against the use of forced ranking, in chapter 3 I'll discuss the cultural aspects that need to be taken into account in deciding to adopt a forced ranking procedure. For now, I'll state the obvious. If seniority is valued more than talent, if conflict is expected to be swept under the rug, if get-along, go-along characterizes the organization's mores, and people at the top are content with the way things are, then forced ranking is not for you. Face the facts: implementing a forced ranking system is a disruptive act. No matter how skillfully the system is designed and installed, the potential for organizational unsettlement is high. I will show you how to minimize this disruption, but don't expect to eliminate it completely.

Forced ranking is also used more frequently in companies that have a strong performance culture and greater leadership support for the importance of performance management as a whole. A 2004 Sibson Consulting state-of-performance-management study of more than four hundred companies found that 20 percent of the companies that were in the top two quintiles in terms of total return to shareholders used forced ranking, while only 14 percent of the companies in the bottom two quintiles used the approach.[30]

Forced ranking is but one element in the organization's entire talent management structure. Frankly, in most cases, organizations will be better served by getting their performance appraisal procedures right than by implementing a forced ranking system—first things first. Performance appraisal impacts everyone in the organization (or certainly should); forced ranking, though, is typically reserved for higher-level employees. Performance appraisal, done right, informs each organization member of exactly what the company's and the immediate supervisor's expectations are; forced ranking only assesses where people stand relative to each other. Forced ranking can validate decisions made in other talent management processes like succession planning, career development, and leadership selection and training. It can tell you, quite accurately, who your keepers are and who would be better off in the service of a different employer. But a forced ranking system alone doesn't tell you what to do to keep your keepers or make them into even more valuable contributors. You need other processes for that.

Finally, and most important, forced ranking is most successful when it's positioned and used as a talent management technique and not a turkey-targeting exercise. The one important aspect of forced ranking that Professor Scullen and his fellow researchers didn't consider is the fact that the real benefit to organizations doesn't come from finding and firing the bottom 10 percent. It actually comes from identifying the organization's top talent and nurturing and developing these high-potential individuals. While it wasn't part of their research design, the fact is that companies that use forced ranking as part of their overall talent management procedures find that identifying top talent may actually be more important than taking action on their poorest performers.

A Road Map for This Book

In the following chapters, we will explore the technique of forced ranking in detail. I will tell you why organizations decide to implement a forced ranking system to supplement their existing performance appraisal procedure, and will discuss the pros and cons of doing so. My objective in these chapters will not be to sell the procedure, but will be to demonstrate that forced ranking, used well, can be a highly beneficial process for an organization that is serious about rapidly accelerating its talent management efforts. In many cases, implementing a rigorous forced ranking, relative comparison process to identify an organization's best talent can provide an enormous payoff and will be well worth the effort to do so. More than any other procedure, it can force the truth into the performance management process. But I will also be frank about when forced ranking is the wrong tool for the job.

Chapter 2, Risks and Rewards, will discuss the risks and rewards of forced ranking. I'll tell you about the positive outcomes organizations have gained from their use of the approach. And I'll also be clear about the downsides of the process.

In chapter 3, Getting Started, I will help you make the right policy decisions that will guide the system's operation. I'll show you how to set up a forced ranking system that works—one that is fair and humane, one that produces valid and reliable information and enjoys the understanding and support of organization members. I will describe the cultural conditions that will serve to make the implementation of a forced ranking system successful, and the ones that should warn you away from installing the procedure. I will show you how to make the tough decisions, such as what ranking scheme to use and what criteria to use for doing the rankings. I'll help you decide how often to use the procedure and who should be in the ranking pool. We'll look at who the rankers should be and what you should communicate about the system (including whether or not people should be told how they came out).

Chapter 4, Getting the Mechanics Right, will concentrate on two operational issues: training those who will serve as rankers or assessors, and running the sessions themselves competently. This chapter will also suggest some ways to minimize the potential negative consequences of introducing and using a forced ranking system.

In chapter 5, Forced Ranking—Behind the Scenes, I will show you how the process actually works as it unfolded in a major corporation. You will be part of the creation of a large-scale forced ranking system and observe the actual ranking sessions as they were conducted.

In chapter 6 we will look at forced distribution, a technique that is often confused with forced ranking. With forced ranking, managers are required to evaluate their employees and assign them into predetermined categories based on their performance, potential, and promotability. Forced distribution, on the other hand, is a technique used as part of a company's performance appraisal process that provides that only a certain percentage of employees are allowed to get the highest rating and that some minimum number must be assigned to the lowest categories of performance. In this chapter I will make clear the difference between these two often-confused procedures and demonstrate how to make a forced distribution requirement work effectively.

Finally, in chapter 7, Getting the Truth into Performance Management, I will look closely at the conventional performance appraisal process, and I'll show you how to get it right. The objective of forced ranking, as the book's subtitle indicates, is to make performance management work. Whether or not a company chooses to use a relative comparison procedure as part of its overall performance management practices, almost every company employs a conventional performance appraisal system. This chapter will show you how to effectively employ one of the newest techniques in performance management: rater reliability or calibration sessions, aimed at making sure that there's a level performance appraisal playing field. Also, I will show you how to build top management support for performance management. We will look at ways to make a conventional performance appraisal system operate superlatively well.

But the greatest value of the book for many readers may be in the appendixes. I will give you the actual scripts that I wrote for a client company's managers to use in discussing the results of a forced ranking procedure with their direct reports. I'll also provide the FAQ document that I developed with another client that used it to explain the process to all the employees who were to be involved. I'll provide copies of the memos written by the CEO of a large organization, communicating his support for the process. By giving you these, I'll eliminate the need for you to figure everything out for yourself.

One of the greatest concerns invariably expressed about forced ranking is the potential the system has for generating lawsuits. In the final appendix, I will analyze the legal aspects of forced ranking.

A Concluding Note

A national discussion was sparked when GE's CEO Jack Welch, in his final shareowners' letter, argued not only for evaluating employees on a relative basis—person-to-person comparisons—but also for systematically eliminating the lowest-performing segment of the population.

The rationale seems unassailable—in every group there will always be those who perform better than others, and routinely removing the C players and replacing them with, hopefully, A and B players, will increase the overall vitality and competitiveness and success of the organization. And while it may be initially painful to those who are identified as being in the lowest category, ultimately they too will benefit, for they will either improve their performance and join their colleagues as fully successful members of the team, or they will leave the organization and find more congenial employment opportunities elsewhere.

Of course, managers should be doing this pruning and weeding routinely, using the performance management tools that organizations have long provided. But too many managers display a reluctance to make meaningful differentiations among the troops, preferring to live in a Lake Wobegon cocoon where all the children are above average. Certainly, few people who have spent any significant time working for large organizations—or small organizations, for that matter—would argue that there is a certain percentage of people in any company who function more as anchors than as sails—a certain percentage that the organization (and their fellow employees) would be better off without.

But requiring relative comparisons—asking managers not to assess how well Sally did in meeting her objectives, but rather how well her performance compares with that of Mary and Bob—strikes many as somehow unfair. Isn't it possible, they argue, for a manager to assemble a team of highly talented and highly motivated performers, and through exemplary leadership enable all of them to surpass the goals no matter how high they are set? And isn't it just as possible for a skilled teacher, given a classroom filled with bright, motivated, and energetic students, to have demanding expectations and still discover at the end of the semester that every single student has in fact earned an A?

Certainly it's possible. But while it's possible, it isn't common. What is common is the fact that the quality of performance varies, and varies significantly, in both the classroom and the workplace. What is being asked in relative comparison approaches—forced ranking systems of any kind—is that managers look at the performance of their subordinates in both absolute and relative terms. There are good reasons to insist on differentiation, if for no other reason than to ensure the universal expectation that people get what they deserve. Forced ranking generates differentiation and accountability. Used well, it is a fair and valid way of making sure that those who contribute the most are recognized for what they've done, and those at the opposite end of the contribution continuum are also recognized appropriately.

2

Risks and Rewards

IN SPITE OF A GREAT DEAL of bad press, forced ranking systems must offer some benefits to organizations or they wouldn't be as popular as they are or have remained in use for three decades or more as they have at Hewlett-Packard, PepsiCo, and others. On the other hand, while many of the criticisms of forced ranking are overstated, there are some genuine and valid reservations regarding the use of these systems. Forced ranking is not for every organization. Obviously, not every company has adopted the approach, and some of those that have used the process, like Dow Chemical, which used a forced ranking process for more than thirty years, have dropped their systems. What are the pros and cons of forced ranking?

Benefits

Let's start the discussion by looking at the benefits and advantages that a well-designed forced ranking system can provide an organization. Companies with a significant amount of experience report that the system has produced several important payoffs—benefits that are difficult to obtain through other talent management approaches.

1. Forced ranking combats artificially inflated performance appraisal ratings and forces the truth into performance management. Bringing the truth into performance assessment may be the greatest benefit of using a relative comparison performance assessment process. In a conventional performance appraisal system, depending on how high or low the bar is set, almost everyone can be rated as exceeding expectations. That's not so with forced ranking. Only 25 percent can be in the top quartile, no matter how well everyone does at meeting their objectives.

Just how valid is this concern over ratings inflation? Frankly, nobody knows. There just aren't any hard data available. But it's observed and complained about constantly. Camille Olson and Gregory Davis, the authors of a study on forced ranking systems published by the Society for Human Resource Management (SHRM), provide a telling example: "Typically, with traditional individual performance appraisal systems, managers assign a rating to employees. Many companies have found that these ratings are inflated with a disproportionate percentage at the highest levels. For example, before Ford implemented its forced ranking system, 98 percent of its management employees were routinely ranked as fully meeting expectations under its former appraisal system."[1] A 2003 Sibson Consulting study, "The Rewards of Work," attempted to compare the attitudes and values of high performers versus those of low performers, but struggled to find a way to ensure accuracy when the data on quality of performance came from self-reports: "The research literature has long demonstrated that people tend to inflate estimates of their own performance," the authors stated in their analysis of the data. "Decades of research have shown that most people tend to view their own performance as 'above average.'"[2]

Managers in general are exceedingly reluctant to finger any of their subordinates as being less than fully satisfactory. Organizations are rife with stories about individuals who were allowed to keep performing at marginal levels for years—sometimes even to retirement—because a series of spineless managers never had the courage to call a spade a spade. While this conspiracy of silence may have avoided the need for someone to have an awkward half-hour conversation, it also allowed an individual to remain a noncontributor for years.

It is this genuine unfairness that a forced ranking process can overcome. The individual who might have had a prosperous career with another organization (or with her original organization if she had decided to change and upgrade her performance as a result of getting an honest assessment of the perceived low quality of her work) has in effect been seduced by silence into staying in a job where her opportunities are secretly limited because senior managers have little confidence in her ability to advance. Worse, if managers don't tell poorer performers that they are simply not meeting expectations, the message to everyone else (who always are aware of who's cutting the mustard and who's not) is that "around here, they let you get away with anything."

Almost every HR professional can tell horror stories about some manager, finally fed up with a subordinate's shoddy performance, at long last demanding that he or she be terminated. A brief review of the individual's personnel file, however, reveals a lengthy history of superior performance appraisals. The frustrated manager is told that he must go back and start over at square one.

The presence of a forced ranking process helps ensure accuracy in performance evaluation. The authors of the SHRM study mentioned in chapter 1 point out that a great benefit of the procedure is that it helps ensure a level playing field. "Ranking helps ensure a fairer distribution of pay and other rewards across the entire organization based on relative performance. Using a forced ranking system for pay distribution, i.e., requiring a fixed percentage at the top and bottom, ensures that the organization will have more money for the top performers and that poor performers are not over-rewarded."[3]

But even if managers universally did an outstanding job of providing straightforward and candid feedback about how each individual performed against the expectations of the job, that's still only half the story. The other half is how well the individual performed compared with the performance turned in by others. Forced ranking creates a supplement to the existing performance management system that serves to confirm or deny the information provided by that system.

While managers may find it difficult to have straightforward conversations with poorer performers, the failure to differentiate alienates high performers. One common complaint about forced ranking is that it may have the potential to adversely affect the morale of lower-ranked employees. While this is true, too often it's easy to forget that it's more important to ensure a high level of morale among the most productive and most talented employees than to ensure it among the bottom group—or the employee population as a whole.

It may seem harsh, but organizations would be wise to pay less attention to the morale and the complaints of poorer-performing members of the team. It may well turn out that if C players are unhappy, that's a good sign that the organization is doing something right. On the other hand, if A players are dissatisfied, that portends serious problems for the company, since these are the people who will find it easiest to pack up and move down the street to a new employer who genuinely values—and rewards—the disproportionate contributions they make.

2. Besides forcing the truth into performance management, the forced ranking process forces information out in the open. "Whether you like it or not, you are being evaluated and ranked by your management and your peers every day," a manager told me. "The difference is that in a forced ranking organization, you will know exactly how you are perceived by your management. That perception may or may not be accurate, but at least you will know it and will have the opportunity to try to change it. In nonranking organizations, you will probably never know where you stand until you are passed over for promotion, not given a key assignment, or laid off."

The manager who said that was on to a genuine truth about the process. Ranking happens all the time in an organization, mostly in informal conversations around the water cooler or in similar venues. In these offhand discussions there are no ground rules, there are no common criteria, there are no well-thought-out mechanisms that must be followed. That is certainly no way for critical organizational decisions to be made.

What forced ranking does is force rigor on an otherwise careless and casual process by helping to ensure that all perspectives are considered, all information is put forth, and all dubious judgments have the chance to be challenged. Do you want fairness to prevail in your decision-making process? Forced ranking may be the best way to guarantee that fairness exists.

3. Forced ranking is a valuable tool to supplement an organization's overall talent management efforts. Forced ranking requires organizations to acknowledge that talent variations actually do exist. While this observation may seem obvious, a great many managers are reluctant to admit that there actually are talent variations and that those variations are significant. There are some managers who simply are not able (or not willing) to accept that some people do perform significantly better than others. It takes the rigor of a forced ranking process to wake them up to reality.

The truth is, talent does make a difference. Disregarding the benefits to be gained by identifying poorer performers, the research clearly suggests that the payoff for clearly differentiating between those who are fully successful performers—the organization's solid B players— and those whose performance is genuinely outstanding—the A players—is enormous. "In every field and every company, you will find star performers," says Robert Kelley in the study he made of the top talent at Bell Labs. "Whether it be money managers or people managers, Silicon Valley software developers or Hollywood film producers, scientists opening new horizons or salespeople closing deals, about 10 to 15 percent of all people will outperform their peers by a wide margin and rise into the star ranks."[4]

British organizational psychologist Adrian Furnham wrote that variances in productivity across workers average about two to one: that is, good workers produce about twice the output of poor workers. But that's for *all workers*. "As the work becomes more complex, the productivity ratio becomes even higher, so that a good physicist produces much more than twice the output of a poor one."[5]

The output difference between the middle and the top rank of performers may actually be much more than Furnham's reported two-to-one ratio. In fields like computer programming, an eight-to-one difference between the productivity of stars and average workers has been reported.[6] And even higher ratios have been described. San Francisco State University's Dr. John Sullivan, who has focused his research on assessing the importance of finding and building talent in organizations, notes that top performers produce as much as ten times more than the average worker (while requiring nowhere near a ten-times pay differential). Sullivan accounts for the vast differential in performance by the fact that, besides simply doing the job better, top performers generate most of the new ideas and innovations and are likely also to help others become better because they serve as trainers, mentors, and role models.[7]

In addition to differentiating talent, a forced ranking process helps a company make more accurate cross-department comparisons than its regular performance appraisal system ever could. Overall, is marketing a stronger department than manufacturing? Looking at the performance appraisals generated by the managers in these two groups will leave you clueless. But a forced ranking procedure, where the members of the marketing department are compared with their colleagues in manufacturing against important, organization-wide criteria, can provide revealing insights into where the talent truly lies.

A well-designed forced ranking process can also provide the organization with useful data on the ability of managers to spot and champion talent. This is a genuinely compelling benefit of using forced ranking, and it's one that is only rarely recognized by organizations. Consider this: not only are valuable data generated about the quality of performance of the population under review, but equally valid and important data are also generated about the people who are doing the reviewing. Are managers able to articulate exactly why one of their subordinates belongs in a particular category? Are they able to come up with convincing examples? Do they argue persuasively in favor of their best, or do they go through the exercise in a perfunctory manner? Do they argue excessively to protect a favored buddy from assignment to a low category? Do they yield their point of view too easily, or hang on too long to an obviously untenable position? Do they know their people well enough to apply the organization's criteria to their performance accurately by providing specific examples? To what extent have they gotten to know people in other parts of the organization? How much attention are they paying to talent in other departments? Do they remain engaged when the discussion shifts to individuals outside their chain of command? Are they sensitive to the importance of diversity and the nuances of language? Are they willing to challenge other managers who, they believe, are overinflating their assessments of their troops? Do they take the process seriously?

The rigor of the ranking process helps overcome the problem of managers who are unable or unwilling to identify and deal with poor performers. Ranking provides upper-level managers with a means to determine which lower-level managers are most and least effective in accurately evaluating employee performance and managing talent. This is critically valuable information.

If, as Andy Pearson and Jack Welch and Bill Gates and Larry Bossidy and a host of other CEOs argue, the most important job of the organization's senior executive is to ensure a cadre of superior talent throughout the ranks, there may be no better way to find out who shares this belief and is capable of acting on it than by watching the performance of managers as they are participating in a ranking session.

Forced ranking creates a forum for serious conversation about performance. There is typically no organization-wide opportunity for discussion about performance in most companies. Of course, performance is discussed in performance appraisal discussions, but that's a one-on-one meeting between manager and subordinate. And performance may also be discussed in management training programs, but that's an artificial classroom-style setting typically conducted by people outside the participants' chain of command. And performance may also be discussed when a manager consults with HR about a specific issue, but again it's a limited forum.

But when the time for the forced ranking (or "talent assessment" or "leadership assessment") sessions comes around, everyone at a certain level on up in the organization will be intently focused on performance and potential and talent. Simply having a forced ranking system communicates that talent management is high on top executives' agenda.

4. A forced ranking procedure can reduce favoritism, nepotism, and promotions or other organizational rewards based on factors other than performance. Forced ranking can be the antidote to favoritism, unwarranted preferential treatment, and decision making based on backroom political machinations. It also helps eliminate seniority as a driver of organizational rewards.

Opponents of forced ranking often argue that the procedure is an excessively political process, where managers make mutual back-scratching deals to guarantee that their favorites end up in the top buckets. This certainly is possible. System designers and session facilitators must be sensitive to the appearance of political trade-offs and guard against its occurrence.

But too many organizations allow their managers to operate their departments as fiefdoms, looking the other way while those managers promote their personal favorites and award them the plum assignments, while simultaneously thwarting the desire of the most talented members of the team to move to more challenging and better-rewarding opportunities elsewhere in the organization. Frankly, forced ranking is one of the most effective techniques to help organizations confront and eliminate this shabby political operation. Done right, forced ranking ensures that the criteria for making important decisions and the judgments and actions that result are held up to the light of day.

A forced ranking process also helps to identify the criteria or competencies that are critical to organizational success and that should be used for making these decisions. One of the earliest and most important tasks in designing an effective forced ranking system is to identify the assessment criteria that will be used. Since the ranking process will compare the performance and potential of people from different organizational units, the criteria selected for the assessment must be important on an organization-wide basis.

One of the most important side benefits of creating a forced ranking system is that it requires the organization's senior management to articulate a small number of critical factors that they expect of every member of the enterprise and establish the way in which these factors will be measured. Many organizations have determined a set of core or universal competencies that they expect to see demonstrated by everyone on the team. Using these competencies as assessment criteria in the forced ranking system will dramatically reinforce the message that the executive team is serious about their importance.

5. Forced ranking provides a sound and defensible rationale for all important personnel actions—including pay raises, promotions, bonuses, developmental opportunities and assignments, layoffs, and terminations. A large number of personnel decisions are continually being made in organizations—who should get salary increases and how big those increases should be, who should be promoted when opportunities arise, who should be let go when business declines, who should be groomed for future advancement, and many others. While there is universal agreement that organizations should operate as meritocracies (except where prevented by union contracts or civil service regulations that require these decisions to be made strictly by seniority and time-in-grade), how should organizations decide where the merit really lies?

Conventional performance appraisal mechanisms fail to do the job for several reasons. First, there is the universally acknowledged problem of ratings inflation and the resulting lack of real differentiation.

Second, standards and measures aren't uniform across the organization. As a result, employees who work for bosses with high expectations and tough standards are at a disadvantage compared with their counterparts working for easy graders. From our schooldays, we know that a B from Professor Smith was harder to earn than an A from Professor Jones. Likewise, in our organizations, a middle rating of Meets Expectations from one manager may reflect a far higher level of performance than a rating of Superior from his counterpart across the hall. But when the hard-earned Meets Expectations is blindly compared with the easily awarded Superior rating without reference to the evaluation criteria and who it is that's making the evaluation, the lesser of the two performers is likely to get the greater reward.

Forced ranking can help prevent this. With a relative comparison process, the odds go up that true talent will be identified, that the most worthy will get the greatest rewards, and that those who contribute the least will be first in line when the ax has to fall.

6. Forced ranking jolts managers and organizations out of complacency. One of the best ways of kick-starting a shift to a performance-oriented culture is to announce that the company will be implementing a forced ranking process. While certainly the introduction of a relative comparison talent assessment process must be carefully communicated, just telling the managerial staff that they will be expected to engage in forced ranking sessions will rivet their attention and convince them that the top dogs are now serious about building a talent-centered organization. Forced ranking immediately heightens awareness of the importance of high performance and instantly starts to cultivate a corporate meritocracy. As Colleen M. O'Neill, talent management leader for the consulting firm William M. Mercer, points out, it's a great tool to use when you want to get people's attention and say, "New day, new rules."

Certainly, the implementation of a forced ranking process may generate some anxieties among employees, given all of the pessimistic publicity characterizing the procedure as one that fosters a hyper-competitive, dog-eat-dog, every-man-for-himself work environment. Certainly, few people would willingly choose to work in such an intimidating environment, and few employers would actively seek out the kind of egomaniacal cutthroats who would thrive in such a system to staff their enterprises. But the presence of a well-designed forced ranking system does have an appeal to large numbers of individuals who genuinely do want to be recognized for their talents and contributions and are willing to run the risks of being assigned to a lower group in return for the assurance that the organization they work for is truly concerned with talent.

In addition, it is also widely accepted that highly talented entrants to the professional workforce with lofty career ambitions may be particularly attracted to a GE or a PepsiCo or a Goldman Sachs or a Microsoft directly as a result of its highly competitive culture. They realize that while they may not make it to the top there because of the tough competition, the preparation and experience they will gain in a few years of employment at one of these talent meritocracies will be a significant résumé builder that will have a significant payoff for the entire life of their career.

With all the concerns and complaints about forced ranking—some valid, some not—there is no argument that the goals of forced ranking are worthy: to recognize and retain top performers, and to improve or remove the least productive members of the organization.

Forced ranking helps make sure that the people who contribute the most to the organization's success and who appear to have the greatest potential for doing so in the future are identified, rewarded for what they have already done, and provided with the chance to do even more. The process also confronts those who are contributing the least with the fact that they must either change or find more congenial employment elsewhere.

Forced ranking helps ensure the fulfillment of a basic human demand—the demand that people get what they deserve.

Risks

While an intelligently designed and skillfully executed forced ranking system can produce the benefits I just described, the press rarely reports this. Most articles in the mainstream media and business magazines have focused on the negative side of the process: the lawsuits lodged against the process, the complaints of unfairness coming from those who failed to be ranked in the top categories, and various design and execution flaws of companies' forced ranking systems.

While the benefits of using a relative comparison, forced ranking process are real, there are some genuine concerns and downsides about forced ranking that need to be addressed. Here I will discuss several important ones.

1. The process may produce culture shock and generate an environment where competition trumps teamwork and corporate goals are suboptimized. The process may promote excessive competition instead of collaboration and collegiality. This is one of the most frequent concerns raised about the forced ranking process. The consulting firm Linkage, Inc., states the case directly: "Competition may prompt hard work and high performance in a Darwinist 'survival of the fittest' fashion. Yet the literature reveals a number of less positive outcomes when employees are pitted against each other. This competition can provide disincentives for employees to help each other."[8]

Organizations, especially those with rich histories and strong cultures, cannot realistically expect to achieve a cultural change in performance orientation overnight, especially through a highly uncomfortable process such as forced ranking. Moving from a culture that may be highly paternalistic and characterized as "best effort" to one that is tough-minded and results-driven will certainly cause internal turmoil.

"Imagine thousands of highly tenured employees finding out that after 20 or 30 years of being assessed as good, hard workers, they are now just B players or, even worse, C players. Imagine managers who have been providing less-than-robust evaluations through a somewhat rote process suddenly being asked, with very little training, to rigorously assess and rank employee performance. The implications of this shock are very clear in terms of morale, productivity and loyalty," the authors of a Sibson Consulting analysis correctly assert.[9]

Organizations that consist of thousands of highly tenured employees who have enjoyed years of less-than-accurate performance evaluations would be well advised to be cautious about implementing forced ranking or any other potent performance management system— provided that their objective is to keep things just the way they've always been. But when those companies realize that having "highly tenured" employees who have not been told the truth about their performance may be detrimental to maintaining a competitive position, the benefits to implementing a rigorous talent management process may well outweigh the culture shock that will accompany the implementation of a robust performance evaluation process.

Certainly, the implementation of a forced ranking procedure will impact an organization's culture. What remains to be seen is whether that culture change will be beneficial to the organization and its members; whether it will increase the odds that the company will be successful. If the goal is to change the culture from one of entitlement to one that is demanding of high performance, carefully implementing a forced ranking process can be one of the best ways of bringing that new culture about.

The fact is that while there are many anxieties expressed over the possibility of a forced ranking system turning the enterprise into a Darwinian Survivor game, the people who actually administer forced ranking systems report little evidence of this actually happening. For the most part, forced ranking systems tend to be used in organizations where there is already a healthy degree of competition as part of the organization's vital essence. The forced ranking system is simply another manifestation of a vigorous meritocracy at work.

Moreover, the concern about generating excessive competitiveness can be allayed by including an element like "teamwork" or "cooperation" as one of the ranking criteria. MetLife's approach illustrates how the concern can be handled: "At MetLife, the focus is on individual performance, but it's not okay to step on people's toes," Lisa Weber, executive vice president of human resources for MetLife says. "You must rate high on partnership and teamwork. If you're a great performer but a terrible team player, you won't do well."[10]

2. Resistance—some managers and some employees may resent and resist the process. Employees may become demoralized. One of the biggest concerns over forced ranking involves managerial and employee resistance to the procedure. Certainly, discussing performance honestly is often an uncomfortable process. If in the past managers have been able to avoid delivering honest and tough-minded assessments by giving everyone an above-average performance appraisal rating, once forced ranking arrives on the scene that stratagem may no longer be possible.

Part of the cause of the resistance to forced ranking results from the use of insensitive labels for the different categories or buckets into which employees are to be assigned. If the label requires a manager to identify an individual as an unacceptable performer (like Sun's Underperforming or the fairly frequent Needs Improvement), then of course the forced ranking process will be a hard sell. While managers will freely admit that some of their subordinates perform better than others, they'll argue strongly that none of their people are Underperforming or Unacceptable. It's important to strive for neutrality in labeling the different groups. The best approach? Probably to use the terms A, B, and C players.

It's understandable that people who end up ranked in a lower category may well be demoralized. Part of the solution to this concern is to make good decisions about what will happen to those in the bottom bucket. To unilaterally terminate them, particularly in the first or second iteration of a forced ranking process, will undoubtedly bring about demoralization in the group to be let go, and will likely breed resistance and resentment even from those placed in higher-rated categories. The people who are being terminated aren't just poorer-performing coworkers. They are also friends and people with whom strong relationships have been developed, often over many years.

Even when the focus of the organization's forced ranking process is to encourage growth and development without any requirement that those ranked in the bottom category will be terminated, it is important to be particularly sensitive to the possible stigmatization that even an accurate assignment of an individual to a lower category can produce. The risk is not so much that the person is miscategorized, but rather that having been accurately categorized, the individual will lose the motivation to change and move up.

But if there is some demoralization, consider who it is that's demoralized. As Andy Pearson, one of forced ranking's firmest advocates (and a believer that those ranked in the bottom quartile should be quickly exited out of the company) asserts, the demoralization risk is greater if a rigorous forced ranking process is not used: "Some managers might object that this relentless scrutiny—and the inevitable firings—will demoralize employees. My experience suggests precisely the opposite. Top performers relish the challenge of meeting ever higher goals. What does demoralize them is a climate that tolerates mediocrity; under such circumstances, they may slow down their work to the tempo of the organization—or they may leave the company."[11]

And just the name *forced ranking* carries with it some negative emotional baggage. "If the objective is to eliminate a fixed percentage of the workforce," the authors of the Society for Human Resource Management study note, "employees will feel increasingly insecure about their employment. Even if that is not the objective, employees will feel increasingly insecure because of misperceptions arising from the adverse publicity surrounding 'forced ranking.'"[12] As we'll discuss later, there are good alternatives to the name *forced ranking* that may make the approach more palatable when it's being introduced to an organization for the first time.

3. **The judgments made in forced ranking or similar relative comparison procedures are necessarily subjective and speculative and therefore inappropriate.** This is one of the most frequent criticisms made of the forced ranking procedure or any process involving relative comparisons. Of course, the "subjectivity" charge is also leveled at any judgment made in the course of regular performance appraisal systems when the manager evaluates the individual's performance in any way other than comparing the number of widgets produced with the number of widgets assigned.

The source of the discomfort with the process's apparent *subjectivity* results from a misunderstanding of the meaning of the term. In common parlance, people tend to use the term *objective* to mean quantifiable, capable of being counted or specifically verified against some absolute and fixed standard. The corollary to this belief, of course, is that anything that is not quantitatively or numerically measurable—any decision that is a function of an individual's judgment or opinion unsupported by provable facts—is therefore subjective.

This belief, while widespread, is simply not true. What does the word *objective* mean? While quoting a dictionary definition rarely settles any argument, in this case the dictionary definition of *objective* is instructive. A check of the dictionary definition reveals that objectivity has nothing to do with quantifiability:

Objective: a. Uninfluenced by emotions or personal prejudices: an objective critic. See FAIR. b. Based on observable phenomena; presented factually: an objective appraisal.[13]

Objectivity does not involve countability. It means being uninfluenced by emotions or prejudices and basing one's judgment on observable phenomena, like a person's job performance, which continually is under observation.

What any talent management system demands is thoughtful, well-informed, mature judgments made by honest and skilled appraisers. Managers constantly make tough decisions based on always limited, frequently incomplete, and often contradictory information: which projects to fund, which to shelve, which to kill. Whom to hire, whom to reject. Where to build a new store or factory. What colors will appeal to the teenage buyer eighteen months from now. Forced ranking is simply one more example of the kind of tough decisions based on limited data that managers are required to make. Evaluating potential and performance is not the solving of an algebra problem. It does not involve a condition where if we identify all the variables and unknowns, then we can apply a formula to come up with a provable right answer. "Going the extra mile for a customer" can't be reduced to a quantitative, numerical description, but it can certainly be recognized and described and used as the basis to say that Bob is better at it than Jane is.

Richard Goodale once ran the U.S. Army's forced ranking procedure. He writes:

> What I learned from the experience is that forced ranking, when made against established and organization-sensitive criteria, and supported and tempered by human judgment, can be a very useful and humanitarian way of helping some of us imperfect humans accomplish the very difficult task of making decisions that will affect the future of some of our fellow humans.
>
> If we believe that one of the most important raisons d'etre for having leaders in the first place is that hard decisions need to be made, always with imperfect information, we should support (and strive to perfect) any tool, like ranking systems, that help such decisions to be made with intelligence and compassion.[14]

Another trepidation regarding the objectivity of a forced ranking system involves the possibility that an individual's rank may be influenced more by his boss's persuasive skills and horse-trading than by his actual performance and potential. "If you force percentage rankings, you are still dooming a certain percentage of employees to be rated in the lowest category, often based on the effectiveness of their boss's presentation in a session where everyone is looking out for his or her staff," an HR manager observes. Her observation reflects a legitimate concern. If the assignment to a particular group results not from the employee's actual performance and potential, but from an assessor's skill in making the case for the most appropriate categorization, then the integrity of the system will be destroyed.

Byron Woollen of Worklab Consulting echoes the concern:

> Some companies require that their managers meet as a group and reach a consensus on each report's ranking. A senior HR professional for a large financial services company reported that during their forced ranking meetings, there is a considerable amount of back room deal making whereby one manager may agree to support the ranking of an employee in exchange for that employee's manager reciprocating in kind. This practice leads to employee anxiety over the integrity of the system and whether his/her manager has sufficient influence, or has prepared sufficiently, to secure a high ranking for him/her.[15]

For system integrity to be ensured, there are safeguards that must be built into the process. Later, in chapter 4, we will explore in detail exactly what needs to happen in order to make sure that the allocations are made based on the qualities of the individual under assessment and not the persuasiveness of the presenter; there are a couple of steps that organizations can take to defend against assessor glibness or political machinations exerting excessive sway:

- Raise the issue directly as part of the assessor training program.

- Demand that assessors present evidence and specific observations to defend their judgments.

- Set an expectation that other participants in the assessment sessions will challenge any recommendation on assignment to a category that is not sufficiently backed up by facts and evidence.

- Sensitize session facilitators to the possibility of deal making and dubious salesmanship substituting for tough-minded judgment.

Another concern with the objectivity of forced ranking involves the fact that the process focuses not only on assessing the individual's performance—evaluating the past—but also on assessing his potential—predicting the future.

Accurately assessing an individual's future potential is certainly a precarious undertaking. Determining someone's degree of untapped capability is a voyage into the unknown.

But there are indicators that suggest what the future may hold. Certainly, the best predictor of future performance is past performance. The individual's ability to take on new challenges, particularly when she's been dumped into sink-or-swim, take-charge situations, is an excellent gauge.

One limitation on conventional approaches to performance management is the fact that they are restricted entirely to historical data. "How well did Diane do in achieving the targets that were set twelve months ago?" is certainly an important question, but it's not the only question that should be asked in a comprehensive talent-management effort. "How well will Diane do in the future, working with different people, given fewer resources and higher demands?" is a much tougher question to answer. But it's a question that should be addressed, even if the answers are harder to come by and the confidence in their accuracy is necessarily lower.

"A lot of companies are ranking based on current performance," according to Susan Gebelein, executive vice president of HR consulting firm Personnel Decisions in Minnesota. "That's wrong. So much of an employee's value is in his or her potential—which can also be measured in a ranking. But a lot of managers aren't very good at seeing potential."[16] The fact that they're not very good at seeing potential—and a great many managers aren't very good at it—doesn't argue that they shouldn't be asked to get better.

A final concern about the degree of objectivity in ranking sessions involves the concern that rankers participating in those sessions may not know employees well enough to make good decisions. "In order to accurately identify a bottom 10 percent, the employee group must be large and random enough for a meaningful bell curve distribution," writer Del Jones points out. "The problem is that no one supervisor has intimate knowledge of the work habits of 100 or more workers. When groups are made smaller, good workers in superior departments will wind up in the bottom 10 percent, while mediocre workers in an average department will squeak by."[17]

Jones is right, and he goes on to explain that most companies combat this problem by having several bosses meet, discuss their subordinates, and negotiate a top-to-bottom ranking from the larger universe. In companies that apply the forced ranking procedure well, the final ranking decision is typically made after an intense discussion among the individual's immediate supervisor, other managers who regularly have contact with the person under review, still others who have had limited but revealing experiences, and finally other individuals who may not have had any firsthand experience with the reviewee but engage and challenge the managers who have in order to make sure that the system's rigorous expectations and standards are being applied consistently across the board.

Bill Ault, a fifty-four-year-old Ford Motor Company software developer and a plaintiff in the Ford suit, was quoted in Jones's article as complaining that nine of the twelve managers who voted him into the bottom 10 percent "didn't know me from Adam."[18] Ault may well be correct, but it's also likely that the three who did know him, and who evaluated him under the watchful gaze of the other nine, made a well-justified and correct decision, under the observation of nine others who had a responsibility to make sure that the process operated the way it was designed.

4. A forced ranking system may influence managers to concentrate only on developing their stars. In a thoughtful article objecting to the process, Edward E. Lawler III put forth the caution that the use of forced ranking systems may cause managers to pay a disproportionate amount of attention to their top performers: "Forced ranking systems also influence how managers develop their employees. It hardly makes sense for managers to invest in developing individuals who are marginal performers when they believe that, in a relatively short time, they will have to eliminate them. Instead, they invest development dollars and personal effort in individuals who are likely to survive the annual assessment and firings. The result is the best get better, while the poor performers have little chance to grow and improve."[19]

Of course, Lawler is correct. Managers certainly will invest their development time and dollars in those from whom they expect the greatest return, and it would be indeed folly to invest anything in those from whom only a marginal return is expected.

But is that wrong? Should a company's development resources, always scarce, merely be allocated at random? Or should they more wisely be targeted toward those who the organization believes will produce the greatest return? One of the objectives of a forced ranking procedure, in almost every organization that has adopted the approach, is to make sure that limited development resources are invested in those who will benefit the most, and in return will then benefit the organization the most. That means necessarily that those ranked in the bottom category will get less developmental attention. And most organizations will argue that that's the way it should be.

But Ed Lawler's reservation about the possibility of forced ranking's building an unproductive "star system" is echoed by Malcolm Gladwell. In "The Talent Myth," his cautionary *New Yorker* article raising concerns about the advisability of excessively concentrating organizational efforts on developing a cadre of outstandingly talented individuals, Gladwell attributes much of the cause of Enron's fall to its inordinate focus on talent. He raises a disturbing question: "The reasons for its collapse are complex, needless to say. But what if Enron failed not in spite of its talent mind-set but because of it? What if smart people are overrated?"[20] What the war for talent amounts to, Gladwell asserts, "is an argument for indulging A employees, for fawning over them." He warns of the danger of organizations being deluded by narcissists, whose charm, energy, and self-confidence may garner more organizational rewards than their actual accomplishments warrant.

Gladwell quotes the observation of Richard Wagner, a Florida State University psychologist, about the difference between a school culture, where individual effort and achievement is paramount, and work cultures: "In terms of how we evaluate schooling, everything is about working by yourself. If you work with someone else, it's called cheating. Once you get out in the real world, everything you do involves working with other people."[21]

The flaw with the Talent Myth, Gladwell argues, is the erroneous assumption companies make "that an organization's intelligence is simply a function of the intelligence of its employees. They believe in stars, because they don't believe in systems." He argues that the opposite may be true: "Groups don't write great novels and a committee didn't come up with the theory of relativity. But companies work by different rules. They don't just create; they execute and compete and coordinate the efforts of many different people, and the organizations that are most successful at that task are the ones where the system is the star."[22]

There is a genuine risk that a forced ranking system can result in an excessively talent-focused culture where only individual excellence counts and being a good team player is disdained. To some extent this risk can be moderated by making sure that the criteria include the degree to which the person excels not only as an individual but also as a member of a larger whole. But the risk of creating a counterproductive "star system" is genuine.

5. A forced ranking process may unfairly penalize managers and departments that adhere to high performance standards and act to remove poor performers in advance of ranking sessions. While it's unlikely that a manager will deliberately hold on to a poor performer in order to have someone to throw to the lions in the company's annual forced ranking process, there is a significant risk that those organizational units that do a stellar job of performance management year-round will be penalized if this effort is not recognized in all the company's talent management procedures.

In every company there are some organizational units that are acknowledged pockets of excellence. Everyone who's been around for a while has discovered, for example, that the talent pool in the Western Region is deeper than it is anyplace else in the company. It's the Western Region's district managers who are always selected for promotion to zone manager in other parts of the company, and who invariably succeed in their new positions. It's the Western Region where corporate chooses to roll out new initiatives first, since the likelihood of both ultimate success and high user acceptance is greater there than anyplace else. Western Region managers are the first to offer candidates for corporatewide focus groups and project teams, and the people they appoint to those teams end up doing the lion's share of the work. And it's the Western Region that hesitates the least in cutting itself loose of those who appear to be employment mistakes.

When the time for forced ranking comes around, should the Western Region be asked to assign as many people to the bottom bucket as every other region in the company?

If it is, the company is doing a great disservice, not only to the managers and employees in the Western Region, but also to the integrity of their talent management practices as a whole. The allocation of talent in a forced ranking process should mirror the actual distribution of talent in the organization as a whole. In any company there are, in fact, pockets of excellence, just as there are pockets of patchiness. If the leaders of the best-managed arms of the organization are not recognized by being allowed to have a disproportionate number of people in the top category (just as the leaders of the worst-performing units should be expected to provide a much greater share of bottom-ranked individuals), then skepticism and cynicism about the validity of the company's talent management systems will grow.

6. Forced ranking is not a sustainable process. It's simply impossible to keep "raising the bar" indefinitely. Almost everybody agrees that the typical corporation has a certain number of under- and nonperformers, and that a year or two of good, fair ranking can weed them out," writes Andy Meisler. "After that, though—especially if a company is cutting its workforce—something else happens. Former A's will become B's and former B's will become C's. Upwardly mobile B's will displace A's; recovering C's will replace B's. Not the healthiest of situations."[23]

GE and a very few other companies are unusual in having been able to sustain a forced ranking system over a period of many years, particularly given the mechanism of their systems, which provides that the people ranked in the bottom category will leave the organization and be replaced by (hopefully) better, more talented performers. But for other companies that don't have their history of the use of a forced ranking system or their long-standing highly competitive culture, is there a limit on how long a literal "rank and yank" system can be sustained?

I believe that there is a limit to forced ranking's usefulness within a company. On one hand, it is certainly possible for an organization to maintain a forced distribution expectation in its performance appraisal system over a great many years (i.e., a requirement that only a certain number can be awarded the highest performance appraisal rating and that a minimum number must be rated in the lowest categories). There is, however, a natural limit on how long a forced ranking system can be made to operate, particularly if the rules of the system require that those ranked at the bottom be purged and replaced with superior talent.

If the policy states that those who are ranked in the bottom bucket must leave the organization, then the churn that Andy Meisler described in his article will occur within the span of a couple of years. In year one of the system, the company will remove and replace the C players, and most would agree that they are people who need replacing. Assuming the exit process is humanely handled, this will generate a significant organizational benefit. In year two of the system, those who were ranked at the bottom end of the B category the first time around are now likely to be tagged as C players and replaced. In year three, those who originally were good solid B's will have moved down to the C level as the curve has moved up.

While the bar is perhaps moving higher and higher, it is becoming more and more difficult to sustain this continual raising. Within another year or two, people whose performance today is fully satisfactory will be led to the gallows. It is at this point that major problems with morale and resignation are likely to arise.

To put it bluntly: in the first year of a forced ranking system, the obvious fat will be removed. In the second year, the interstitial fat will be removed. In the third year, however, the company will be removing muscle, and by the fourth year, it's bone. This is not a sustainable process.

This observation has recently been confirmed through the mathematical simulation described in chapter 1. The closing paragraph of the Scullen study of forced ranking systems published in the journal *Personnel Psychology* references a statement I made during the course of a *Workforce Management* magazine interview on forced ranking: "I think that after about three iterations, forced ranking loses its effectiveness."[24] Referring to my statement, the authors say, "If he is right about that, and we think he is, then the long term viability [of a forced ranking system] may be questionable."[25] Their simulation indicated that most of the gains companies received from implementing a forced ranking system were achieved in the first three to four years of operation. Their math squares with my experience.

When I conduct executive overviews for the senior management teams of organizations that are interested in learning more about the forced ranking process (and about best practices in performance management in general), my recommendation on installing a system is almost always the same. I tell them this: if forced ranking seems right for you, make the investment necessary to do it right. Try it for one year and assess the results. They'll probably be beneficial. Assuming that they are, tune the system up based on your first year's experience and use it again a year later. Again assess the results. But before using it a third time and certainly before moving to a fourth iteration, test very carefully all the outcomes from the system with an eye toward concluding, "It did what we needed it to do. It's time to move on to other things."

7. Forced ranking isn't appropriate for an organization that already consists entirely of all-stars. Whenever there's a discussion of forced ranking, it's inevitable that one of the objections raised is that while the procedure may be appropriate in general, it just isn't appropriate when all of the people being ranked are exceptional performers. I recall a conversation with a few executives during the break in a presentation I was making for a large chemical company at their annual senior management retreat. One of the executives was objecting to my generally sympathetic report on the benefits of forced ranking.

"Forced ranking won't work for my team!" he told me. "I've got three people on my team, and they're the equivalent of Einstein, Newton, and Galileo."

"Don't listen to him," his colleague standing next to him quickly put in. "What he's really got is Larry, Curly, and Moe."

Even among Einstein, Galileo, and Newton there are differences in achievement and contribution, as Charles Murray has demonstrated in his book *Human Accomplishment*.[26] And there's probably some performance difference in the least capable of performers, even the Three Stooges.

What this objection to forced ranking highlights is one of the most common misunderstandings about the process—the belief that in a ranking procedure, the people assigned to the bottom are necessarily poor performers. This is simply not true.

Listen up: the purpose of forced ranking is to identify the *relative difference* in performance or contribution or potential among a group of people. This examination of relative difference is appropriate whatever the overall composition of the group under review may be. In the team that wins the World Series or World Cup, all of the members are outstanding athletes who would greedily be sucked up by almost any other team in the league. But some members of the winning team are better than others, even though all of them are among the best in the world.

I see this error being made by otherwise knowledgeable people whenever they discuss their reservations about forced ranking. They assume that people assigned to the bottom bucket are "unacceptable" performers, or "unsatisfactory," or "need improvement," or some other absolute comparison label. This is a mistake.

Here's a real example of this error made by an executive of Dow Chemical, a company that successfully used forced ranking for several decades. In "Forcing the Performance Ranking Issue," Steve Constantine, Dow's director of HR development and workforce planning, is quoted as saying, "Dow recruits the cream of the crop. To then say that a certain percentage of them are poor performers, even if the department and the company are meeting goals, did not make a lot of sense for us."[27]

Well, of course it doesn't make a lot of sense—they're *not poor performers*. What they are is simply less talented, or possessing lower potential, than the rest of their world-class colleagues.

This objection to forced ranking always posits a situation in which the hapless manager is forced to sit in judgment of his team of what he believes to be incredibly skilled organizational Green Berets, each one doing a brilliant job, and force-rank a portion of them into a dunce category. This is not what is happening. Talent variations do exist, even among real Green Berets. As a whole, the Green Berets may well be the ultimate military organization, but some demonstrate more courage under fire than others. Some make better judgments about how an attack should be planned, about which informants are double agents, about which hill should be taken. So while everyone in a small department may indeed play a unique role well and deliver fully acceptable levels of performance, some play their roles better than others and offer more potential to play bigger and more challenging roles.

8. Forced ranking—comparing one individual against another—is somehow unfair. The concern underlying this objection to the

forced ranking process is that the use of the approach is simply evidence that management isn't doing its job in the first place. If management met its responsibilities by hiring only talented people, and made sure that supervisors gave their subordinates both appropriately challenging assignments and straightforward performance feedback, and provided opportunities to all for development and growth, forced ranking would then be unnecessary. And further, that absent these behaviors on the part of the enterprise's leadership, the attempt to improve organizational performance on the backs of the employees by fingering and sacking the least productive members of the group represents an unfair and dishonorable practice.

Underlying this "unfair" objective is the mistaken belief that almost any worker is salvageable, and that organizations, once having accepted a person into membership in the organizational family, should be barred from cutting the family ties unless the individual has repeatedly proved to be incapable of meeting even minimal standards of performance.

This is nonsense. Companies aren't charities, and there are limits to what an organization can do to improve the performance of its members. While it makes good economic sense for an organization to develop its assets to make them as productive as possible, it also makes good economic sense for companies to jettison those assets that are generating the least return.

Is it fair to compare the performance and potential of one member of the enterprise with that of others? With limited ability to provide the organizational rewards of training programs and developmental assignments, is it fair not to direct these rewards toward those who will benefit the most? If companies do have to downsize, is it fair to throw out strong performers and retain marginal ones? If companies do that, and make layoff decisions on bases other than performance and potential, isn't that unfair to their customers? And if companies treat their customers unfairly, isn't the job security of the remaining workers thereby jeopardized?

Dr. John Sullivan, professor of management at San Francisco State University, warns that HR departments too often adopt, in his words, a socialistic rather than capitalistic approach toward the management of human resources. They are, he argues, too often the advocate of the weak rather than the strong, spending too much energy to ameliorate poor-performing employees and managers "despite the fact that human resources has no statistical evidence or metrics that show that focusing on poor performers results in them ever becoming top performers."[28] They offer progressive discipline and second-chance programs for those employees who consistently fail, says Sullivan, "but they offer little in the way of programs that support or improve the productivity of top performers."

Finally, in summarizing his list of indicators that human resource departments lean toward socialism, Sullivan notes one other telling characteristic of a socialistic bent: "Striving to eliminate any 'special treatment' means turkeys and eagles get the same treatment."[29] Forced ranking does make sure that turkeys are distinguished from eagles and that they receive different treatment. Is this unfair? Perhaps, but those who would object to this differentiation are likely to be labeled by Dr. Sullivan as "HR socialists."

9. Mistakes are inevitable—you're bound to miss a few late bloomers and overrate a few glib duds. Mistakes are indeed inevitable, as they are in every area where managers—or human beings in general—are asked to make important decisions with only limited data available. Companies make mistakes all the time in hiring people who turn out to be not as good on the job as they were in the interview. They make mistakes in rejecting candidates who actually would have turned out to be exceptional performers. They make mistakes in all personnel decisions because the "right answer" can never be known in advance. But the fact that mistakes may be made doesn't justify abandoning the process.

Ed Lawler summarizes the challenge here:

> Because employee performance patterns in organizations often do not follow a normal distribution, identifying poor performers using a forced ranking system is fraught with difficulties. First, a very real danger exists that some satisfactory employees will be misidentified as poor performers. For example, some divisions, departments or teams are always staffed better than others. In those areas, individuals who are satisfactory or even outstanding performers on a company-wide basis may be judged to be underperformers just because they happen to be among a group of very good employees.
>
> The right thing to do is to strengthen weak areas where there are a large number of poor performers by replacing them, rather than

removing the "the worst of the best" from areas dominated by high performers. Most forced distribution systems do not produce this result
because every area, regardless of the quality of its employees and its performance, is required to make the same percentage of cuts.[30]

Lawler's observation that some divisions may be staffed better than
others is obviously correct, and his recommendation that when there
are large numbers of poor performers they be booted en masse, while
probably difficult to pull off, may well be the right thing to do. But his
report that most forced ranking systems require every area to make the
same percentage of cuts just isn't true in this author's experience. I find
that almost every organization with a well-designed forced ranking
system does not require the burden to fall equally on outstanding
departments and mediocre ones alike—and shouldn't. Instead, in most
cases the organization recognizes that there are indeed organizational
units that are talent-rich and others where real talent is scarce, and
those units that have continually done a poorer job of demanding performance excellence are required to assign a larger percentage of their
populations to the bottom category, simply because they have larger
populations of poorer-performing individuals who deserve to be there.

Mistakes are indeed inevitable. The answer is not to abandon the
process, but to improve the policies and operating practices of the
forced ranking procedure, and the training and assessment skills provided to the rankers, so that more and more accurate assessments are
made with every iteration of the process.

**10. Lower-ranked employees who are members of a protected
class may believe that the ranking procedures produce illegally
discriminatory results.** This final concern may be the most important in causing organizations to hesitate about designing and
installing a relative comparison, forced ranking procedure.

As we will see in appendix C, where I will explore the legal aspects
of the forced ranking procedure, there is no law that prohibits an
employer from making relative comparisons of the employee group.
The problems arise in the use of the results of a forced ranking process,
particularly when members of a protected class are disproportionately
represented in a lower category.

The Linkage, Inc., study addressed one cause of the high-profile
concerns about forced ranking: "Why does forced ranking lead to

adverse reactions in employees more than other performance evaluation techniques? The answer to this question is not entirely clear from the literature. One conjecture is that forced ranking causes employees to feel they are being assigned to non-contestable labels versus more descriptive and constructive feedback. Such labels can carry tremendous consequences for an employer when used for decisions regarding layoffs and firings."[31]

The phrase "non-contestable labels" suggests two immediate areas where improvements or clarifications in companies' forced ranking systems will lessen the likelihood that people will believe that the system generated illegally discriminatory results. First, exercise caution in deciding on the labels to be used for the different categories in the forced ranking system. There's a big difference between telling someone who's always received fully satisfactory performance appraisals that she "ended up in the lowest quartile in a comparison with all of her peers," and telling the same individual that in spite of all those years of acceptable appraisals, she's now considered a "poor performer."

Second, consider providing people with the ability to contest the assignment they receive in the process. How should this "appeals process" be structured? We'll consider that question in chapter 4, which focuses on how to set up a forced ranking system that works.

A Closing Word

Over the past few years, hundreds of articles have been published about the use of relative comparison processes—forced ranking systems—in American organizations. Almost uniformly, these articles have focused on the problems and downsides of the approaches. They highlight errors made in systems design and the lawsuits that have sprung from the application of forced ranking system results. Too often they are sprinkled with a one-sided collection of quotations from disgruntled employees and plaintiffs' attorneys. No wonder so few organizations are willing to go on record about their use of the system and the beneficial results it has produced for them.

Forced ranking systems are not panaceas. But every organization that is concerned with ensuring a comprehensive talent management process should well consider implementing a procedure that examines each individual's relative contribution as well as their absolute contribution. Doing so ensures a more well-rounded view of performance and increases the odds that performance excellence will be recognized and rewarded.

But before an organization can realize the rewards of a forced ranking system, it needs to know how to establish a system that works. In the next chapter, I'll explain how to get started.

3

Getting Started

THE OPERATION, IMPLEMENTATION, and mechanics of a forced ranking system must be clearly thought out and skillfully implemented if the procedure is going to be genuinely effective and accurate in identifying the relative contributions made by organization members.

Start with the end in mind. If the organization's only goal is to achieve a fairly limited and clear-cut purpose, like determining how a pot of money available for bonuses should be divvied up among a half-dozen people, it's not hard to assess the relative contribution to overall success each member of the team made. But if the goal is bigger—like identifying the quality of talent throughout the organization—and the population is larger than a mere half dozen, then it's important to think through all of the issues that will affect the system's success. In this chapter, we'll identify the operational issues involving forced ranking, see what alternatives are available, and look at the most effective ways of creating a forced ranking system.

In discussing forced ranking in this chapter, I'll be considering only formal forced ranking procedures that are separate from the organization's performance appraisal system. As we noted earlier, when they talk about forced ranking, many people also include the notion of *forced distribution*—the requirement that performance appraisal ratings meet a predetermined outcome or distribution of scores. That's not our issue here. I'll cover that procedure in Chapter 6 when we explore how to use a forced distribution of appraisal ratings to make conventional performance appraisal systems work more effectively. In this chapter, we'll look at how to create a distinct forced ranking system that operates independently of the company's performance appraisal procedure.

First Things First—Is Your Company Ready?

Forced ranking works well in some cultures, not as well in others. But there are some cultures where the introduction of a forced ranking procedure may not be appropriate at all. "Forced ranking doesn't work well for standing teams," argues Lisa Sprenkle, formerly of Andersen. She offers as an example a major European retailer whose strategy emphasizes teamwork on the sales floor. "Alternatively, project teams, in which groups disband, re-form, and are results-oriented, find that forced ranking works extremely well. Product-design teams and professional service teams follow this model."[1]

What are the cultural attributes that will guarantee the failure of a forced ranking system? If the following characteristics are true of your company, then you should treat forced ranking like poison ivy:

- Employment is considered to be for the duration of one's career.

- Promotions and other organizational rewards are based as much on longevity as on performance.

- Maintaining an atmosphere of niceness is a core cultural value.

- Compassion rather than toughness is the primary response to performance failures.

- Stability is valued more than innovation.

- Length of experience is more important than quality of performance.

- Employees are not used to receiving frank feedback about the quality of their performance, and managers are not encouraged to provide it.

- Senior leadership of the organization wants to keep things just the way they are.

Certainly, this list does not describe the culture found in most organizations and the kind of culture most senior managers want to build or encourage. The fact is that while implementing a forced ranking system should be approached with the same degree of care and circumspection that would be used when installing any potentially disruptive technology, organizations may well be surprised at the high level of acceptability they encounter when introducing a forced ranking system, assuming that the system has been well designed and well communicated. There is a hunger among people for accurate information about their performance. It is likely that every member of the organization is eager to know both what is expected of him and how he is doing at meeting those expectations. Conventional performance appraisal systems answer the first question. Forced ranking can help deliver an honest answer to the second question.

Listen to what Camille Olson and Gregory Davis say in their legal analysis of forced ranking systems: "The leadership of an organization can better sell a ranking program if it is responsive to the needs and desires of the people who will be ranked. Organizations should start by surveying their work force to assess whether employees will support the introduction of forced ranking. A work force that has concerns that top performers are not being recognized, concerns that there are inadequate systems in place to identify developmental opportunities for employees, and feelings that low performers go unrecognized and are allowed to demoralize others in the work force will be more accepting of a relative performance assessment system."[2]

Do a Performance Management Audit

In addition to doing a culture check, it's important to conduct a specific audit of the organization's current performance management practices and results. In conducting this audit, raise these kinds of questions:

- How good a job are managers doing right now at using the company's current performance appraisal system? Are there up-to-date appraisals for almost every employee, with reasonable explanations for the few who do not have recent evaluations in their files? Are appraisals complete and filed on time? Do you get 100 percent uncomplaining compliance?

- How good a job are managers doing right now at talking to their people? Are people getting a clear, unequivocal message about how they are doing, their career prospects in the company, their strengths and weaknesses? Do managers have the courage to have the tough conversations that effective talent management processes, whatever they are, demand?

- Are there particular pockets of leniency or toughness in the organization? In other words, is the average performance appraisal rating given to employees in the sales department about the same as the average rating of employees in manufacturing and accounting, or are some departments far more strict than others in handing out high ratings?

- Is there any evidence of adverse impact in current performance appraisal ratings? Before installing a forced ranking system, it would be wise to check whether employees in a protected class are receiving disproportionately high or low performance appraisal ratings.

- Do performance appraisal results seem to correlate reasonably well with business results? That is, if the Eastern Region of the company is universally acknowledged as the strongest of all, and the results produced by Eastern Region employees are typically better than those produced by people in other regions, are performance appraisal ratings significantly higher for employees in the Eastern region than they are for employees in other parts of the company? (Interestingly, this author's experience is that there is often an *inverse correlation* between performance appraisal results and business results—those organizational units that deliver the best results often have lower-than-average overall performance appraisal ratings, suggesting that managers in these high-performing units have a high level of performance expectations and a toughness about awarding top ratings.)

An Executive Overview

An effective way to begin the introduction of a forced ranking system is to provide an executive overview for the senior management group.

The objective of this presentation, provided by either an external expert or an internal senior human resources manager, is to give the senior leaders of the organization all of the information they need about the forced ranking process so that they can make an informed decision about whether going forward with implementation is appropriate, or whether some other performance management process or tactic is a better way to meet their goals. The individual presenting the overview should describe the experiences of organizations that have adopted a forced ranking approach and the business outcomes it has produced for them. The presentation should lay out all of the decisions that need to be made in creating a system that is specifically suited for their organization, honestly reviewing both the potential risks and rewards and describing various implementation alternatives.

The purpose of the executive overview is not to sell the top management team on the idea of proceeding with a forced ranking system. Rather, it's to provide them with an educational forum, an opportunity to get all of their questions answered, to express openly the doubts and concerns that many of them unquestionably will have. The overview presentation can ensure a common base of understanding among the top management group, so that they make a wise decision about whether to proceed.

Designing the Forced Ranking System

There are a great many critical administrative decisions that must be made in creating a forced ranking process—items like who should be in the ranking pool, how small groups will be handled, what ranking scheme will be used, whether top management will be included in the population to be ranked, what will happen to those ranked at the bottom, what development or other plans will be instituted for those ranked at the top, what information should be given to people about how they came out, and so on. For the system to be successful, all of these questions need to be answered.

One of the first decisions to make is simply what to call the procedure. As we've noted, the term *forced ranking* is often used in a pejorative context. The name alone is enough to cause an adverse reaction from people whose knowledge of the approach comes only from headlines about lawsuits.

Does it need to be called anything at all? Well, yes. If a forced ranking, relative contribution process is going to be a significant aspect of a company's talent management process, it needs to be called *something*.

GE calls its procedure "Session C." Other companies refer to their "talent management process." Texas Instruments refers directly to using a "top ten/bottom ten" approach. One organization I worked with to create a forced ranking system referred to its approach as the "Leadership Assessment Process."

Forced ranking is often used as an element of an organization's succession planning process. In this case, it may be appropriate simply to refer to the procedure as an element of succession planning.

Call it what you will, but make sure that everyone knows what it is that's being referred to.

What Ranking Scheme Should Be Used?

There are half a dozen sorting schemes used by companies for their forced ranking processes. For example, GE, Sun Microsystems, and several other companies use a 20-70-10 (top 20 percent, vital 70 percent, bottom 10 percent) ranking scheme. Texas Instruments and Capital One use a "top 10/bottom 10" approach. Years ago when I worked for PepsiCo, we used a quartiling approach, where managers were asked to identify the top 25 percent, the next 25 percent, the third 25 percent, and the bottom 25 percent. When Dick Brown took over as CEO of EDS a few years ago, he installed a quintiling system—top 20 percent, and so on. Before it disintegrated, Enron used a complex six-level system. And some organizations, for small groups, use a straightforward rank-ordering procedure: 1, 2, 3, 4, 5, . . . and so on.

20-70-10. The best-known approach is that used by GE and trumpeted by Jack Welch. On an annual basis, senior executives get together for a full-day Session C meeting. It's held in April at every major business location. Armed with binders that contain complete dossiers on everyone to be assessed—photograph, time in position, performance appraisal history, long-term potential assessment, perceived strengths and weaknesses, and self-assessment—managers review, analyze, and debate the quality of talent under review. Each person is evaluated not only on an absolute basis in terms of their delivery of results, but also on a relative basis against GE's four Es—high *energy* level, the ability to *energize* others around common goals, the *edge* to make tough yes-and-no decisions, and the ability to consistently *execute* and deliver on their promises.[3] Diversity concerns are factored into the discussions, but the emphasis is squarely on talent and stretch.

These sessions can be heated and emotionally intense—jobs, careers, opportunities, promotional possibilities are on the line. Pluses and minuses, strengths and weaknesses of every individual under review are honestly and minutely analyzed. The outcome: a decision about whether the individual belongs in the top 20 percent of the executives under review, the vital 70 percent, or the bottom 10 percent.

The GE model was also adopted by Sun Microsystems. In March 2001, Sun Microsystems launched a ranking of all forty-three thousand employees. The categories are 20 percent Superior, 70 percent Sun Standard, and 10 percent Underperforming.

In making the assessments, Sun divides the employee population into groups of about thirty. Those who end up in the bottom are given ninety days to improve. If they remain in the bottom 10 percent, they get a one-time chance to resign and take severance pay. Those who choose to stay are given another chance, but "if it doesn't work out," they will be fired without severance, spokeswoman Diane Carlini says. "This ensures that employees who elect to stay are committed to get better."[4]

The 20-70-10 ranking scheme has some obvious advantages. First, it's tried-and-true. Many companies have settled on this distribution scheme, and their experience is beneficial to others. GE, in fact, originally ranked employees on a 1-to-5 scale but revised its rating scheme after discovering that almost everyone except the top 10 percent felt demoralized. By providing that the vast majority, 70 percent, would get the middle grade (and rewarding some of them with stock options), it made the process more palatable.[5]

Second, a 20-70-10 ranking scheme inherently recognizes that there are more people at the positive end of the curve than there are at the lower end. Using a ranking scheme that allows for twice as many people to be put in the top category as in the bottom category appeals to the belief of most organization members that the talent pool in their company does not mirror a standard bell-shaped curve; that there are more great performers than there are weak ones.

Quartiling. Thirty years ago, when I headed the training and development function for Frito-Lay, we used a process that was remarkably similar in its structure to that of GE and Sun, but with a significantly different outcome distribution. On an annual basis, well after the performance appraisal process had been completed, senior managers gathered for manpower reviews. In these sessions information about the performance and potential of each individual being reviewed was presented, discussed, and debated. The rigorous process was supported by a spreadsheet of information on each person that extended almost three feet across the conference table. (Colloquially, it was referred to by session participants as the "BAF"—the "big-ass form.")

The outcome, though, was not a 20-70-10 allocation. PepsiCo at that time used quartiling. The entire population of managers and executives under review was assigned into one of four equal-sized buckets—top 25 percent, next 25 percent, third 25 percent, and bottom 25 percent. Andy Pearson, PepsiCo's president at the time and the primary driver of the process, argued the importance of the rigorous process in a *Harvard Business Review* article in which he discussed the need for top executives to demand frank and honest talent assessments from the senior managers reporting to them. He talked about the need for a hands-on approach to talent management from the top: "Going through the process, unit by unit and manager by manger, is obviously hard work, but there is no easy way to establish and enforce tougher performance standards and focus everyone's attention on management development. I should add that the work is not only time-consuming, but also emotionally charged. It leads to heated discussions, especially early on, when standards are likely to differ widely."[6]

But the problem, Pearson points out in explaining the rationale for the quartiling approach, is that unless they are forced to do otherwise, managers, even at very senior levels, are likely to inflate the ratings of those on their team:

> You must be willing to engage in frank, tough-minded discussions of each manager's weaknesses—and you must convince each person to use equal candor with subordinates. You are likely to find that many executives are initially either unwilling or unable to give you useful staff evaluations. For example, a division manager might say that everyone in the division is doing a pretty good job. If this happens, you will have to

bear down and force the manager to draw distinctions—say, to identify who the single-best performer is. It is also helpful to ask the executive to categorize the managers into four groups, from poor to superior, and then ask for a specific plan for the people in each group. Always focus first on the bottom group. The manager should specify who should be replaced, who should be reassigned, and when these decisions will be implemented. Rooting out the poorest performers will foster a climate of continual improvement. If everyone in the bottom quartile is replaced, the third quartile becomes the new bottom group and the focus of subsequent improvement efforts.[7]

The quartiling approach (25-25-25-25) offers some significant benefits:

Quartiling forces harder decision making. The 10 or 20 percent of employees who are truly water walkers are usually fairly well known and relatively easy to identify. The bottom 10 percent are also fairly easy to spot. It's harder to identify the top and bottom quarter of the population, and for the half that are in the middle, to determine whether they're in the top or bottom half.

Quartiling reduces weak managers' ability to wiggle out of the process. If a top 10/bottom 10 approach or a 20-70-10 scheme is used, a spineless manager can lump all her troops in the middle and be done with it. Quartiling forces real decision making. There's no obvious middle into which a weak manager can dump everyone and be done with it.

Quartiling is unexpected. Most managers at senior levels are probably somewhat familiar with forced ranking and have heard references to either a top 10/bottom 10 approach or the 20-70-10 system. When managers discover that the company plans to use a quartiling process, they are likely to give their decisions about who's where more attention.

Quintiling. Quintiling, a similar procedure that substitutes five equal-sized buckets for PepsiCo's four, was adopted by data services company Electronic Data Systems (EDS), which Ross Perot founded. EDS regularly divides its employees into five groups, or quintiles, the *Dallas Morning News* reported in an article describing the company's use of the procedure in order to make layoff decisions. "Those in the highest quintile are rewarded with better compensation and resources to do their jobs, while those in the lowest group are encouraged to improve or leave."[8]

10/10. A 10-80-10 distribution is demanded by many organizations, including one of America's largest manufacturers, a major credit card firm, and numerous others. Here managers are required to identify the top 10 percent, the middle 80 percent, and the bottom 10 percent. In these organizations, the system's intent is to spotlight that small minority of employees on both tails of the bell curve who either have the highest potential for rapid development and promotion or who must immediately move up or out.

However, one large technology firm that had been using a 10/10 approach for several years switched in 2004 to a scheme that mirrored a 20-70-10 approach. The change happened when HR managers from different divisions discovered in comparing notes after their units had completed their forced ranking sessions that several groups of rankers independently reported that the process worked better for them if they identified not only the top 10 percent but also the next 10 percent of their talent. They then made the new "top 10, next 10, bottom 10" allocation official.

1 to 5. At Microsoft, employees are ranked from 1 to 5, the majority receiving a grade between 2.5 and 4.5. While no absolute percentage distribution is officially required, managers must meet a bell-curve expectation. "Under a performance and compensation approach that Bill developed in Microsoft's early days, managers give employees numerical performance ratings, which closely follow a bell-shaped curve," according to Bob Herbold, Microsoft's former COO. "The system ensures that star employees are disproportionately rewarded, and it forces managers to constructively deal with poor performers."[9] (But even at Microsoft, universally acknowledged as one of America's toughest-minded talent meritocracies, Herbold often found the forced ranking process a hard sell to reluctant managers. "They would frequently contend that the bell-shaped-curve approach is unfair, even with some built-in flexibility in meeting target percentages for each rating. Since the company hires the cream of the crop, these managers maintained, everyone should get a high rating.")[10]

MetLife also uses the 1-to-5-scale approach to relative comparison. MetLife measures employees and managers by comparing each person to others who are on the same level. Employees are measured on a 1-to-5 scale. The company then calculates which employees are at the top, in the middle, and at the bottom.[11]

In spite of the controversy over forced ranking, MetLife is sticking with the system, according to senior vice president of HR and chief learning officer Deb Capolarello, since the company does a good job of explaining to employees what they need to do to improve their performance. "As an employee, you want to know where you stand, how you did, and how you can improve," she says, adding that her system does just that. "Employees are rated one, two, three, four, or five. A four or five employee can receive about 40 percent in total compensation more than a three."[12]

Stack ranking and totem poling. An alternative forced ranking approach is to actually make the relative comparison individual by individual. In this case, managers are asked to look at their team and identify who's number 1, who's number 2, and so on until the bottom of the stack is reached. In other words, it's a totem-pole approach, with one (and only one) person at the very top, with one (and only one) immediately beneath her, followed by another one (and only one) beneath him, and so on down the pole.

Rank-order rating is the simplest form of employee comparison: the assessor simply ranks all employees from best to worst. Ranking is typically facilitated by providing assessors with a pack of cards, one for each employee. Deal them out in front of you; put them into the right order.

Rank-order rating has the advantage of simplicity and can be used easily when there is a small number of people to be ranked, all of whom the ranker or rankers know well. Large engineering organizations are likely to use this kind of ranking for all their engineers. But it is difficult to keep the performance of many employees in mind at one time. Using a pure rank-order scheme is also difficult since the procedure usually involves a number of managers ranking their employees separately and then amalgamating their lists into a master list. While this can be done by having all participants meet together with their boss acting as arbitrator, the likelihood of gaining agreement among a number of individual managers on specific rank order is slim.

Finally, anytime there are more than a half-dozen people to be ranked, not only does the number of possible combinations grow exponentially, but the probability of accuracy in any single rating is reduced ("Does George rank 33 or 34 in my group of 41?"—a foolish question).[13]

While rank ordering may be workable if the group is small, it's almost impossibly unwieldy if a large number of individuals are under review. A mathematician will tell you that if a dozen people are in the group being totem-poled, the number of different pole positions will be 12 factorial, or $12 \times 11 \times 10 \times 9 \ldots \times 2 \times 1$, or 479,001,600. Over four hundred million ways to rank just 12 people? Better stick with buckets.

Finally, there are some notoriously bad ideas in the forced ranking toolkit: desert island exercises or lifeboat decisions. In these hare-brained procedures, managers are told to evaluate their troops against the criterion of who they would most like to be stuck on a desert island with or who they would most like to have next to them in a lifeboat. This is silliness. Almost equally silly, but with some redeeming features if explained and used appropriately, is a forced ranking drill with the criterion being the person or people you would choose to take with you if you were forming your own company. The assumption here is that since the evaluator will now, hypothetically at least, be the one whose signature appears on the paycheck, he or she will be more circumspect in selecting only the best to be the recipients. The difficulty, of course, is that the skills required for a brand-new company start-up are not perfectly parallel to those required to keep a Microsoft or Sun or PepsiCo running in top form. Besides, with the eternal shortage of outstanding talent, why would organizations want to plant the seed in the minds of their most gifted that they should be considering leaving the organizational fold?

While we'll say no more about voting for who you'd most like to spend some desert-island time with, note that all the approaches described earlier, bucket-based or individual-based, have a similar goal—to compare the performance of members of a group with each other based on various criteria to determine the relative quality of each individual's performance, contribution, and/or potential. Remember, the issue is relative comparison: it's not how well the person performed her job; it's how well she performed her job compared with how well everybody else performed theirs.

It's also important to recognize that with the exception of individual ranking (totem poling), all the distribution schemes described earlier have one factor in common. Whatever their allotment mechanism—quartiling, quintiling, top 10/bottom 10, 20-70-10, or some other allocation—groups of employees are plunked into various big buckets without any further separation made within the bucket. In other words, if you're a GE manager who's under review in a Session C meeting, and the deliberation about your performance and potential results in your being placed in the "vital 70 percent" category, there is no further formal substratification that determines whether you're at the top of the bucket and almost into the top 20 percent category, or at the lower end of the bucket having just barely escaped being assigned into the bottom 10 percent category. While it's likely that this information will have been thoroughly discussed in the meeting and will be communicated to you when the results are reviewed, the system doesn't demand any finer granularity.

What all of these systems have in common is that they bunch the employee population under review into groups—they don't drill down to the individual level of granularity and literally determine that George is better than Betty but not as good as Bob. But if the organization decides that it will let employees know how they came out in the ranking sessions, it will be helpful to give managers different scripts to use to tell someone who just missed getting into the top 10 category versus announcing the results to another individual who just barely missed being assigned into the bottom bucket. You'll find those scripts in appendix A.

Determining the actual numbers. Another consideration in determining the ranking scheme is not only what ranking format to use, but how the percentages will translate into actual numbers of people in each category. For example, in a group of forty-seven, will there be four or five people assigned to the bottom 10 percent? It's important to get this resolved in advance of the ranking session so that the question about whether there will be four or five people placed in the bottom category is not a function of who the specific individuals are.

How rigidly must the ranking scheme be followed? Some organizations take a hard line and insist that 20 percent, for example, means exactly 20 percent. Their policy is that except for the unavoidable rounding off discussed earlier that is required to translate percentages into actual numbers of people, the distribution requirements be precisely met. Others are more flexible, and argue that it really doesn't make much difference if, in a 20-70-10 scheme, for example, you end up with the top 23 percent and the bottom 8 percent. "There's no point in driving to absolute precision on this," the HR manager of a large technology corporation told me. Their top 10/bottom 10 system in 2004 ended up with an actual distribution of 14 percent in the "top 10" group and 8 percent in the bottom.

In general, I find that it's better to be fairly firm on the requirement that the actual distribution requirements be met, since once you allow top 10/bottom 10 to become "top 14/bottom 8," managers participating in the ranking sessions will push to greatly expand the percentage allowed in the top group and reduce to nothing the percentage required for the bottom. This is particularly true in the first year of the forced ranking system, since managers will be likely to test to see how firm the organization really is about "this forced ranking business." It's also likely that in the first year of operation, there will be little problem in identifying a bottom 10 percent, or whatever the ranking scheme requires. In further years, once those ranked at the bottom have either significantly improved or have moved on to positions that are better fits, and once managers have gained more experience with the process, it may be appropriate to allow a degree of flexibility in meeting the distribution requirements.

What Criteria Should Be Used for the Ranking Process?

"George is better than Mary but not as good as Sam." A true statement? It depends on the criteria being used to evaluate the three of them.

After several attempts, GE settled on the "Four E's" as the criteria against which all of their managers and executives are ranked: High *energy* level, the ability to *energize* others around common goals, the *edge* to make tough yes/no decisions, and the ability to consistently *execute* and deliver on promises. While the Session C discussions cover a lot more aspects of the individual being reviewed, these four attributes are the constant yardstick against which each individual is measured.

For a company just beginning the forced ranking process, one alternative is simply to use the same four E's that GE, the company that has been most successful in using a forced ranking procedure, uses. The benefits of simply taking a cut-and-paste approach are that GE has invested a great deal of intellectual energy and trial-and-error efforts in coming up with these four as workable ranking criteria. The four criteria are unarguably important to the success of anyone in a significant management position. The meanings are easily and immediately understood by almost everyone. Data about the third criterion ("the edge to make tough yes/no decisions") will be reflected by an individual's behavior in the ranking sessions and will thus influence people to increase their toughness in their decision making. Finally, if it's good enough for General Electric . . .

On the other hand, your company isn't GE. Just because these four are right for General Electric doesn't mean that they are right for any other organization. No definitions or descriptions of mastery performance are provided. Borrowing a set of competencies from an unrelated organization, no matter how admired that organization may be, may suggest that your firm can't do world-class stuff on its own. Simply lifting a set of criteria, whether from GE or anyone else, is probably not the right path.

Other organizations use their core values or cultural competencies as the criteria for making ranking decisions. FedEx, for example, has identified nine personal attributes that they define with remarkable specificity and rate aspiring leaders on the extent to which they possess these attributes. The FedEx leadership attributes are charisma, individual consideration, intellectual stimulation, courage, dependability, flexibility, integrity, judgment, and respect for others.[14] If a company has determined a set of leadership competencies or core values, it makes sense to consider using that list as the criteria in a forced ranking process. In fact, there is probably no better way for a company to communicate that it is serious about its competencies or core values than to use them as the primary determinants in ranking the troops.

But the FedEx list is long, as is the list from most other companies that have developed their sets of competencies. It may become unwieldy to use so long a list as the basis for evaluation in a forced ranking procedure, particularly when people are likely to score very highly on one attribute and further down the development scale on another. How do you determine whether Mary should be ranked higher than Jim, when she's terrific at individual consideration but stumbles when it comes to charisma, while he's as charismatic as Al Sharpton but has the integrity of a Bernie Ebbers?

When you look over your company's list of competencies or core values, you may find that the list is just too long to use as is as the criteria for a forced ranking system. Or the competency list may not lend itself to being used as a set of criteria for forced ranking, or may not reflect what genuinely is important for success at the organization today and in the future. But if you have identified a set of competencies, it's wise to see if it can work as the basis for making forced ranking decisions. Using existing competencies, revised to make them work for forced ranking purposes, sends an appropriate message of consistency about what's really important in your company. Developing an entirely unrelated set may send a mixed message.

Check your mission statement, too. It may be that your organization has developed a mission statement or vision and values statement that genuinely reflects the ideals and principles of top management. If you have, then certainly it should be used for forced ranking purposes, since doing so will demonstrate that the organization is serious and is putting its money where its mouth is. Consider the core values statement of InteCap, the international consulting firm specializing in intellectual property and complex commercial disputes. Among them are these five:

Responding to clients' needs is our top priority.

Creativity is an integral part of each assignment.

Teamwork is vital to our execution.

Our firm is designed as a meritocracy for a reason. Professional advancement is based exclusively on engagement performance, leadership abilities, and economic contributions to the firm's success.

Enthusiasm is a necessity to employee and client satisfaction.[15]

Assuming that they're serious, these five core values could easily be recast as criterion statements for evaluating performance and potential in a forced ranking activity.

One of the InteCap values is teamwork. In determining the criteria to use for a forced ranking system, it's particularly important to consider including teamwork or some similar attribute. Not only is teamwork considered a key contributor to success in many organizations, but one of the most consistent objections to forced ranking is that the procedure necessarily damages teamwork and, to believe the more strident adversaries of the process, invariably generates a hostile dog-eat-dog environment where it's every man for himself. For example, *Fortune* magazine columnist Anne Fisher, in her "Ask Annie" column on reader reaction to an earlier article on the GE process, reports, "The consensus: It fosters cutthroat competition, paranoia, and general ill will, and destroys employee loyalty."[16]

Is this true? If a forced ranking system is badly designed and clumsily installed, of course it will generate adverse results, as will the imposition of any other ham-fisted and insensitive procedure. But systems that are effectively designed and implemented generate none of the hysterical reports of hostility and antagonism. I can tell you that in thirty years of working with these systems, I have yet to see one that has the power to create this kind of organizational disruption. But because this is a frequently asserted objection, it can easily be quashed by making teamwork or cooperation with others one of the attributes considered in making ranking decisions.

Another frequent objection to forced ranking is that it merely rewards those who are good at sucking up to the boss, rather than those who genuinely are outstanding performers. Once again, while I have often heard this objection expressed, my experience is the opposite. I have consistently seen individuals under review in forced ranking sessions downgraded in their assessments strictly because they engage in this (to use an old-fashioned term) apple-polishing behavior. Managers can distinguish the suck-ups from those with genuinely effective interpersonal skills, and it's important that the process of comparing one person with another not reward those who advance by playing politics. Peter Drucker said it best:

> Executives often cannot judge whether a strategic move is a wise one. Nor are they necessarily interested. "I don't know why we are buying this business in Australia, but it won't interfere with what we are doing here in Fort Worth" is a common reaction. But when the same executives read that "Joe Smith has been made controller in the XYZ division," they usually know Joe much better than top management does. These executives should be able to say, "Joe deserves the promotion; he is an excellent choice—just the person that division needs to get the controls appropriate for its rapid growth."

If however, Joe got promoted because he is a politician, everybody will know it. They will all say to themselves, "Okay, that is the way to get ahead in this company." They will despise their management for forcing them to become politicians themselves in the end. As we have known for a long time, people in organizations tend to behave as they see others being rewarded. And when the rewards go to nonperformance, to flattery, or to mere cleverness, the organization will soon decline into nonperformance, flattery, or cleverness.[17]

Should the various criteria be weighted? Probably not. While some of the criteria may be more or less important in some positions than others, as a practical matter an absolute weighting system may not lead to the best decisions. More important, assigning weights to the various ranking criteria may reduce the forced ranking process to the solving of an arithmetic problem. Assessors will now have to come up not only with objective analyses of the performance and potential of each individual under review, but also perform a multiplication exercise to determine the person's final standing. Shaky in theory, weighting is almost impossible in practice.

It's possible that when the organization determines the criteria that will be used for a forced ranking process and announces them, people may complain that these expectations are being sprung on them without notice, and, unlike the goals and objectives they were given at the start of the year, they are now being unfairly held to standards of which they were previously unaware. This complaint, of course, has little validity. The criteria that organizations choose for use in a forced ranking process will be those that any reasonable person will understand as appropriate behavioral expectations of a person working for an employer. It is both appropriate and fully legal for any employer to review its workforce and use any reasonable criteria to assess which members turn in the best performance and have the highest potential for making even greater contributions in the future.

The reason for identifying specific criteria against which everyone in the ranking pool will be assessed is to ensure a level playing field, to make certain that similar standards are used in reviewing each individual being assessed. But requiring participants in ranking sessions to restrict their discussions of an individual's performance and potential to only a limited list of predetermined criteria is unnecessarily restrictive. Worse, this rigid restriction is unfair to all of the people being reviewed, since there's a lot more to them—positive and negative—than just how well they do against a set of formal criteria. What else should be discussed besides the formal assessment criteria?

The discussions in a forced ranking session almost invariably include a review of each individual's specific strengths and weaknesses. Since the purpose of a forced ranking exercise is to identify the talent bench-strength of the organization and make sure that appropriate talent management decisions are made, it would be imprudent not to discuss the areas of great strength possessed by each person under review as well as the areas where that person needs to grow and change and develop.

This is particularly true since there will be several people discussing each of the people being ranked in the session. The individual's immediate supervisor will almost certainly be present and, in most cases, will do the lion's share of making the presentation about the person. Other people in the room with experience with the individual under discussion will also have experiences to contribute. Others in the room may not know the person all that well, but perhaps have had one or two telling interactions that shed additional light on performance and potential. There is no better opportunity to get a well-rounded picture of how well the person performs, and how much potential the individual possesses, than by having senior executives talk with each other about their personal experiences with the individual under review.

So in addition to establishing a set of specific criteria for the ranking procedure, rankers should be encouraged to raise and thrash out other performance factors in the discussions that produce the final ranking decisions:

Specific pluses and minuses. In addition to comparing each individual against the set of criteria determined, evaluators should be asked to identify two or three significant strengths of each individual and one or two major liabilities or shortcomings. Everyone has both; most of the population making up any organization's middle and senior management group will have more of the former than the latter. Forcing identification of significant strengths and weaknesses also helps identify the people-reading skills of those making the assessments.

Intellectual horsepower/conceptual thinking ability/smarts. While this is a very sensitive area to consider, psychometric research consistently confirms that intellectual horsepower (IQ) is about the best independent predictor of success in sophisticated and complex jobs. The ranking system participants need to take into account how smart the individual is.

Stretch projection. The evaluators should come to a consensus on the number of major organization levels the individual is capable of moving to. It's important, though, to recognize that projecting any further than two or three years out not only may be unsupportable, it can raise some questions about age discrimination. Asking rankers to consider how far someone can go over the next twenty years does an obvious disservice to those who are in their fifties, compared with those in their thirties. Limiting discussions of potential to a foreseeable two- or three-year window is a wiser course.

Past year's transformational results. The best predictor of future performance is past performance. It's a good idea for the evaluators to identify in their discussions of each person what (if anything) the individual did in the previous twelve months to transform the function or to significantly change the results of his or her unit. This is not the same as how well the person performed against predetermined objectives, which should be captured by performance appraisal results. Here the focus is on the things the person may have done that demonstrate a capability of transforming the job or organizational unit.

A final thought about criteria: do you even need to come up with a set of specific criteria at all? While it is common for an organization to develop a specific set of criteria for its forced ranking process, and it's particularly important when a company is first installing the procedure to have a clearly articulated set of criteria that will be used to compare individual A against B and C, once the use of the process has become familiar and mature, it may no longer be necessary to hold to a rigid set of criteria for assessment purposes. "Our criteria used to be 'flexible, curious, and collaborative,'" an HR executive with a large technology company that has been using the process for many years told me. "Now it's just 'right results, right behaviors.'"

"Right results, right behaviors" is probably the ultimate criterion for any forced ranking system. It's certainly useful to give managers specific criteria that they're expected to use in making their ranking decisions, particularly the first time around. But in the final analysis, all that rankers are being asked to determine is who delivers the best results and has the most potential, and who delivers the least.

How Often Should We Use the Procedure?

In most organizations that use a forced ranking process, the ranking sessions are conducted on an annual basis. They are typically scheduled separately from the company's performance appraisal system. Scheduling the forced ranking sessions to be held at a different time of year from the time of performance appraisal has several advantages. It reduces the apparent workload on managers by separating the two events by several months. It helps to ensure that the rankers focus on the entirely separate questions that the two procedures ask. (That is, performance appraisal essentially asks, "How well did George do in achieving his objectives?" Forced ranking asks, "How well did George do compared with Mary and Bob?" The answers to the two questions can be strikingly different for the same individual.) If the forced ranking process is used to make compensation decisions, it reduces the perceived lockstep linkage between one's performance appraisal rating and one's merit increase percentage, while still reinforcing the notion of pay-for-performance. Finally, forced ranking provides an independent evaluation of the accuracy and consistency of performance appraisal ratings.

The forced ranking system, however, should be well integrated and aligned with other talent management systems and processes, and the data produced by the exercise should supplement and provide useful perspectives for other areas of talent and performance management. As the authors of Sibson Consulting's study of forced ranking note:

> All people-related systems—performance evaluations, development activity, high-potential identification, salary planning, succession planning, advancement discussions and managed attrition—should place people in roughly the same position as would a forced ranking exercise. In other words, consistent performance messages run throughout the various people-related systems. If forced ranking is being used solely as a means to understand which employees fit into which performance buckets, and it is the only tool to do this, then its use is simply a band-aid put in place to correct other deficiencies in the performance management

system. The implicit messages from the results of the process should not contradict the explicit performance messages employees are receiving via other channels. Likewise, there should be clear alignment between the outcome of the forced ranking process and consequences received through other performance management means.[18]

The other issue regarding the scheduling of the forced ranking process involves the company's long-term intentions for the procedure. Is forced ranking intended to be used as a one-time event to achieve a specific end, or does senior management anticipate that this procedure will be a way of life, repeated annually in the future?

One consideration in making the annual event/way of life decision is to recognize that the effectiveness of forced ranking may diminish after several iterations, particularly when the expectation is that those employees assigned to the bottom category will be terminated. Virtually every organization can identify a bottom 10 percent whose departure will be beneficial. The following year, with last year's 10 percent gone, the organization digs a little deeper, and managers become more resistant to cutting loose people who now end up in the bottom group. And as Jack Welch has noted about GE's Session C's: "By the third year, it's war."[19] The senior leadership needs to analyze whether this is a war worth fighting. It may well be that a rigorous forced ranking system has a natural life span of three or four years in most organizations, after which the procedure might be shelved until it's needed again.

Who Should Be in the Ranking Pool?

Should the forced ranking system review everyone in the organization? Only people in exempt or managerial positions? What about professional individual contributors, like engineers, or systems analysts, or HR specialists and auditors? Should top executives be exempt from review in the ranking procedure?

Obviously, the more people who are included, the more complicated and time-consuming the process will be. And while some organizations, like Sun, evaluate everyone on an annual basis, it makes better sense for the forced ranking process in most companies to be limited to those who have the greatest impact on overall organizational success. In other words, start from the top and work down.

Among commentators on the forced ranking process, there is solid agreement that no matter who is included, top management must necessarily be part of the pool. Camille Olson and Gregory Davis, in exploring the legal aspects of forced ranking for a Society for Human Resource Management legal report, write, "In implementing any ranking scheme, an organization must decide who should be included in the ranking, i.e., whether it should include the entire work force, only management, or only above a specific level of management. In explaining the demise of its ranking system, Ford believes that it attempted to include too may employees—18,000 of its managers—in the system. One solution, which may also foster better cultural acceptance, is to first apply the ranking system to top management. After two or three years, if the program succeeds, it can be applied to a larger population of managers."[20] And the authors of a similar legal study, prepared for the Association of Corporate Counsel, give virtually the same advice: "Regardless of your company's purpose in using forced ranking, such a system should be introduced to your workforce gradually, beginning with top management."[21] If senior managers are exempt from the process, then it is likely to be seen as unfair, particularly if there are a couple of senior officers who have been Peter Principled into positions beyond their capability.

How far down in the organization should the process go? It makes sense to answer this question by looking at two things: salary bands and individual professional contributor roles.

Salary bands. Most organizations have developed a salary band structure as part of their compensation system. Starting with the highest salary band, senior managers and HR professionals should discuss and decide the point where forced ranking's payoff is dissipated because of the large number of people involved. By starting at the top and moving down a certain number of salary bands, the organization makes sure that all of the people who have the greatest influence over organizational success are included in the review process. It also demonstrates that the great rewards that are enjoyed by people at the top are accompanied by greater risks, too: at these exalted levels one's performance is subject to even greater scrutiny than it is at lower levels. In other words, people earn the right to be included in a forced ranking process by attaining a certain high level in the organizational hierarchy.

Individual contributor roles. In addition to including the highest-paid members of the organization, who typically tend to be in managerial or executive positions, in most companies there are also a large number of people in specialist, individual-contributor positions: engineers, graphic artists, lawyers, geologists, programmers, and so on. It may be useful to expand the forced ranking process to include people in these positions, particularly when a company has a large number of people doing essentially similar jobs. As I noted earlier, the relative contribution made by a top performer, even in fairly low-level jobs, is significantly greater than that made by his average-performing colleague, let alone that made by a poor performer. If a company has a large population of software designers, for example, it only makes sense for the forced ranking process to assess the relative contributions made by the members of this group.

Another concern with ranking pools involves the size of the pool. If the pools are small—a dozen people or fewer—it's hard to meet a requirement like 20-70-10. On the other hand, if pools are large, the amount of time required for full evaluations of each person under review may become unreasonable.

One solution to the problem of having to review and rank an extremely large number of people can be achieved through "roll-ups," a procedure where ranking decisions made about small groups are rolled up and reviewed by senior managers who look at larger groups and adjust rankings to ensure both an appropriate distribution and assessment accuracy. But rolling up brings with it the concern that decisions about people's relative performance and potential will be made by senior executives who don't actually know them. In analyzing this process for the *WorldatWork Journal*, Michael O'Malley argues that it in fact leads to better decisions being made: "Companies can 'roll up' managers' performance evaluations. This is where evaluations undergo successive reviews at higher levels in the organization. This forces managers to be deliberate and thorough in their evaluations and performance summaries or else risk embarrassment, as they and their reviews will undergo scrutiny by superiors. The process seldom leads to significant modifications in overall assessments partly because the assessments are of higher quality because of the process. The true virtue of performance roll-ups, however, is that [they add] the cost of accountability to managerial judgments—creating more discriminating observations."[22]

Who Should Do the Ranking?

In most cases, it is fairly apparent who should be in the room when the forced ranking discussion is taking place. Obviously, the individual's immediate supervisor will be there, as well as the supervisors of people who hold similar positions. Others who know the person well or have important incidental information to contribute should be there. In addition, there may be others present who may have no knowledge of the person under review. These "strangers" can provide a valuable service by making sure that the rules of the game are followed and by asking for specific examples if generalized assertions about the individual being reviewed are made.

It's also important that the HR manager or specialists serving the functions whose people are being reviewed take an active part. The HR manager's role will be twofold. First, to be a provider of information just as anyone else taking part in the discussion. Second, to make sure that the rules are followed; that inappropriate comments are pointed out and people are reminded of the serious nature of the undertaking; and that serious attention is given to every person under review, particularly when the heavy emotional load that always occurs in a forced ranking session begins to result in rater fatigue.

Since it's hard to wear two hats in a forced ranking session, it's wise to use a separate facilitator to run the ranking sessions. If the facilitator is an expert on forced ranking from outside the company, even better: there can be no arguments that the facilitator unduly influenced the outcome of a discussion in favor of (or against) a particular individual or had any axe to grind other than ensuring a fair and equitable process.

It's likely that many of the participants in a forced ranking session will be unfamiliar with some of the people under review. They are not discharged of any responsibility, however. Even when they have no knowledge of the person being discussed, they are expected to be engaged in the process by asking questions and seeking specific examples. In addition, one of the great benefits of a forced ranking process is that it informs senior leaders about the existence of talent in the organization that they have, until now, been unaware of. Conducting forced ranking sessions opens up opportunities for the most talented members of the organization by exposing their capabilities to executives in other parts of the organization who now can consider them when promotional opportunities arise.

What Information Should Be Provided to Rankers?

In many companies, participants in ranking meetings are given binders with information on all of the executives to be reviewed: brief biographies, a photograph, title, time in position. Other companies add the last one or two performance appraisals (either the complete appraisal or the summary page) and full demographic information.

Since one of the purposes of a forced ranking process, in addition to identifying A, B, and C players, is to make sure that senior managers in the organization have a greater understanding of where the talent in the company is, it makes sense to provide briefing books that are as complete as possible. In this way an executive from another division, listening in on the discussion of an individual whom he does not know, can look at the photo and say, "Oh, yes. That's John Smith. I've met him briefly two or three times. I'm going to pay more attention to him in the future."

But assembling comprehensive briefing books is a major administrative chore. And there's another caution, perhaps excessive, about providing photographs and demographic information. A company that was about to initiate the first iteration of a new forced ranking process asked its outside counsel to review all of its plans to help spot any potential problems. He wrote:

> The step-by-step implementation plan states that a briefing book will include a photograph and demographic information about each of the individuals to be evaluated. Rankers should be reminded continually to make decisions without regard to race, gender, age, etc. and, therefore, demographic information and photograph should not be included. Presumably, each ranker should know who the people are they are evaluating by name, without the need to resort to a picture, but, if for some reason someone did not know and a picture was thought to be useful, that person could be shown a picture or otherwise have the person described to him.[23]

The concern about making sure that decisions made in the process are free of reference to race, age, or gender is certainly legitimate. And one of the least discussed rating errors is "attractiveness effect," the well-documented tendency for people to assume that those who are physically attractive are also superior performers. However, deciding not to provide a photograph or other demographic information under the assumption that everyone who will be discussing the individual will know the individual, and, if that's not the case, a picture can discretely be shown, seems like legalistic overkill. In addition, it negates the benefit of giving people in the ranking session a broader understanding of the talent pool of the company by letting them see what the cream of the crop looks like. It is also possible that by seeing pictures of every person under review, the rankers will be even more sensitive to issues of race and age and gender than they otherwise would be. In any event, this specific issue of providing pictures is one that any organization about to proceed with developing a forced ranking process should review with its legal counsel.

What Should We Communicate About the Ranking System—and to Whom?

Earlier I argued in favor of a "no secrets, no surprises" approach to forced ranking. In spite of the fact that the process has received bad press and while there might be an initial negative reaction to its implementation in an organization, trying to keep the system's existence secret will only serve to exacerbate any concerns about the organization's good-faith efforts to make sure that the most talented contributors get what they deserve. And from a practical point of view, it's probably fruitless to try to keep the installation of a forced ranking system a secret, and the misinformation and rumors surrounding the "secret system" will be far more damaging than the truth might possibly be.

How should the system be announced? If it will not apply to everyone in the organization, it makes little sense to provide a companywide, all-inclusive communications effort, since only a fraction of the employees will be affected by the procedure. However, a companywide communications effort, directed even at those who will be neither rankers nor rankees, can have the beneficial outcome of demonstrating to the people at the bottom of the hierarchy that those at the top are subject to greater scrutiny and to being terminated if their performance lags behind that of others. Either way, it does make sense for there to be a targeted communications effort, coming directly from the top, aimed directly at the two groups with a personal stake in the process—the rankers and the rankees.

A memo or an e-mail will probably be sufficient to announce that the company will be using a relative comparison evaluation system, particularly if another aspect of the total communication plan is the training of those who will participate in the ranking sessions. It's best that the memo to those who will be in the pools of employees being ranked come from the CEO and that it cover the following items:

- A statement that the company has decided to adopt a forced ranking procedure as part of its performance management processes

- The reason why the company has made the decision to use a forced ranking system and the benefits to the organization as a whole and to the individuals whose performance will be reviewed

- The ranking scheme (top 10/bottom 10, 20-70-10, quartiling, etc.) that will be used

- The criteria that will be used to make ranking decisions

- A brief summary of the program's mechanics

- A statement of endorsement or personal commitment to the goals of the forced ranking procedure

The memo to the managers and executives who will serve as rankers (most of whom will probably also be rankees) might cover the preceding items, an announcement of the training planned, and a clear message about how the CEO expects those with ranking responsibility to meet their obligations.

In appendix A, I have provided the actual memos sent by the CEO of a large consumer goods firm to the rankers and rankees to initiate the procedure at his company. While I have changed the name of the company to "Acme Services Company," the memos are the actual ones received by everyone involved in the process.

Should People Be Told How They Came Out in the Process?

There are valid arguments on both sides of the question of "coming clean." The advantages of disclosing ranking results to the individual are these:

- People identified as high-potential may be more willing to stick it out for the long term in spite of short-term career disappointments. It can be an effective retention tactic.

- Being forthright about an individual's high potential may encourage his or her manager to be more forthright about the individual's development needs, shortcomings, and possible derailers.

- There will be a strong natural curiosity that will need to be assuaged since most of the evaluators will also be evaluatees.

- Most organizations and most people feel that being up front about an individual's perceived career potential is simply the right thing to do.

- Telling those who end up in the lowest category exactly where they stand can communicate the need for immediate performance improvement and encourage these people to seek other employment quickly, if the termination of those who end up ranked in the bottom category is not an aspect of the system.

- You might as well—most people figure it out anyway.

There are also some real disadvantages to disclosing ranking results to the individual:

- High-ranked individuals may interpret being placed in the top bucket as a promise or an "oral contract" of promotability or long-term employment. When the person's assessment changes or he is not given an expected promotion, the person may become discouraged, become angry, or initiate litigation. (*Note*: this risk is entirely hypothetical. No organization has ever reported having this happen; no one knows any organization where it actually did happen.)

- The set of requirements, competencies, and talents needed to make it into the top-quartile pool this year may change next year. People may assume that being identified in the top quartile is permanent—"once in, always in."

- Managers are notoriously bad at conducting straightforward performance appraisal conversations, let alone being skilled at delivering important and sensitive information about the results of a forced ranking procedure. They'll probably screw it up.

- It may create a stable of arrogant "crown princes." (*Note*: if this happens—and it's unlikely—it may actually be a benefit in bringing to light a person's true nature quickly. One criterion for continuing to be considered top-tier talent is that the person deal appropriately with the communiqué that he or she has been identified as one of the elect.)

- Greenmail—the individual may use his high-potential status as a high-denomination bargaining chip to force the company to match a competitor's hire-away effort.

Considering all of the pros and the cons, I usually recommend that people be told how they came out in the ranking process, with the caveat that the information about how they came out is confidential and not to be shared with anyone who is not directly involved in the process.

How do you actually do the telling? What do you say to break the news to an A, B, or C player? In appendix A, I have also provided the set of scripts I prepared for use by managers in an organization that I helped to create a forced ranking system. In developing the scripts with the company's management development specialists, we realized that although we had talked generally about "A, B, and C players," the forced ranking procedure in fact produced five different results:

A players—Those high-potential, high-performance employees who ended up in the top 20 percent category

High B players—Those employees who barely missed being named in the top 20 percent, either because they were relatively new in their position, had a significant weakness that required attention in spite of their otherwise great strengths, or were just a tad below the caliber of the solid A's

Solid B players—The great majority of fully successful contributors

B-minus players—Those few who barely escaped being named in the bottom 10 percent category, either because they just missed the 10 percent cutoff or had a significant deficiency that outweighed otherwise solid evidence of strong performance and potential

C players—The bottom 10 percent

When you read the scripts, you'll see that they reflect the fact that the organization for which I wrote them—"Acme Services Company"—had decided that it would proceed with the termination of people who ended up in the bottom 10 percent category. The company offered those employees a generous severance package and included a proviso that the employee could reject the severance deal and try over a three-month period to prove that the original assignment to the bottom 10 percent category had been erroneous, with the risk of receiving a reduced package if he failed.

How Should the Results Be Used?

Be clear on the intent of the procedure, advise the authors of an analysis of forced ranking published by Sibson Consulting: "Clarify the purpose of forced ranking within the context of the company's broader human capital and talent management strategies. For example, forced ranking can be used to determine the top 5 percent of employees based on performance and potential, to pay out a higher percentage bonus to the top 20 percent of contributors, or to identify the bottom 8 percent for wanted turnover. As these examples indicate, forced ranking is more often than not used to determine some sort of consequence, positive or negative."[24]

Ranking by itself produces no value. Only when important decisions are made based on the results of the ranking activity will the process contribute to an organization's success. The senior management team should require the results of the ranking to be used in the following specific areas:

- *Specific and demanding development plans for the top category.*
  Each person ranking in the top category should have a specific development plan written and executed; each boss of these individuals should be held accountable for ensuring the plan's execution. These development plans should focus on giving these individuals fresh assignments and job rotations, not on training programs. High-potential people get stale if they're kept in the same position or functional area too long.

- *Compensation.* The swiftest way to communicate, "We're serious!" about the forced ranking procedure is to link it to compensation. Successful organizations reward the hell out of top performers and deliberately withhold giving increases to the people at the bottom. *Differentiation* is the operative word. At one large financial services company, managers are actively encouraged to "triple zero" those subordinates who have come out in the bottom of their top 10/bottom 10 procedure—no merit increase, no bonus, no stock options. The message gets across.

- *Accountability for retention.* Managers who have top-ten or top-quartile people reporting to them should not only be held accountable (through the performance appraisal system, the next year's ranking activity, and compensation) for executing challenging development plans, they should also be held accountable for ensuring the retention of those people. The unforeseen loss of any top-quartile corporate human asset should be treated with the same degree of seriousness as the disappearance of any other multi-hundred-thousand-dollar corporate asset would be.

- *Up-or-out plans.* For the people identified in the bottom category, each manager must be held accountable for creating and executing plans (including specific dates and outcomes) to replace or reassign each individual so identified.

- *Identification of "corporate asset" jobs.* Some jobs lend themselves to providing excellent development opportunities. These jobs should be identified and considered as corporate assets, to be regularly repopulated with A players.

- *Promotions.* No promotion should be made without a formal review of the ranking results.

Should the bottom 10 percent be terminated outright? In some companies—Sun, for example—separation is the normal outcome of being ranked as a C player. Sun CEO Scott McNealy is known around the company for saying the bottom 10 percent is where you "love them to death." But any workers who don't respond to McNealy's love are offered death in the form of a "prompt exit" severance, which they turn down at their peril, since those who continue to be found wanting face dismissal without compensation.[25] It is this Darwinian approach to forced ranking that has resulted in the ugly "rank and yank" term being applied to the process.

Many analysts of forced ranking argue for a gradual introduction of more severe sanctions for those who end up in the bottom group. "You must consider why your company wants to use forced ranking," suggests the study prepared for the Association of Corporate Counsel.

> The least controversial use is as a check against managers' performance ratings. The most controversial and most risky use is to identify low performers for removal from the company. Because rankings in such a system have significant ramifications, employees are more likely to fear and feel negative about the process. And because a ranking can result in termination, the stakes are high enough to trigger litigation. A less risky use and one that would fulfill your company's retention goals, is to use ranking to identify top performers who will receive higher pay and other rewards. Such a process would engender less employee fear, and the financial stakes of a low ranking would be less severe.[26]

Michael O'Malley's cautionary article, "Forced Ranking: Proceed Only with Great Caution," points out that the need for ensuring accuracy in ranking results varies depending on how the results of the ranking exercise are used: "It might be presumed that one's appetite for exactness will increase as the following performance-related outcomes are added:

- Performance scores are purely informational.

- Performance scores are used to make training and development decisions.

- Performance scores are used to make salary adjustments and bonus calculations.

- Performance scores are used to make employment decisions."[27]

The culture of the organization certainly should influence the decision about how the results of the forced ranking procedure will be used. It would be unwise to attempt to jump-start a historically paternalistic or highly relationship-oriented organization into a results-oriented one by imposing forced ranking and sacking the bottom group. "Such an organization will do better to initially emphasize a dedication to recognizing top performers and offering as many people as possible the developmental opportunities to become top performers," notes consultant Byron Woollen.

As an organization introduces forced ranking, it is often better off using the first years to adjust the system according to the needs of the company and communicating that the rankings are to be used primarily, though not exclusively, to guide development opportunities. This allows an appropriate time for cultural acceptance of the system, after which it is considerably easier to begin to introduce specific compensation criteria associated with various rankings. The emphasis on development and performance also eases the acceptance of lower performers being moved out of the company.[28]

And it may not be necessary to make a formal decision to forcibly separate the members of the bottom group from the organization—frequently they'll do it themselves. One large computer company applied a rigorous top 10/bottom 10 system but took no action with individuals other than clearly telling them that they had been classified in the bottom group. Over the course of the next six months, they found that of that bottom group 30 percent resigned, 30 percent voluntarily requested transfer to lower-rated positions where they would have a greater chance for success, and 40 percent significantly improved their performance. ICI Paints found that the employees in the bottom 20 percent of a forced ranking procedure had a much higher percentage of voluntary terminations following frank feedback about their performance without any suggestion on the part of the company that those employees leave.[29]

Finally, it's important to recognize that an individual who is a member of a high-performing team consisting of unusually talented coworkers is necessarily going to be ranked lower within his work group than another individual who possesses an equal degree of potential and performance but who works in a cadre of sluggards. Forced rankings depend on the relative performance of people in the work group, building a degree of arbitrariness into the system. Achieving the top 10 or bottom 10 percent label depends, always, on the caliber of the other people on the team. A top 10 percent performer in a mediocre group will become an average performer in a strong group. The same is true for the bottom 10 percent. If organizational selection systems are well implemented, the lowest 10 percent of the organization could still be acceptable. Forcing such people out of the organization may be perceived as unnecessary and draconian, with debilitating morale consequences.[30]

Should There Be an Appeals Process?

Should those individuals ranked in the bottom category have the right to appeal the decision? On the surface, the obvious answer would seem to be "Of course!" in line with our notions of fairness and justice. It's possible that a mistake could have been made.

The difficulty is that, unlike appealing a performance appraisal rating by saying that there were factors that the manager failed to take into account in making the absolute comparison judgment about how well the individual performed, in this case the employee appealing the forced ranking decision must argue that she is not only good but in fact is better than others who were ranked higher. To do this, she'll need to know who it is that was ranked higher, and exactly how she compared. That's a sticky wicket, since issues of privacy and confidentiality are bound to be violated if all of the information is released.

There's another problem, too. Let's say that Jane is assessed in the bottom 10 percent and, once having been notified, asks for a chance to improve her performance so that she's no longer in the bottom 10 percent. She is allowed a period to demonstrate this improvement and she does so. But all she's done is displace someone else out of the B category and into the C bucket. Now that person will want a chance to prove the assessors wrong, move up, and displace someone else. It's a vicious cycle.

It's rare for organizations to allow a formal appeals process for the rating an employee receives in a conventional performance appraisal system. The reason for not allowing an appeal is not to mindlessly back up a supervisor who might well be mistaken or even malicious. Rather, the reason that an appeals mechanism is rarely provided flows from the nature of performance appraisal itself. What is a performance appraisal? It is a formal record of the supervisor's *opinion* of the quality of the employee's work. To allow an appeal is to permit the employee to argue that the supervisor should have a different opinion. Perhaps the supervisor should have a different opinion, but who's to judge? Allowing an appeal, while noble in intent, is an unworkable mechanism.

The same problem arises in conjunction with allowing appeals of forced ranking decisions. There is no logical basis for determining that the decision was faultily made and should be reversed.

More challenging is the fact that allowing appeals simply generates churn at the bottom of the barrel. The employee who was ranked as a C player appeals, works hard to improve, and displaces a low B player into the C category. That person now appeals, works hard, and displaces someone else. There's no end to the constant churn, and no real organizational improvement.

A better approach is to forgo appeals if there is no direct action taken as a result of the person's being assigned into the lowest category. Nothing has been lost, and the individual has gained important information about how his or her performance is viewed by senior managers in the organization. The message is, here's what we think, get to work, better luck next time.

But if the bottom group is to be demoted, be terminated, or face some other adverse consequence as a result of ending up being in the bottom group, the organization will surely be preparing some kind of severance package. Consider allowing the individual the chance to reject the package and prove the assessment wrong by demonstrating exemplary performance over a fairly short period, perhaps ninety days, after which the individual's performance will be reassessed against the other employees who constituted the original ranking pool.

But here's the kicker: it's not enough to get sufficiently better as to displace someone else into the bottom category. What the organization will expect to see, the individual is advised, is that your performance over this ninety-day period *leapfrog* you over the others who were originally ranked higher—not just improve a little bit but demonstrate a dramatic difference. If you're able to demonstrate that, you'll be considered a solid B (or whatever the designation is) until the next round of ranking sessions. But should you fail to demonstrate that, the individual is advised, this severance arrangement that we're offering right now will no longer be available, and you'll be terminated with a much leaner package.

I have provided in appendix A the script to use for announcing the results of a forced ranking process. In the script for announcing the outcome to a C player, a person who ended up in the lowest category in the case where the organization had decided to terminate those individuals who were so ranked, I have provided the actual words to use in explaining this option to an individual.

Forced Ranking and Compensation

In addition to identifying the distribution of talent within the organization so that high-potential individuals can be recognized, developed, and retained and low performers can be encouraged to improve or find other jobs more in line with their talents and goals, forced ranking is also commonly used to make compensation decisions. When the bucket of money is limited, as it always is, it's important that dollars be distributed to reinforce a meritocracy rather than just handed out on a random basis.

But it's not uncommon for the results of a forced ranking exercise to vary significantly from the results delivered by the organization's performance appraisal system. One of the primary forces driving the use of forced ranking is the lack of meaningful differentiation produced by companies' performance appraisal systems, where managers are notoriously reluctant to rate anyone as Needs Improvement or any rating less than satisfactory. Forced ranking addresses this issue by ignoring whether the individual failed to meet expectations, met expectations, or exceeded expectations (which is frequently a function of the toughness or leniency of the performance standards managers set), and asking instead about the employee's contribution relative to others. The result, however, may turn out to be that the employee is rated quite high in the conventional performance appraisal process but far lower in the relative comparison procedure. If the results of the forced ranking/relative comparison process are used to allocate merit increase or bonus dollars, there may need to be some explaining done of why a high performance appraisal rating didn't generate an equally high increase or bonus award. These problems are highlighted by the authors of the SHRM legal report:

> If forced ranking is used primarily for pay distribution purposes (and not to eliminate employees), employers will likely have to deal with possible inconsistency between employees' rating and their ranking for purposes of determining pay. For example, an employee in a high-performing work group may receive an average performance rating, but be ranked at the bottom of his or her group and, thus, receive an insignificant or no pay increase. Additionally, some organizations have suffered for tying their ranking system too rigidly to compensation.

When no discretion is left to managers, there is no way to distinguish between an employee who is ranked in the middle but is on the rise from another employee who is an average performer and shows little potential for advancement.[31]

Putting It All Together

Developing a sophisticated forced ranking system, as we've seen in this chapter, involves a great deal more than simply marshaling the organization's executives and asking them to sort the population into different buckets based on their performance and potential. A ranking scheme needs to be determined, criteria established, pools established, evaluators identified, and information provided to all who are affected by the system. Good decisions need to be made about what criteria the assessors will use to make their decisions and what the outcomes of the ranking exercise will be.

But even when these requirements have been met, two other major activities must occur. First, the people who will serve as evaluators or assessors in the ranking sessions must be trained in how to carry out their responsibilities in an objective and ethical way, and the ranking sessions must be conducted. In the next chapter, we'll look at exactly how to do both of these jobs well.

4

Getting the Mechanics Right

IN CHAPTER 3, WE reviewed the policy decisions that need to be made in developing a forced ranking system. Whatever the policies may be, two operational components will always be critical to the system's ultimate success: training those who will serve as rankers or assessors, and running the sessions themselves competently. This chapter will concentrate on these two issues, as well as suggesting ways to minimize the potential negative consequences of introducing and using a forced ranking system. Make no mistake: as important as it is to design wise policies, the success of a forced ranking system will be determined by the quality of execution.

Training Assessors

Training the managers and executives who will participate in forced ranking sessions serves several purposes, in addition to the obvious one of giving them the skills they need to make good decisions in determining the performance, potential, and relative contributions of the various people under review. Training can serve as a necessary pressure valve, allowing reluctant or resistant managers a forum in which they can vent their gripes and reservations about the process in a way that doesn't affect the outcomes. Training can help ensure that everyone knows the ground rules and operational mechanics. Training can communicate the intention of top management to build a performance-oriented culture, an intention that is greatly reinforced when top managers themselves attend the training program or, even better, conduct a part of it.

Training can also serve to build a positive understanding of the appropriateness of using a relative comparison process as part of the organization's overall mix of talent management and performance management processes. Many managers will be familiar with forced ranking only from having read the headlines about lawsuits and articles condemning the process. They need to be told the other side of the story.

Finally, the training process can help ensure the defensibility of the process if questions or challenges are ever raised.

In Advance of the Training Program

Many organizations create "briefing books" providing performance and demographic data on all of the individuals who will be reviewed. These may (and probably should) contain copies of the last one or two performance appraisals and the type of information that would appear on the person's resume. A photo is useful for those participants in the ranking session who may not have direct experience with the individual but are learning about the depth of the talent pool in the company. It's helpful to prepare the briefing books in advance of the training sessions and provide them to the participants, with the request that they review the material relating to their direct reports to ensure accuracy and completeness.

In addition to making sure the data is up-to-date on their own subordinates, assessors should be requested to identify those other individuals who will be reviewed in the session with whom they are sufficiently familiar that they can participate knowledgeably in the discussion. *Participate knowledgeably* does not mean that the assessor has the same intimate and exhaustive details of the person's performance and capability that the individual's immediate supervisor should be expected to possess. It means that the assessor is able to make informed contributions about the individual's performance and capabilities against the criteria that have been determined, or can contribute experiences, examples, and anecdotes that will support a high or low ranking.

Further, for each of his or her direct reports who will be evaluated, the assessor should make preliminary bullet-item summaries of that person's performance and potential, strengths, and development needs. These lists will be further refined after training, but making them up in advance will start the process of thinking through the distribution of talent in his or her work group by each person who will be participating in the ranking sessions.

If there are specific criteria that will be used in the ranking sessions, each participant should also be asked to identify which of the criteria represents the area of greatest strength for each individual to be reviewed, and which criterion most represents an area in need of development.

Other preparation activities might include asking participants to read an appropriate article about forced ranking or performance management or talent development, perhaps with a request to identify elements of the article that the person found most useful or with which the individual most strongly disagreed. In addition, each participant might be asked to come prepared with any questions that he or she wants answered in the course of the training program.

Finally, each participant in the ranking session might be asked to make a preliminary identification of *benchmark individuals*. These are the people who appear to be unquestionably in the top 10 or bottom 10 percent (assuming a top 10/bottom 10 ranking scheme is to be used) and who in effect define what *top 10* or *bottom 10* represents. As we'll see, it's helpful to start the ranking discussions by coming to agreement on the benchmark individuals at both ends of the spectrum, who then can serve as comparators when other individuals come under review.

Overview of the Forced Ranking Process

The training program for those who will be participating in the ranking sessions needs to cover three areas:

The *why* of the process (why the organization decided to proceed with a forced ranking process, why it's a good idea, why they should take it seriously).

The *what* (what forced ranking is all about, what has happened so far, what will happen when the ranking sessions are completed, what their responsibilities are, and what the specific mechanics of the process are—where the sessions will be held, how they will be run, how long each session is expected to last, etc.).

The *how* (how to assess performance and potential, rating errors and how to avoid them, how to deal with disagreements over assessments, how the forced ranking process interacts with other performance management efforts, how to discuss the process with their subordinates).

Timing and Content

People are busy, and the people who will be participating as assessors are particularly busy since they are the senior managers of the organization. About two to three hours should be sufficient to cover the what and why of the procedure, fine-tune their skills in performance and potential assessment, and answer the questions they will raise.

When I conduct training programs for managers who will be acting as assessors in their company's forced ranking sessions, I usually follow the following agenda:

Background. What their company's forced ranking process is all about.

Rationale. Why the company has decided to embark on the program, and what it expects to get out of it.

Outcomes. What will happen when the process is over. This is the place where I discuss in detail the company's plans for those who end up in the bottom ranking category and what the responsibilities are of those managers who have subordinates identified in the top ranking category.

Events to date. What has happened so far.

Mechanics. How the process will actually work—the step-by-step plan. (Expect lots of questions here.)

Skill building. Developing the ability of the assessors to make good ranking decisions.

Q&A to close.

Building Assessor Skills

The primary skill required to be a good assessor is behavioral observation. Typically, I provide the criteria that the organization has determined and ask the participants (typically working in teams) to develop a list of examples of behaviors that they would accept as indicators that the person excelled in this area. It's also helpful to ask for a list of behaviors that would indicate a deficiency, too. This helps to ensure not only that they have a shared understanding of what such frequent ranking criteria as "high energy level," or "passion for results," or "execute with excellence" mean, but that they are able to describe specific examples in behavioral terms.

It's not enough just to be skillful at identifying and describing examples of the forced ranking process's criteria in behavioral terms. Participants also need to be able to assess whether the individual under review, taking the specific criteria and other factors into account, is an A, B, or C player. That's more difficult, and it can't be done in the abstract.

The most useful technique I've found to get people to make A-, B-, and C-player decisions, using real people that they know but still maintaining appropriate confidentiality, is to ask them to write down the initials of every boss they've had since they began working. Start with your current boss's initials, then those of the previous one, and keep on going back as far as you can remember. Most managers who have spent much time in large organizations will be able to develop a list of a dozen or more bosses without difficulty. Now identify the one or two that you would classify as A-player bosses, and the one or two that to you represent a C-player boss. Next, without necessarily revealing who the individual is (since it's entirely possible that a participant will have identified her current supervisor as an example of a C-player boss), discuss with your team how you happened to decide on who was an A and who was a C. I press them to continue providing behavioral examples, not just emotional reactions, and then ask whether they found any correlation between the criteria their company is using for the forced ranking activity and the criteria they personally used in determining their A- and C-player boss examples.

The Behavior/Results Matrix

Another useful technique to help participants in the ranking training program fine-tune their assessment skills (and, more subtly, to demonstrate to them how pervasive their tendency toward grade inflation may be) is to draw the results/behavior matrix on a flip chart (see figure 4-1).

In using this matrix, I begin by writing the words *Results* and *Behaviors* on the flip chart and explain that these are the two components of job performance. I then draw the nine-box matrix and explain that for each of the two factors, a person's performance can either exceed his boss's expectations, meet the boss's expectations, or fail to meet expectations. I then number the nine boxes to indicate the nine possible combinations of performance.

At this point I throw out some examples to the group and ask them which of the nine boxes best describes the individual's performance. First, consider the supersalesman who invariably beats quota, but does so in a way that pisses off both his customers and his coworkers. His sales colleagues actively avoid him because he's braggadocious and steals their leads; his customers buy from him only to be rid of him.

FIGURE 4-1

The results/behavior matrix

	Results		
	Exceeds	Meets	Fails to meet
Exceeds	1	2	3
Meets	4	5	6
Fails to Meet	7	8	9

(Behaviors labels the vertical axis: Exceeds, Meets, Fails to Meet)

But he always exceeds quota, no matter how high it's set. Which box best represents his performance?

Box 7, of course—he exceeds expectations as far as the results he produces, but fails to meet expectations as far as his behavior is concerned.

Now consider good old Joe, the company sweetheart. Joe is a model of courtesy and cooperation. He gets along with everyone; he's never met a stranger. Joe's always the first to volunteer when a nasty job comes up. But no one ever takes him up on his offer, because no matter how simple the task, Joe will find some way to screw things up. Which box?

Box 3, of course. While he exceeds expectations in terms of behaviors, he fails to meet when it comes to results.

At this point the matrix is clear to all. I then ask them to write down the initials of each of their direct reports (to preserve privacy) and then for each person, write down the number of the box that best describes that person's performance in terms of how well he or she does in meeting your expectations in terms of their results and behaviors. Once everyone's done, I ask them where their results clustered.

The frequent response is that a lot of people are reported to be 1s with a smattering of 2s and 4s. At this point I explain that the matrix exercise they just went through is not an inquiry into the quality of performance of their subordinates. Instead, it is an analysis of how tough or lenient their expectations are. If they report a preponderance of 1s (and 2s and 4s), what that indicates is that their performance expectations of their staff are too low—they're easy graders. The ideal response is to have most people clustered around the 5 position. This represents a manager who has tough and demanding performance expectations coupled with a team of talented people who are capable of performing—in both behaviors displayed and results achieved—at the high level that the manager has set.

Integrating Performance and Potential

The focus of conventional performance appraisal systems is exclusively historical. The manager is asked to assess how well Harriet did in demonstrating the competencies and behaviors her company expects, and how well she achieved her goals and met her job responsibilities in the past twelve months. Forced franking adds a second dimension. In addition to evaluating the quality of her performance (relative to others, in this case, instead of against job expectations), the manager is now also asked to assess her potential, her stretch. Among the factors that will be important in accurately making this difficult but necessary assessment will be such intangible but describable aspects as her conceptual thinking ability, how she's done when confronted with the kinds of challenges that arise frequently in higher-level jobs, and certainly her own expressed interest in moving up.

Another matrix that is useful to help rankers understand the relationship between performance and potential, and to guide them toward the appropriate actions to be taken as a result of the assessments they will make, is the performance/potential matrix (figure 4-2).

There are certainly many other techniques that will help a manager become adept at behavioral observation and differentiation. Intertwined with whatever skill-building activities the assessors participate in, however, needs to be an ongoing message about the importance of sticking with the observable and being sensitive to not doing or saying

FIGURE 4-2

The performance/potential matrix

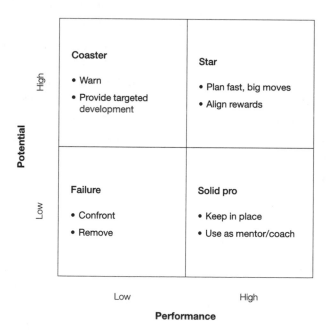

anything that could reflect poorly on the organization if outcomes of the process are later challenged. But soft-pedal the EEO component— the assessor skill-building session isn't another diversity training program, and providing anything more than a brief reminder of the company's commitment to diversity is probably overkill.

Another topic that might be productively covered in the assessor program is what participants should say to their subordinates about the forced ranking procedure. A large manufacturing firm made the following statement in both the assessor training program materials and in the memo to assessors about the process: "Since the fact that [*name of company*] is using a Leadership Assessment Program is not confidential and we have communicated both the nature of the program and the criteria that will be used for assessment, we encourage all assessors to invite their direct reports who will be assessed to submit any information they wish to supplement the information that assessors already have." This is an excellent example of no secrets/no surprises at work.

Dealing with the Outcomes of the Forced Ranking Procedure

One of the first questions raised in the training program usually involves what the managers' responsibilities will be if one of their subordinates is identified in the bottom ranking category. The answer, of course, will depend on what the organization's intentions for the process are. If the organization is using forced ranking only as a tool to identify high-potential employees and no action is planned for the rest, then there will be little for the managers of non–A players to do. On the other hand, if the organization intends to release those assigned to the bottom bucket, then it will be the responsibility of the immediate supervisor to break the bad news and shepherd the individual out the door.

An unfortunate tendency in training managers, however, is to focus too much attention on their responsibilities when they have a bottom-bucket subordinate. Not nearly enough attention is paid to the responsibilities of those managers whose subordinates are identified as top-bucket, A players. There's a lot more to do than just passing on congratulations.

Many companies have strong expectations of the managers of A players. They expect the manager of a high-potential individual not only to work with him or her to develop genuinely meaningful development plans (not just sending the individual off to some training program or university advanced management curriculum) but to work consciously to increase the degree of challenge and responsibility and opportunities for achievement in the existing job until the person moves to a higher-level, more demanding position. Managers of these top-talent contributors are also held accountable for retaining these corporate assets, and can expect serious consequences in their own performance appraisals and bonuses if they permit an A player to leave for a "better opportunity." At Texas Instruments, Cypress Semiconductor, and many other talent-valuing organizations, a manager who allows a high-potential employee to leave can expect to get a call from the president or CEO asking, "Why did you let her get away?" That's a call no manager wants to get.

A Word About "Objectivity"

Invariably, a concern is raised by participants in training programs (as well as many other people) about whether a forced ranking process is "objective." The widespread assumption is that only those things that are directly countable or scientifically provable or numerically quantifiable are objective, and that the opinions and judgments of managers about their subordinates' performance and potential are by definition "subjective."

That's not true. As we discussed in chapter 2, *objective* means, "Uninfluenced by emotions or personal prejudices: *an objective critic.* Based on observable phenomena; presented factually: *an objective appraisal.*"[1]

Forced ranking systems actually serve to increase the objectivity of the employee review process by systematizing the complex job of assessing talent. A great benefit of forced ranking systems is that they clarify the criteria the organization uses to assess performance and potential, and then force managers to focus on only those criteria in making their judgments.

Employee ranking requires tough decisions in an area where solid, unarguable, quantitative data simply don't exist, particularly when one is assessing the individual's potential and promotability. The employee ranking process requires the exercise of honed, objective managerial judgment in a situation where the data are always incomplete and often contradictory—the same managerial judgment that we applaud and reward when it is applied in other areas. But managers make tough decisions based on limited data all the time: which projects to fund, which to shelve; when to react swiftly to a competitor's move, when to let time take its course. Just because the decision isn't based on countable units doesn't mean that the decision isn't objective. Such highly valuable skills as sensitivity to nuance, or the ability to transform adversaries into allies, or the willingness to go the extra mile for a customer, can't be reduced to a quantitative, numerical scheme. Employee ranking is not the same as solving an algebra problem—it can't be reduced to a mathematical algorithm. Hard decisions need to be made in organizations. The data are always imperfect. The forced ranking procedure helps managers make these hard decisions with intelligence and compassion—and with objectivity.

Preparing for the Ranking Session

It's wise to schedule the training program and the ranking sessions as close together as possible. Skills atrophy, and high interest in the upcoming ranking sessions can dissipate if too much time elapses between the training and the ranking sessions themselves.

In preparing for its first iteration of a forced ranking procedure that was planned to be an annual component of a large corporation's talent management process, the HR staff and I worked together to prepare a Frequently Asked Questions document that was handed out at the training program. The FAQ document was also provided to all employees who would be reviewed in the program. In the week between the training session for rankers and the ranking sessions, managers were asked to invite their subordinates who would be in ranking pools to review the FAQ document, submit any information they felt would be helpful to those who would be discussing their performance and potential, and raise any further questions about any issues about the process that concerned them. A copy of the FAQ document, revised only to remove any identifying references to the organization, is included as appendix B.

Kicking Off a Forced Ranking Session

When managers gather to review individuals in a forced ranking session there's likely to be a significant amount of tension and discomfort, particularly if the organization has not previously used a relative comparison process. It's helpful for someone to review the purpose of the procedure, go over the ground rules and expected outcomes, and remind participants of key points that were covered in the training program.

One of the important "ground rules" involves note taking. Since notes taken during the session could later be subject to discovery if there is any legal challenge raised, companies should consider limiting the note taking to people who are sure to be sensitive about not including anything in session notes that might later indicate that decisions were made on the basis of a protected category, particularly age. In this regard it may be helpful to use an external facilitator to run the session and to have an HR specialist or member of the company's legal staff serve as a note taker and question answerer if any uncertainties arise. And the note taker should be advised to take particularly good notes on the decisions that led to individuals' assignments as A or C players, since that information will become useful later in arranging appropriate development or improvement plans.

While some organizations use software to facilitate the assessments made in their forced ranking assessment meetings, a relatively simple, low-tech, but visually dramatic way to get the session started once the overview of the session has been provided is to have the names of all of the people who will be discussed in the session already written on sticky notes and placed alphabetically on a flip chart on the side of the room. On the front wall facing the group, post additional large flip chart pages that indicate the rating categories the company has decided to use, with space for the sticky notes to be put in the appropriate category (figure 4-3).

FIGURE 4-3

Forced ranking flip chart arrangement

Top 20%	Vital 70%	Bottom 10%

Note that in figure 4-3, the amount of space allotted to each category is an approximation of the 20-70-10 ranking scheme being used.

In starting out, it's helpful for the facilitator to write the total number of people who will be reviewed in the session on the flip chart and then the specific number that the percentage figure represents. In this way, participants will know exactly how many sticky notes must ultimately end up in each category.

In determining how the percentages will translate into an exact number of people for each category, it will be rare for the percentage figure to equate to a whole number. In other words, if there are 47 people under review and the company is using a 20-70-10 scheme, will there be 4 people or 5 people who must be assigned to the bottom group? It's important to make this decision in advance of knowing who the fourth and fifth "worst" individuals in the group are, so that decisions are not made on the basis of the personalities involved.

It's also wise to allow some liberality in determining the way percentages translate into actual numbers of people to be assigned to each category. Continuing the example of a ranking session with 47 people being reviewed, there's little to be gained by insisting that the bottom 10 percent category of 4.7 be rounded up to 5, or arguing that the top 20 percent of 47 be limited to only 9 since arithmetic provides that only 9.4 people can be in the top category. Be generous—set the number that must fall in the bottom category at 4 and allow 10 to be ranked in the top 20 percent. There is enough resistance to the forced ranking process without adding mathematical foolishness to its adversaries' arsenal of complaints.

Once the target numbers have been decided and written down, rankers can be asked to go to the flip chart holding the names of each person to be reviewed on sticky notes, peel off the ones for each of their direct reports, and then place each one in the appropriate position on the main flip chart to indicate their opinion of where the individual belongs. This can be done either by having all participants move the name notes simultaneously or by asking those participants who feel that they have a benchmark individual (a person who is manifestly and unarguably in either the top or bottom category) to start by putting the sticky notes of the proposed benchmark individuals in the appropriate place on the main flip chart.

The advantage of having everybody move the sticky notes at the same time is that the initial distribution is immediately apparent as soon as they've moved the notes and sat down. And it could well be that in this first identification of top 10/bottom 10, the distribution comes out exactly as required. Highly unlikely, of course, but still possible.

Whatever the formal ranking scheme the company may have decided on (top 10/bottom 10, 20-70-10, quartiling, rank ordering, etc.), invariably the discussion focuses on distinguishing A, B, and C players. And in using the simple sticky notes and flip chart technique described here, my experience is consistent: assessors will invariably place their sticky notes not just in one of the ranking categories but along a continuum to indicate that while Betty may be in the same "vital 70%" category as Bob, her sticky note is properly positioned just outside the "top 20%" area, while he is far down, approaching the "bottom 10%" group.

I have found that it's wise to allow and even encourage this kind of continuum thinking. As discussed in chapter 3, in writing the scripts for managers to use to announce the results of a forced ranking exercise to their subordinates, I found that I needed to write five scripts and not just three for the three formal ranking categories the company had settled on. Instead of identifying A, B, and C players, the executives of that firm had comfortably allocated the troops into A, B+, solid B, B−, and C categories. The goal of the process is to let people know where they stand. The more precision we can bring, the more valuable the information. (The scripts are contained in appendix A.)

Starting the discussion by identifying benchmark individuals provides several benefits. First, it clearly defines what a top-ranked candidate offers that others do not. If there is agreement, for example, that Fred unquestionably belongs in the organization's top 10 category, then it will be easier to assess others since there is now an accepted standard of comparison or reference point. In addition, since the organization's stars tend to be well known, it's likely that not only Fred's boss but many other participants will be able to provide telling examples and illustrations of exactly why Fred is where he is. Discussing clear, behaviorally-based examples from the start will help later as other, more difficult-to-assign candidates are under review. Finally, as Andy Pearson, the former president of PepsiCo and a long-time advocate of the forced ranking process observes, "By comparing people with star performers, you start to set higher standards and expectations."[2] And that's the purpose of forced ranking—to encourage higher goals and expectations throughout the organization.

The Role of the Facilitator

Using an effective facilitator is critical to session success. And while internal training or organization development (OD) specialists often have the finely developed facilitation skills that leading a forced ranking session requires, attempting to use an internal facilitator can throw up a serious stumbling block. First, the internal facilitator is typically not at the same organizational level as the participants in a forced ranking session. It's common for all the evaluators in a ranking session to be at the vice president level. If the facilitator is a person who works for a person who works for a vice president, the hierarchical differential will make it difficult indeed for the facilitator to confront a session participant who is obviously attempting to exercise political power to sway colleagues toward the decision he wants them to make. Memories are long, and the internal facilitator will still be around after the sessions have been concluded.

Second, and more important, it's likely that the internal facilitator will know many of the people being reviewed. Even if there is no concern about the integrity of the person who is serving as session facilitator in maintaining absolute confidentiality of all things discussed, participants may still regulate what they say because it will be heard by a colleague of the person under review. Forced ranking discussions need to be open, honest, and freewheeling; anything that inhibits that process makes the sessions less valuable. A facilitator from outside the organization, one who knows none of the people being reviewed and has no stake in seeing any particular result come about, will be far more effective.

The facilitator of the session has several responsibilities:

- To kick the session off, review the ground rules, and explain the process the group will follow in coming up with its assessment.

- To pay attention to time and provide routine time checks. It's useful at the start of the session to announce to the group what the average time per person being reviewed might be (divide the number of people being reviewed into the total number of minutes scheduled for the session). Warn the group that it's easy to spend a lot of time discussing individuals early in the process and then sacrifice important discussion toward the end, when time is short.

- To encourage the active engagement of all meeting participants throughout the session. Forced ranking sessions are grueling and intense—people's careers are on the line. It's easy for a participant to mentally check out when the individual under discussion is one with whom she's not familiar, and abandon the responsibility of asking probing questions and testing that similar standards are being applied to all. Sometimes calling a short stretch break can help when several participants have emotionally, intellectually, or even physically removed themselves from the process.

- To be sensitive to common rating errors arising in the discussions. *Central tendency*, where the rater evaluates everyone in the middle, is not uncommon among weak managers who resist the process by placing everyone in the B category, figuring that as long as they're not rated as C players, no one will complain very loud. *Recency effect*, where only examples of behavior in the last few weeks are discussed, is another common rating error. Finally, a subtle rating error that often arises is the *Similar-to-me effect*, where the rater unconsciously evaluates subordinates with similar styles or characteristics higher than even more effective individuals with different approaches. As Robert Kelley and Janet Caplan wryly observe, "Some managers still wonder whether high productivity is due only to individual work style and motivation. In many cases, they're looking for a justification for their own style. 'Clean desk' people want to believe that being organized leads to higher productivity. 'Sloppy desk' managers, however, view their style as evidence of the creativity that translates into high performance."[3]

- To have a well-honed sense of the hidden agendas and unspoken deal making that can swirl through a session, and the guts to confront the possibility of collusion directly.

Probably the biggest responsibility of the facilitator is to help the group think through the rationale for placing people in the appropriate position. The quality of questions the facilitator asks the group will help them focus on the individual's capacity and potential and teach them about the kinds of issues they should be considering as they look at the talents of their own people.

Leadership experts Melvin Sorcher and James Brant offer a small sampling of the questions one might ask of a particular individual under review:[4]

Describe the candidate's integrity:

- Have you ever known him to shade, color, or withhold information? If so, what were the circumstances?

- Does he give credit to others when appropriate?

- Does he stand firm in his opinions, or does he move with the winds of politics? Can you give examples?

Describe how the candidate communicates information and expectations:

- How persuasive is he in getting his ideas accepted?

- Does he command the respect and attention of senior executives?

- Does he tailor his message to the needs of his audience? Examples?

- Is he intellectually aggressive without offending?

Describe how the candidate reasons and analyzes issues:

- How well and how quickly can he assemble and integrate a diversity of information?

- Is he logical, and how does he demonstrate sound judgment?

- When confronted with an ambiguous or complex situation, does he procrastinate? Or does he make decisions too quickly? Give an illustration.

- Is he more of a tactical or a strategic thinker?

- Does he have a vision for the company, and has he demonstrated that he can move a business into new areas?

- How well does he anticipate trends and translate them into the organization's long-term objectives? Examples?

Describe how the candidate runs his immediate work team:

- Has he demonstrated the ability to assemble a good team? Explain.

- Is he threatened by people who are more experienced, smarter, or better technically?

- How well does he work with people who have different styles and skills?

- Does he always surround himself with strong people who will be candid and tell him what he needs to know instead of what he wants to hear?

- How does he motivate others to accomplish things independently of him? Can you give examples?

- Does he delegate authority and responsibility or just tasks?

- Is he sometimes needlessly interested in certain activities? Or does he perhaps have a tendency to relinquish too much authority to others?

Finally, there is one important role that the facilitator should *not* play. The facilitator should not be the person who moves the sticky notes up and down the flip charts as assessors change their mind and revise their opinions as the session progresses. Participants will demand that the facilitator shoulder this easy and obvious administrative task. Don't do it! The person moving the sticky note or adjusting the position in a software-aided procedure should always be the immediate supervisor of the individual under review. No one else should touch it.

Wrapping the Session Up

Frankly, I have found that it's rare for a forced ranking session to end at the official stopping time. Discussions are often passionate, and there's a great deal of work to be done. But it's worthwhile pushing through to completion rather than setting a time to get back together and attempt to continue anew after a significant break. The energy will be lost.

As things are coming to a conclusion, it's important to ask the group to check the names posted on the flip chart or projected on the screen by the software program to make sure that the final positions are accurate. Are they exactly where they should be, not only in terms of being accurately placed as far as the formal rating categories are concerned, but also along the imaginary continuum that always seems to arise as managers make finer and finer distinctions about the distribution of talent in the organization? If the rankings are being made using computer software, the program will remember the final ranking placements. If sticky notes are placed on flip chart paper to indicate the individual's category, taking a picture of the flip chart at the conclusion of the session with a digital camera can be a handy way to record accurately the final placement.

As the session ends, remind the group of the importance of holding all the results—and the discussions that generated those results—confidential. Managers should be instructed not to let their subordinates know how they came out in the ranking process, since the results won't be official until they've been reviewed by the human resource or legal departments to make sure there are no glaring issues of adverse impact. In addition, a post-session review may indicate that someone who should have been assessed wasn't considered, or someone else was reviewed in two different sessions. These kinds of administrative slipups do occur, and it's always best to wait until the election is certified before announcing the winner.

It's also useful at the close of the session to remind the group of any next steps and to conduct a quick "lessons learned" debriefing session, particularly if this ranking session is one of the first in a series that will occur.

Minimizing Potential Negative Consequences

By taking into consideration all the issues raised earlier, and tailoring the recommendations to exactly fit the culture and the needs of your organization, you'll end up with a forced ranking process that produces an accurate picture of the relative distribution of talent in the organization with minimum resistance or concern. But there are a few other items to consider in designing an ideal system.

Communicate. Let everyone who will be involved in the process know what's happening. There are many ways to communicate the company's decision to institute a forced ranking process, but everyone who's affected—either as a rater or as a ratee—needs to know what's going on and why.

Aim your communication efforts at those in the top group. At the start, probably most employees who will be reviewed in the ranking pool will believe that they are top-tier players, in the top 20 percent, or the top quarter if quartiling is the ranking scheme being used. But their self-perceptions may be unrealistic. As business etiquette consultant Barbara Pachter points out in exploring why executives can't see their problem behaviors, these top dogs are no different from anybody else. "I've given fifteen hundred seminars to over one hundred thousand people, and no one in any of my classes has ever admitted to having bad behaviors. It's always the other guy. It's the same psychology that makes everyone think they're better-than-average drivers. Many people are worse than average, by definition. But they'd never admit it to themselves. So the starting point is for businesspeople to acknowledge that, chances are, they're making etiquette mistakes they're unaware of and that they'd want to correct if only they knew about them."[5] One of the great advantages of a coerced ranking process is that, assuming it is run well and is marked by candor-filled discussions about the outcomes of the assessment process, people will find out about areas where they need to improve.

Depending on the ranking scheme, three out of four, or eight out of ten, will ultimately be disappointed when they learn they've not been ranked in the highest group. But the positioning of the initial communication needs to stress that the company is entering into this process to enhance the career possibilities of top-tier players, not as a turkey-ousting procedure. The themes to be communicated might include such messages as these:

- People earn the right to be included in the ranking procedure by dint of their having already been appointed to important positions in the company.

- It's a means to identify and ensure the swift promotion of top talent.

- It will help the company create a talent-rich management cadre.

- It will increase the probability of genuinely effective development plans being created and carried out.

- It will ensure that people who don't share the same talent and energy as the majority of managers are confronted with the need to change or leave.

- It will help make sure that people get what they deserve.

Provide training and coaching to evaluators on how to do the job. Managers are notoriously reluctant to meaningfully differentiate the relative performance and potential of their troops. The two ways to overcome this problem are first (and most important), through top management's insistence that it be done and that tough-minded standards be applied; second, through providing managers with good coaching and training so they have no excuse not to do what they're expected to do. This training and coaching requirement can be satisfied through some of these activities:

- As discussed, conducting a short (about two- to three-hour) session for groups of raters that covers why the company is using the process and how to evaluate potential, promotability, and strengths and weaknesses using the organization's criteria

- Providing specific written instructions for how the ranking sessions will be run

- Providing training in how to communicate ranking results and create development plans

Provide a skilled internal or external facilitator at each ranking session. This person's job will be to ensure that procedural requirements are being met and that tough-minded standards are being applied.

Monitor for results. In addition to the obvious need to monitor the results of the rankings against EEO categories for legal defensibility reasons, there are several other tests that should be applied to make sure the results are relatively accurate:

- Are there significant differences in rankings between one department and another? (E.g., 35 percent of people working in department X were ranked in the top quarter, while only 15 percent of people who work in department Y were ranked there.)

- Are people from work units that are universally known to be talent-rich or poor-performing appropriately represented in the top and bottom categories? It is a serious mistake to demand that, for example, a top 10/bottom 10 scheme be rigidly followed in two different departments, one of which is recognized throughout the organization as a repository of stars, while everyone knows that the other is populated entirely by flops and washouts.

- Is there an appropriate distribution of rankings at different job levels? In other words, is the top quartile overly represented by higher-paid individuals, while the bottom quartile contains mostly people in lower-level jobs?

- Are people who are ranked in the lowest quartile genuinely at the bottom of the performance curve, or are they simply the people who are the most obvious targets (close to retirement, already accepted a job outside the organization, brand-new to a position, recently deceased, etc.)?

Ensure that the company's performance appraisal procedure is first-rate. Finally, remember that, in most cases, ranking and succession planning typically affect a small number of employees, even exempt employees. Performance appraisal affects everybody. Ranking gives top management information that they can use for ensuring the achievement of strategic plans. Performance appraisal gives individuals the information they need to ensure personal and organizational success. If ranking is going to work optimally at a company, it's important that the company's performance appraisal process be world-class.

In the next chapter, I'll show you how the process unfolded in one major corporation.

5

Forced Ranking—Behind
the Scenes

IN JUNE 2002, I completed a major forced ranking project with one of America's best-known consumer goods companies. From the start, the company—anonymous at its request—did everything right. We'll call it Acme Services Company.

Why did Acme decide that forced ranking was the right approach? Almost three years before, a new CEO had been brought in from the parent company for a turnaround. He found:

- While the company was highly profitable, market share had been flat for the past several years.

- The company had a culture best described as high tenure, best effort, get along, go along, don't make waves.

- Performance appraisals were regular and routine, but leniency was common. Almost everyone was rated in the top two of the five categories. In addition, in sales, the one department where there initially appeared to be more differentiation in perfor- mance appraisal ratings than in others, all the lower ratings were concentrated among the salespeople themselves. Middle managers got higher ratings, and all the senior sales executives uniformly were rated in the top appraisal category. This in spite of the fact that sales had been flat for several years and the sales department was universally considered as one of the company's poorest-performing units.

- The company's succession-planning process included all the accepted standard features. But two contradictory problems were obvious: first, the same candidates were rated as highly promotable year after year without anything happening; second, key organizational slots were rarely filled by the candidate that the succession-planning list recommended.

In addition, a recently appointed performance improvement manager with two decades of field HR experience wanted to explore forced ranking as a way to overcome the functional silos and lack of performance management toughness that characterized the organization.

The process started with my presentation of an executive overview of forced ranking for the company's top brass. This three-hour presentation gave the company's senior leadership a firsthand view of the procedure as it works in several different organizations. We reviewed the research data that demonstrated a high degree of correlation between excellence in performance management and excellence in business results. We discussed the experiences—positive and negative—of companies that were using forced ranking as part of their talent management practices. A surprising amount of time was spent on clarifying the difference between developing a formal *forced ranking* system like the ones used by GE or Sun or PepsiCo, and requiring a *forced distribution* of scores on Acme's existing performance appraisal system. A significant amount of time was devoted to discussing the cultural impact that the initiation of a forced ranking process would have. We concentrated on exploring the key components of the system that, assuming the senior leadership decided to proceed with the process, would make Acme's forced ranking process exactly appropriate to the culture they wanted to create and the CEO's objectives.

As a group, the senior leadership team analyzed six areas critical for system success:

- *Criteria for evaluation.* Since we would be assessing leadership and future potential, they realized that they would need to identify some standard yardsticks that would apply to individuals across all organizational units. After several iterations, a list of four emerged that everyone agreed were appropriate and measurable: execute with excellence, passion for results, succeed with people, and make tough decisions. The first three criteria were lifted directly from the company's "Values in Action"; the final one was not only incorporated in one of the other values but would also be measurable in part by the way in which the person participated in the process as an assessor. In addition, they decided that raters would be told to also consider each individual's performance history and perceived potential over the next two or three years, along with intellectual horsepower and demonstration of teamwork/collaboration with others.

- *Organizational level.* How far down in the organization would the ranking process extend? Where would you reach the point of diminishing returns? And would this executive group also be included in the forced ranking population? To make sure that the forced ranking process would have the biggest impact, we decided that only the company's top executive and vice presidential group (forty-seven individuals) and the people who reported directly to them (one hundred eighty individuals) would be included in the ranking process. This meant that the CEO and I would meet for him to rank his seven direct reports. This group of his direct reports would then meet with him to assess the pool of VPs; and the VPs, along with their bosses and the CEO, would meet to assess all the remaining managers.

- *Ranking scheme.* Curiously, at the end of the executive overview, there were two sets of opinions about what the best ranking scheme to employ would be. Some of the group preferred adopting a quartiling approach (25-25-25-25) on the basis that this would prevent the possibility of some of their conflict-averse managers from dumping all of their direct reports in the middle category. Others, a slightly larger group, argued for a top 10/bottom 10 approach. A week or so after the meeting, the CEO made an executive decision that the company would use the same ranking scheme that GE had made popular: top 20 percent, vital 70 percent, bottom 10 percent. All the other executives quickly got on board with this decision.

- *Confidentiality and communications.* To what extent would the company publicize the fact that it was embarking on a forced ranking system? Would assessees be told how they came out in the forced ranking process? The group decided to publicize the program to all exempt employees, even the ones who weren't included in the ranking process. This decision resulted from a conclusion they came to during the executive overview that they would start at the top of the organization and then, assuming success with this population, expand the program in the second year to include all exempt employees. "No secrets, no surprises," was the mantra.

- *Procedure.* How exactly would the ranking sessions be run? How long would they last? What would be the roles and responsibilities of each participant? And how would rankers be prepared so that they could do their job knowledgeably and accurately? We decided to conduct mandatory three-hour training sessions for all rankers and to hold the ranking sessions offsite—both good decisions. We also decided to run two sessions a day—a bad decision, it later turned out, since time pressure to complete analyzing all the individuals under review forced us to spend less time on identifying developmental ideas for the A players and replacement plans for C players than we would have liked.

- *Outcomes and consequences.* What will happen once the ranking process is complete? What will we do with those who are assessed to be the company's A players? More worrisome to the group, what will we do with those identified as Cs?

A significant amount of discussion swirled around that last question, what will happen to the bottom-ranked individuals? The immediate assumption was that they would be involved in a development effort to move them up, into the B-player ranks. I pointed out that, unfortunately, the usual effect of initiating development efforts with this group is merely to churn the larger population. People who are rated as Cs are developed until they move up a bit and displace some bottom-end Bs. These new entrants to the C ranks are then developed until they move up and displace others . . . a never-ending nasty cycle.

A better solution, I argued, was to do what everyone knew was right for them in their specific situation: to reserve intensive development efforts for the A players who would enormously benefit both themselves and the company, and to remove C players from their jobs, placing them either in other jobs within the company that they could unquestionably handle with a high degree of competence, or arranging for them to leave the organization and find a more appropriate position elsewhere.

Did this mean summary terminations? No. But it meant that anyone identified in the bottom group would be removed from his position and either moved to another job that he could handle in an outstanding way or exited from the company in a dignified way with a generous separation package. When separations were deemed necessary, they would be done over time—a brief period of time—but long enough to make sure that the company wasn't damaged by important work left undone or that the morale of the great majority of employees wasn't wounded by seeing coworkers treated without compassion. Once this decision had been made, the HR team developed an attractive severance package to be offered to those who would end up in the bottom group.

Finally, the company decided to include a form of appeal process. They decided that if an employee disagreed with the outcome of the ranking session, he or she could reject the severance package and over the next ninety days attempt to demonstrate that the assessors had been wrong and that he truly was in the solid B category. If this happened, then the record of the initial C assessment would be expunged, and he would be dealt with the same as anyone else who had initially been placed in the vital 70 percent category. But if he failed, he was told that termination would occur, and the severance package would not be as generous as the one offered at the conclusion of the initial rankings.

Figuring Out the Nuts and Bolts

The program was well publicized to everyone who would be directly affected as an assessor or assessee. Each individual was assured that not only his final ranking but also his strengths, weaknesses, and development needs (including disagreements) that emerged in the group discussion would also be shared.

Every assessor got a briefing book with complete job histories and demographic data on the individuals being assessed, along with the last one or two performance appraisals. The briefing book opened with a one-page cover sheet that detailed the individual's complete employment history (both with the company and previous jobs), educational background, pay grade and salary, time in position, performance appraisal summaries, skill assessment, photograph, and the result of the last succession-planning discussion. Each one went through a three-hour training program that reviewed the spirit, intent, and mechanics of the program, along with intensive skill-building activities. A sample activity: write down the initials of every boss you've ever had in your career, from your first part-time job in high school up to the one you've got now. Pick the A and the C—the best boss and the worst. Now assess that boss against the four leadership criteria. What made him or her an A player or a C?

Finally, the CEO sent everyone involved in the procedure two e-mails in the two weeks before the meeting. In the first, addressed to every one of the people who would be reviewed in the ranking sessions, he said, "The purpose of this process is to identify the top 20 percent of our leaders whose career development should be accelerated, the middle 70 percent whose solid contributions are critical to our success, and the lower 10 percent whose talents are not fully leveraged here, and who could probably be better utilized elsewhere." His e-mail continued:

> This program will benefit everyone who is involved. For those 90 percent of Acme managers who will end up being ranked in the top two groups, the ranking process will confirm the importance of their contributions. For those ranked in the top 20 percent, this program will highlight the talent they bring to Acme and accelerate their development. And for the 10 percent who are ranked in the bottom category, this process will allow the person to move to a job that better matches his or her skills, whether inside or outside the company.

In the second e-mail, with the subject line "My expectations," he provided a blunt message to all assessors:

The future of the company's leadership rests with the employees that you identify as the top 20 percent. Use care, be deliberate, be selective, and be "executive" in these identifications. I want the best identified so that aggressive development can be created and implemented for them. We must also identify a full 10 percent of our lower performers. That said, I am prepared to work with you to ensure that all employee separations which become necessary through this process are accomplished in an orderly manner.

Finally, he concluded that e-mail to assessors with some bullet points:

- I fully expect that each of you will continue to prepare for the sessions as you have been instructed. Get your thoughts together and talk to the employees who report to you who will be assessed. Get their viewpoints on how they feel that they have performed to the criteria.

- Think out of your functional silos. Demand that your fellow assessors provide clear examples of excellence when they describe an employee.

- Ask questions . . . reach in to zones of discomfort.

- There will be a minimum of 10 percent lower-echelon individuals identified. The number could be greater in any given session *but not less*. I have heard talk that there may be less . . . let me be clear, *there will not be*. I recognize that this is a difficult task, but it has to be done if we are going to raise the bar for executive leadership at Acme.

- Planning for what the development plans for the top 20 percent is going to look like is under way at this time. While the architecture for this development is being finalized, I want you to know that I expect each of you to take a major and fundamental role in this endeavor. The development of our top 20 percent is a strategically important undertaking for which many of you will be held directly responsible.

An "Orderly Manner"

One of the early concerns of the executives who would be participating in the ranking session regarded what would happen to those subordinates who were identified as C players—the bottom 10 percent. They and their colleagues had decided that these people would not be merely advised of the fact that they were identified in the bottom group or be given a year to shape up, but instead would be moved out of their positions. Most of them probably knew before the sessions even began who their C players were. They also knew that these were good people, many of whom, through no fault of their own, had been promoted over their heads, and almost all of whom had been faithful and diligent workers for many years. They were not "poor performers"—the company's true poor performers had been let go in the course of two reductions in force over the previous two years. They were people who simply didn't have what it took to move the company from where it was to where it needed to be in order to survive in a highly competitive environment.

Complicating the situation was the fact that many of the potential C players were working on important special projects or assignments that they were capable of handling in an excellent way. Managers were concerned that they would be forced to remove someone from a job prematurely, without allowing for important projects to be completed or for replacement candidates to be identified. We realized that not telling them how they came out until their project was completed and a replacement was in the wings was both ethically and operationally unworkable. It would be wrong not to let people know how they came out as soon as the sessions were completed—we had pledged that we would do so. Besides, the anxiety produced by forcing people to wait for the news would have an intensely negative effect on both morale and productivity.

Instead, managers were told that first, they would be able to replace anyone they let go as a result of the ranking sessions. (One of the biggest resistances to forced ranking arises when managers are not allowed to replace individuals who are terminated as a result of ending up in the lowest category. Managers are much more willing to identify and remove poorer performers if they know they can immediately replace the person with an outside hire.) Second, we told them to work out a plan for the individual's orderly transition out of the job (and out of the company if no appropriate internal position could be found) with the full involvement of the employee himself and the HR specialist for the department.

Inside the Assessment Meetings

The assessment meetings took up most of a week, with each meeting running up to eight hours. At first we thought it would be feasible to conduct two assessment sessions per day, morning and afternoon, for two different groups. But the intensity of the meetings coupled with the large number of people to be assessed caused many sessions to run long. The quality of discussion of the performance and potential of any individual was never sacrificed; only the extended discussions of development needs for A players and appropriate placement for C players had to be shortened.

Meeting mechanics were simple. In each session, the name of each manager to be assessed was written on a 4 × 6 sticky note and arranged in alphabetical order on blank flip chart pages posted on a side wall. In the center of the room, facing the group of assessors, was a blank piece of graphics paper, five feet high, ten feet long. Lines divided this paper into three segments. The only words on it were *Top 20 percent*, *Vital 70 percent*, and *Bottom 10 percent* at the top of the appropriate section, together with another sticky note that provided the exact number of people who needed to be assigned into each category.

After a quick review of the mechanics for the session, the rationale, a few ground rules, and the key points from the training sessions, came the final instructions about the required meeting outcome: "Your job is to discuss each individual fully, then move each name from the alphabetical list to the appropriate position as an A, B, or C player."

In the first session, after a minute or two of hesitance and shuffling, the assessors decided to move all of the names from the alphabetical list to the initial position at once and not one at a time. Each boss went up to the flip chart, peeled off the names of his or her subordinates, and stuck them in the A, B, or C area.

In the first assessment session, thirty-seven people needed to be slotted as As, Bs, or Cs. After the assessors sat down, the numbers weren't close. Thirteen names had been placed in the A area, twenty-six were tagged as Bs, and the C territory was empty. For the first of several times in the session, I reminded them of the outcome required: seven As, twenty-six Bs, four Cs. Then they started talking.

This group of Acme's vice presidents began their discussion by reviewing a person who had been proposed as a top 20 percent individual. "If this were my company, would I want this guy on my team?" the head of manufacturing asked of this apparent high-potential benchmark A player. "I'm going to throw the first turd on the table," he continued. "He doesn't belong in the top 20 percent. He's no A."

The sales head came in. "I want him on my team," he said. "On my B team."

The man's boss—after several other participants put forth the argument that this individual, long considered a high-potential employee, actually had less stretch than had been assumed—got up and moved his name out of the A ranks. "But he's a high B," he said as he moved the sticky note to just the other side of the line.

"There's no such thing as a 'high B!'" the manufacturing VP responded. "A B is a B is a B."

The first argument erupted. Very quickly the assessor group further refined the middle category into B-pluses (those who just missed being classified as As), B-minuses (those who barely escaped the C category), and the great majority of good solid B performers. And this made sense, since the conversations that would follow the assessment meetings would be different depending on whether a B player just barely missed being named an A or whether the individual just barely escaped a C-player designation. (See the scripts in appendix A for what to say to A, B, and C players.)

The discussions concentrated on the requirement that they make their judgments based on the four criteria that the executive group had selected: execute with excellence, passion for results, succeed with people, and make tough decisions. But other factors continually came in. One manager was new to a job and, somebody argued, was a B by default. "Not true," another said. "We are looking at an individual's innate skills, and they aren't going to change because of a new job."

Pruning the list of A players was tough, particularly since everyone agreed that these managers were all among the best in the organization. But the rules couldn't be changed. "Look," somebody explained. "We've got a shelf that holds seven bottles. It doesn't matter how hard we work or how beautiful the bottles are. We can only put seven bottles on the shelf!"

Assigning people into the C category was equally difficult, even when there was common agreement that an individual did not measure up to the rest of the team. "I don't want to have to shoot myself in the foot and get rid of somebody that I don't have a replacement for," the head of IT said. "Does it mean we have to terminate?" "Will this be a hollow exercise if we don't terminate?" the CFO responded. The ensuing discussion brought out both the fact that while terminations would result, they would be arranged so as to cause minimum disruption to everyone involved, and the observation that some departments that had done a good job of moving quickly on marginal performers stood at a disadvantage compared with those that, until now, had tolerated mediocrity. "But a C is a C, wherever he is," another said. The outcome was that one department that had never been seen as particularly tough-minded or demanding ended up contributing almost all the C players to the list.

Every individual was discussed fully, though some required far more time than others. The solid B players were usually identified and slotted with just a few minutes of review. The longest discussions involved those who had generally been accepted as high-potential promotion candidates, when the discussions around the table revealed that not everybody agreed with what had preciously been the accepted view.

"I'll be straight," the chief operating officer said to the VP of HR about one individual who for years had been seen as the obvious replacement candidate for the VP of HR's position. "She's not an A player and she's not going to get your job. She's not proactive. She may be a strong manager, but she's not a leader. I'm not going to say never, but it's a long, uphill fight. She needs to work on her bedside manner. You have turned her into a very competent professional, but she's not on track for your job."

The sensitivities that surround personnel discussions throughout organizations showed up here, tempering the blunt frankness that characterized all the sessions:

"Would you give her the Western Region job?"

"Yes, I probably would."

"If she were a white male, would you give her the job?"

"Well . . . "

"She is disorganized in her style of thought. If she were a white male, we wouldn't be having this conversation. She is a solid B. Promoting her is not the right thing for this organization." A pause. "Am I damning her too much?"

"No. She's a B."

Besides identifying the company's top talent, the vital majority, and the also-rans, the intense forced ranking discussions also caused senior management to look at development in bigger ways than training seminars and university executive programs. "Are there jobs in headquarters that we can use as development experiences for these guys in the field that we just don't see?" the VP of HR asked.

The head of operations responded. "We've got a couple of jobs that might be possible to use as eighteen-month rotation assignments."

"There's another issue, though," another participant said. "We've got some people who are doing a good job but aren't going anywhere and aren't going to move. These people are slot blockers."

A name of a slot blocker surfaces. One of the executives talks about him in a way that makes him sound like an obvious C player, a man that needs to be replaced. "But telling him that he's a B will be a real shake-up for him," his boss replies, still convinced that his subordinate is a candidate for an A ranking.

"So would telling him that he's a C and he's out," another responds.

The matter is settled. "I don't think it's healthy for anyone to be in that job forever," the VP of HR says. The individual will be told that while he was ranked as a B player, the organization will be looking for another assignment for him because his job is too important to have it permanently filled.

The Results

The immediate result was that the task was completed successfully. Each group of assessors assigned the appropriate percentage of individuals to the various groups. But more than that, they achieved in every case a genuine consensus on the leadership potential of each of the company's top 227 leaders. The ranking session results were reviewed by the CEO and both the company's inside and outside legal counsel to see if the outcomes produced any issues of disparate impact. None were found and no legal challenges resulted from the separations that resulted from the process.

For each of the C players, a full discussion was held during the ranking session about whether there actually was an appropriate job match for this person somewhere in the company or whether it would serve everyone's interests best if the person left to find other opportunities elsewhere. For some, there was an obvious better fit within the organization. For the majority, the company's generous severance package, combined with outplacement and other help, made the transition to a new employer easier. For some A players, specific developmental assignments were discussed; for others, the development plan was figured out over the following weeks with the individual's active participation.

Perhaps the greatest additional benefit resulting from the process came in the comments made by many of the managers and executives as, exhausted, they left the room at the close of the session: that they had for the first time truly understood the depth of the company's top-talent pool and recognized where leadership peaks and valleys existed. The company's annual succession-planning event had never generated the depth of analysis or the candid scrutiny of talent that the forced ranking session had produced

Forced ranking can't substitute for other organizational processes. An effective performance appraisal process that focuses all organization members on key goals and competencies should be in place before a forced ranking procedure is initiated. Because of forced ranking's sensitive and controversial reputation, wise decisions about tailoring the procedure to the organization's specific culture need to be made from the start. The process needs to be toughly managed, since the temptation to bend the rules will always be present. But as Acme Services Company demonstrated, if a company wants to jump-start a genuine leadership development process, and move quickly toward muscle-building the organization, forced ranking may well be the best tool around.

Forced Ranking and the Small Company

I'm sure that the impression I've given in this chapter is that forced ranking is a procedure undertaken only by the big guys—*Fortune* 500

companies and similar-sized firms. I have discussed conducting training programs and utilizing external facilitators. I described how Acme
put together briefing books and made provisions to keep those rankers
who may not know a particular person being reviewed engaged with
the process. I talked about a process used in a company employing
thousands of people to rank the top 227 executives. But is all this activity necessary when it's a small company that is using forced ranking?

No, it's not. Recently, on a Monday morning, I got a phone call
from the HR director of a local company with about one hundred
thirty people. We'll call the company TechCorp. She told me that after
two years of the president's urging his VPs to toughen up their performance standards and take action to replace subpar performers, his
CFO had decided (at long last) to fire the manager of accounting and
replace him with a stronger individual. This decision gave the president the stimulus to decide that a more thorough housecleaning was
needed and demand that the HR manager create and execute a forced
ranking system specifically to identify and terminate the weakest 10
percent of the company's employees. Learning about my work in this
area through her company's employment attorney, she was calling me
to ask for help.

After a short meeting with her the next day to review some of the
basic concepts of forced ranking and to learn more about the president's expectations, I suggested that she review our discussion with
him. I said, "Ask him if he'd like to meet with me to talk about the
possibility of my working with them to design the system, make sure
it did what he wanted, and was defensible in the event any challenge
later arose to the terminations he was planning."

That was Tuesday. She called back on Wednesday asking if I could
meet with her and the president at 1:00 p.m. Thursday—the next day.
I said I'd come over a little early so she and I could come up with a
game plan for my meeting with him.

That game plan went out the window when he and I started talking.
He knew exactly what he wanted. He said that he had told his five
VPs that they were to come into the conference room where we were
now meeting at 1:30 p.m. (it was now 1:05 p.m.). He told me that he
wanted me to tell them how to do forced ranking to identify the bottom 10 percent so they could be terminated and wanted her to make
up a list of all the people in the company and have it ready to hand

out to the vice presidents the next day. And, he said, they were all going to be involved in a conference call at 2:30 p.m., so I only had an hour to get them on board and explain how the process would work.

In the twenty-five minutes I had before the company's five VPs walked in, the three of us hammered out the details of their forced ranking system:

1. Instead of just identifying and terminating the worst 10 percent of the TechCorp employee population, they would approach it as a talent identification process and identify their best performers as well as those on the bottom.

2. They would use a top 20 percent/vital 70 percent/bottom 10 percent ranking scheme.

3. They would separate the total employee population into two different lists: one of exempt employees (about a hundred, primarily engineers) and the other of nonexempt employees (about thirty, primarily secretaries and administrative assistants). Each VP would independently rank both groups.

4. For each group, each VP would conduct the top 20/vital 70/bottom 10 analysis on the entire list, including both his own direct reports and those people who worked for the other VPs. They would do this over the weekend. On Monday morning, they would meet and compare lists, thrash through any disagreements, and come up with a final 20/70/10 distribution for the president's review.

5. On Monday afternoon, the VPs would meet with the president and the HR manager, review their recommendations, and make any final adjustments to the list.

6. People who were ranked in the bottom 10 percent would be terminated from the company. But a specific departure plan would be created for each individual, taking into account the projects the individual was currently working on, to minimize disruption, and the individual's history with TechCorp.

7. A generous severance package would be tailored for each departing individual.

8. The HR manager would work with each of the VPs on development and retention plans for those identified in the top 20 percent.

9. The use of the forced ranking process would be considered "company-confidential" information and not discussed with employees.

10. I would write and provide them with scripts to advise those employees who ended up in the bottom group that they would be leaving the organization and how the termination process would work.

At 1:30 p.m. the vice presidents walked in. We had quickly duplicated copies of the overview materials I had brought with me to go over with the president. I handed them out. I went over the rationale for forced ranking and explained the basic principles (two of the five had earlier worked for large corporations and had participated in a ranking process; the other three were familiar with forced ranking from their business reading).

We established the criteria they should use to make the decisions. I drew the two matrixes I provided in chapter 4 (see figures 4-1 and 4-2) on the conference room's whiteboard. I suggested that besides making their decisions based on current performance and perceived potential, they also consider two additional factors: effectiveness of execution and intellectual horsepower. We went over the mechanics and timetable. We talked about how to make good ranking decisions. At 2:30 p.m. we were done. Their forced ranking system had been designed. They left for their conference call; I drove back to my office.

The following Tuesday, the HR manager called. The process had worked perfectly. The VPs had come to agreement without difficulty, the president concurred with their recommendations, and all of them felt significantly enlightened by having to identify the top 20 percent. The scripts were just what they needed. The TechCorp forced ranking process was a smashing success.

All the publicity about forced ranking has focused entirely on America's household-name companies and left the impression that it's a technique for only giant corporations. Granted, designing and installing a forced ranking procedure is usually a major organizational change requiring the efforts of many people over a period of several weeks or months, as we saw with the example of Acme Services Company. But it doesn't have to be that way. It particularly doesn't have to be that way in the small company. Forced ranking can be an appropriate talent management process for any company of over a hundred or so people to consider. It can happen fast, and it can be done right in a very short period of time (as the leaders of TechCorp demonstrated).

In chapter 6, we'll examine a technique called *forced distribution*, which is often confused with forced ranking. I'll explain how forced distribution is different and how to make it work effectively.

6

Forced Distribution

THERE IS LITTLE ARGUMENT that those who contribute the most, have the greatest potential, and shoulder more than their share of the load, should be more generously rewarded. Likewise, almost no one would dispute that those who contribute the least should be encouraged to either increase the quality of their contribution or find employment at another organization, where their talents and contributions are more in line with the organization's expectations. "Executives owe it to the organization and to their fellow workers not to tolerate nonperforming individuals in important jobs," notes management authority Peter Drucker. "It may not be the employees' fault that they are underperforming, but even so, they have to be removed."[1]

The challenge—how do you figure out who's in which group? If conventional performance appraisal systems were actually used as they were designed to be used, the need for any more rigorous procedure would be minimal. Most appraisal systems ask managers to identify their distinguished performers, their solid steady-Eddies, and their also-rans. But, as we've seen, too many managers would rather fudge the facts and inflate their ratings than face having the hard conversations that truthful performance assessments often require.

As we've discussed, the familiar performance appraisal system can fail if managers set their goals soft and have performance expectations that are low. To drive rigor and truth into performance appraisal assessments and discussions, many organizations today employ a technique called *forced distribution*, the setting of maximums and minimums in performance appraisal ratings to ensure that there is differentiation.

One of the most common misunderstandings that arise when people talk about performance management involves the difference between forced ranking and forced distribution. While most people in organizations are familiar with the term *forced ranking*, it turns out that they use the phrase to describe two very different processes. In some cases, they are referring to the procedure I have devoted this book to, the process in which managers are required to evaluate their employees and assign them into predetermined categories based on their performance, potential, and promotability. In other cases, they use the *forced ranking* term to refer to a requirement in the company's performance appraisal process that allows only a certain percentage of employees to get the highest rating and requires that some minimum number must be assigned to the lowest categories of performance. And sometimes they mean something else entirely.

Here's a personal example of the multiple-meaning confusion I've described. Within the same month recently, I was invited to spend a day providing an executive overview to the senior leadership teams of two large corporations on the subject of forced ranking. My assignment, as I understood it (and my clients seemed to be very clear in spelling out their expectations for the day as we discussed them in our telephone conversations in advance of the engagement), was to discuss the use of the forced ranking procedure that this book has concentrated on describing. From our conversations, it was clear that my job was to describe the ways in which companies like Sun and PepsiCo and GE were using the forced ranking technique I've described in this book, analyze the pros and cons of the approach, and then in smaller sessions with their senior HR managers, review their own forced ranking process with the goal of fine-tuning it.

That's what I thought. But in both cases, when I arrived on the scene, it turned out that there was a significant amount of confusion and misunderstanding—on my part, on the part of the senior executive who engaged me, and on the part of the members of the executive team I was to address—about precisely what we were talking about. In the first organization, an entertainment colossus, the organization's objective was actually to tune up its performance appraisal procedures. In doing so, it was considering giving managers some fairly rigid guidelines on what the company's top executives felt an appropriate distribution of appraisal ratings would look like. In the second case, a large telecommunications firm, the company for the first time in several years had a few extra dollars it could put into a bonus pool. It was considering using some kind of quick totem-pole forced ranking process to make the best decisions about who should get bonuses and how the dollars should be allocated.

With both organizations, the day I spent with them ended up being highly productive. All of their goals got achieved. Both times, however, we spent a short period at the start of the day awkwardly sorting out exactly what we were talking about when we used the same *forced ranking* term to mean quite different things.

Forced ranking and forced distribution are two different processes. In this chapter, we will discuss the forced distribution of appraisal ratings and examine how this technique can be introduced and used effectively in a traditional performance appraisal system.

What Is Forced Distribution?

Forced distribution is a procedure that involves tweaking the rules of the performance appraisal system to either request or require a certain distribution of performance appraisal ratings. Figure 6-1 highlights the key distinctions between the two approaches as they are commonly used in organizations.

How Forced Distribution Works

Consider a company that has a five-level rating scale—Distinguished/Superior/Fully Successful/Needs Improvement/Unsatisfactory. Unhappy with the fact that every year almost everyone in the firm is rated in the top two categories, management adopts a policy that restricts the number of people who can get the top rating, and requires a certain amount of lower-level ratings. Its forced distribution scheme might look like figure 6-2.

FIGURE 6-1

Forced distribution versus forced ranking

Forced distribution

- Forced distribution is a component of an organization's performance appraisal policies and procedures.

- The purpose is to ensure differentiation by requiring that appraisers meet a predetermined distribution of performance appraisal ratings.

- The distribution of ratings may either be required ("forced") or recommended ("guidelines").

- The focus is on *absolute comparisons:* managers are required to assess how well people performed against their goals and objectives.

- It is a *person-to-standard* evaluation.

- The forced distribution procedure is used by a large number of organizations, public and private.

- Sample distribution requirement:

Distinguished	Maximum of 10%
Superior	20–30%
Good Solid Performer	50–60%
Needs Improvement	10–15%
Unsatisfactory	Minimum of 5%

Forced ranking

- Forced ranking is a management system that typically operates independent of and in addition to the organization's performance appraisal procedure.

- Assessment criteria are usually different from those used in performance appraisal.

- The assessment focuses on both performance (past) and potential (future).

- The procedure is used almost exclusively by private sector organizations.

- The focus is on *relative comparisons:* managers are required to assess how well people perform compared with others in the organization.

- It is a *person-to-person* evaluation.

- General Electric is the most famous proponent; many other companies, large and small, use the technique.

- Sample ranking schemes: top 20%/vital 70%/bottom 10%, or quartiling, or top 10/bottom 10.

If rigidly enforced, the new policy will ensure that there is differentiation in performance appraisal ratings. But two major problems immediately arise with the proposed distribution scheme in figure 6-2. First, there is no flexibility in the percentages of ratings allowed. As a result, the manager of a low-performing group is required to assign 5 percent of her subordinates into the Distinguished category and another 20 percent into the Superior category, when, in truth, hardly

FIGURE 6-2

Sample forced distribution rating scheme

Distinguished	5%
Superior	20%
Fully Successful	50%
Needs Improvement	20%
Unsatisfactory	5%

any of them deserve even a Fully Successful rating. Likewise, the manager of a group of all-stars is restricted from giving appropriately high ratings to his outstanding cadre of performers. And exactly half of the people in each group, regardless of either the relative or absolute quality of their performance, will be rated as Fully Successful.

Another problem with the proposed distribution scheme is that it exactly mirrors a bell-shaped curve. Regardless of how well people in the organization actually perform, in this example the manager is required to allocate performance ratings to fit a Gaussian statistical model. But a pure bell curve is almost never accurate in describing the distribution of human performance. For a legitimate bell-shaped Gaussian curve to be valid, two conditions must be present. First, there must be a sufficiently large population under assessment. While the company as a whole may have enough people to support the math behind a bell-shaped curve, individual work units of four or eight or a dozen employees just aren't large enough for a bell curve to be valid.

More important, in addition to a sufficiently large population, there must be a *random distribution* of the elements that make up that population for a bell curve to be valid. But the employee population of an organization is never the result of random distribution. Companies don't hire people at random, selecting, say, every fourteenth applicant. Instead, they sift the applicant pool carefully to identify the most promising. Companies don't promote people at random, selecting people for advancement by lottery or on an alphabetical basis. Instead, they promote the best talent they've got. Almost every company provides training programs and developmental experiences to enhance the quality of talent and performance throughout the organization, thus further de-randomizing the population. And in spite of the complaints detailed earlier that they don't do it fast enough or soon enough, organizations still weed out and terminate some members of the workforce whose performance is simply unacceptable.

Thus a pure bell-shaped curve is almost never an appropriate model for the distribution of scores in a performance appraisal system. The distribution must take into account the fact that there will always be a positive skew—an appropriate positive skew—caused by organizational efforts to improve the quality of the employee population.

A better approach might be to allow some flexibility in the allocation of ratings, and allow a positive ratings skew to reflect the reality that the members of the organization are not performing at random. Upon reflection, our hypothetical organization that wants to ensure a degree of differentiation in its performance appraisal results might alter its first draft of the proposed distribution scheme and propose a model that more accurately reflects the reality of human performance (see figure 6-3).

Now, instead of requiring that exactly 5 percent of all employees be rated Distinguished regardless of the actual level of their performance, the revised distribution scheme allows managers to place up to 5 percent in that category—but there's nothing that says that anyone must be rated Distinguished. At the other end of the scale, the requirement has also been adjusted to provide a range of 2 to 5 percent of employees who are expected to fall into the Unsatisfactory category. There must still be some Unsatisfactory appraisal ratings assigned, but the requirement has been significantly reduced.

Instead of the rigid and fixed percentages that were required for each of the three middle performance appraisal ratings in the initial

FIGURE 6-3

Revised forced distribution rating scheme

Distinguished	5% maximum
Superior	20–30%
Good Solid Performer	50–60%
Needs Improvement	10–15%
Unsatisfactory	2–5%

model, ranges have now been provided. This will increase the flexibility of the system and allow managers of particularly poorly performing or high-performing work units to reflect that fact in the appraisal ratings they assign to their team members. Finally, the rigid bell-curve requirement has been adjusted to allow twice as many people to be assigned to the rating category one step higher than the middle rating than to the category a step lower than the middle. In other words, 20 to 30 percent of all employees can expect to receive a Superior rating, while only 10 to 15 percent of all employees—half as many—are expected to fall into the Needs Improvement category.

But some important questions still need to be addressed:

- Is this distribution scheme appropriate for an actual organization?

- How well will the system described actually meet the needs of the two managers described earlier, one who is saddled with a bunch of goof-offs and goldbricks, the other with a cadre of champions?

- How should it be applied to a work unit with a very small population? For example, if there are only three people in the department, does that mean that no one can be rated Distinguished?

- Should the distribution percentages merely be suggested, with flexibility allowed for individual managers to vary from the ranges if they can present a compelling case for variance, or must the distribution requirement absolutely be met by all?

- When, if ever, should exceptions be allowed? If a manager can demonstrate through hard business results that her team has outperformed any comparable unit in the organization, should she be allowed to award a greater percentage of higher ratings? And if another manager's unit produces only mediocre results, should he be prevented from awarding a Distinguished or Superior rating to anyone on the team?

- How do you control for variations in the standards and expectations of various managers? In one department, the manager may evaluate a subordinate with a 98 percent customer satisfaction

score as Needs Improvement; in the next department over,
the same 98 percent customer satisfaction score may earn the
employee a Superior rating.

- Who will police the system, making sure that the guidelines are
followed? Is that line management's job? Is it HR's? And what
happens if the policeman is asleep on the beat and allows variances to get by?

- What will happen when a manager (or a whole department)
ignores the guidelines? Will managers have to take their
appraisals back and assign a different rating (provoking morale-
destroying, buck-passing whines from spineless managers to
their subordinates, such as "I really rated you Superior, but
personnel forced me to lower it to Fully Successful"). And what
will happen if the manager has already had the performance
appraisal discussion with the individual when the variance from
the guidelines is noticed? Will she still have to go back and
change it?

Getting Forced Distribution Right

The most common reason that companies adopt some kind of forced
distribution requirement for performance appraisal ratings (whether
rigidly required or more loosely offered as "guidelines") is that their
compensation system employs a pay-for-performance philosophy and
relies on performance appraisal ratings as the basis for distributing merit
increases. When performance appraisal ratings determine the amount
of merit increase an individual will get, managers are under pressure to
rate everyone as high as possible in order to maximize the dollars flow-
ing to every member of the team. Top executives and compensation
specialists want to see managers make significant differentiations among
their subordinates, reflecting the quality of their performance; managers, however, routinely discover that their lives are less stressful if they
prevaricate about the quality of Suzie's performance on the official form,
award her as big an increase as they can, and then deal with her performance deficiencies on an off-the-record basis.

While adding a forced distribution requirement to a performance
appraisal system may solve the ratings-inflation problem, it may also
produce some adverse side effects. Requiring managers to meet a

forced distribution will lead to the identification of more underper-formers, acknowledge Camille Olson and Gregory Davis, the authors of the legal report on forced ranking prepared for the Society for Human Resource Management (SHRM). "But it will do so at the risk of creating perceptions of arbitrariness and demoralizing managers and employees who do not buy-in to the system." They offer an alterna-tive suggestion:

> To the extent an organization's real objective is to better reward top per-formers, it could set a percentage for high ratings only and thereby minimize the antagonism of low-ranked employees. But rather than requiring managers to hit fixed percentage targets, more flexible per-centage goals might be established. Then, over time, it may be possible to force managers to identify an increasing number of poor performers.[2]

Other authors simply reject out-of-hand the notion that providing managers with guidelines or requirements for the distribution of performance appraisal ratings can be a useful way to address the perennial ratings-inflation problem. Alfie Kohn, a vehement foe of any rewards-based structure and an opponent of competition, whether in companies or in educational institutions, argues:

> If bonuses are to be handed out at work, they should be available to any-one who meets a given standard instead of making each person an obstacle to the others' success. Likewise the tendency of some classroom teachers to grade on a curve is nothing short of immoral: it gratuitously limits the number of good grades just so the result will conform to an arbitrary, fixed distribution (few grades that are very bad, an equally small number that are very good, and a lot that are mediocre). This requires making meaningless distinctions between essentially compara-ble performances so that only a few students will receive a top mark. More important, it turns students into rivals, creating an atmosphere of hostility and sabotaging the possibility of cooperation that leads to higher-quality learning.[3]

Notwithstanding Kohn's fervor, he seems to have his facts wrong. The distinctions in job performance aren't meaningless. As we saw earlier, the distinctions between good and bad performers (let alone the distinctions between good and great) are significant, and certainly worth the efforts to identify and retain those who deliver outstanding performance. And this author's experience is that the "atmosphere of hostility and sabotage" that Kohn warns against is rare. When such an atmosphere is present, it tends to be caused by factors far more malev-olent than the distribution procedures required in a once-a-year performance appraisal system.

A more rational trepidation about the appropriateness of providing distribution guidelines is voiced by the distinguished author and researcher Ed Lawler. "I believe that the forced distribution approach is a bureaucratic solution to a serious leadership failure," he writes. "It ignores the reality that in some work groups there are no poor performers and in others there are no good performers. It causes man-agers to disown the appraisal event and to essentially say, 'I was just following the rules.'"[4]

Lawler's right, of course. In some work groups there are no poor per-formers, and in some there are no good ones. But these tend to be the exceptions. For the most part, within any given group of people there will be some who excel and some who lag, with most meeting the expectations that have been set. And tough-minded reviews of all performance appraisals and ratings conducted by the organization's senior leadership, with seemingly inflated appraisals routinely kicked back for rework, will be the best solution to the ratings-inflation con-cern. But even that won't stop weak-willed managers from telling underlings, "I put you in for a superior rating, but the big boss kicked it back."

Forced distribution requirements can have an appropriate place in the design of performance appraisal systems, particularly when they are structured in such a way as to recognize that in any work group there are likely to be many more good performers than poor ones, and they provide a mechanism for managers of exceptional work teams to secure an exemption from the guidelines' requirements through demonstrating genuine excellence in business results.

What Are Appropriate Distribution Guidelines?

Earlier I listed a series of questions that need to be addressed to make the requirement that there be some distribution of ratings workable. Here are some suggestions that will be useful in determining whether to have a distribution requirement in your performance appraisal sys-tem and how to make it most effective.

Get wide input on what the appropriate distribution should be.
This is an issue that should be discussed widely, and nonsupervisory employees should be included in those discussions. I have consistently found that the great majority of employees agree that there is a wide distribution of performance among their coworkers. They also feel that it is appropriate for a performance appraisal system to provide guidelines to their supervisors on what an appropriate distribution of appraisal ratings should be.

In working recently with a large financial services company to help create a new performance appraisal system, I addressed over a dozen employee meetings that involved hundreds of the workers in sessions aimed at introducing them to the new procedure. After talking for a few minutes with them about quality variations in peoples' performance, I asked them to work in small teams and quickly answer two questions: first, should the company provide a set of recommended guidelines for the distribution of appraisal ratings, or should it let every manager decide for himself what appraisal ratings to award to members of his work unit? Second, if they felt that there should be guidelines provided, what should the guidelines be?

Altogether about three dozen teams of nonmanagement employees took part in these informal team discussions, and overwhelmingly the teams came up with the same answers. Yes, there should be guidelines provided. And second, the guidelines should reflect a bell-curve distribution in their performance.

By discussing the purpose of providing guidelines, and by letting people have input to what the guidelines should be, the probability of acceptance escalates enormously.

Provide guidelines, not rigid requirements. Allow some flexibility in the distribution expectations. In GROTEAPPROACH, the Web-based performance management system my company has developed, clients can determine whether they want to show a recommended distribution and what that distribution should be.[5] Our default recommendation is illustrated in table 6-1.

This set of guidelines provides for twice as many people to be rated in the Distinguished and Superior category than in the Needs Improvement and Unsatisfactory categories. It provides a range and not a fixed requirement at every rating level. It provides for a reasonably normal distribution but one with an appropriate positive skew. And finally, as the heading indicates, the distributions displayed are not rigid requirements but instead represent the "likely percentage of employees" that will end up in each area.

Allow managers to vary from the guidelines—but don't make it easy for them to do so. It will be rare for managers of troubled units to complain that the guidelines suggested in table 6-1 force them to award an undeserved high performance appraisal rating to too many of their poorly performing subordinates. It just won't happen. But it's entirely possible that managers will complain that the guidelines prevent them from awarding enough high ratings to all the members of their disproportionately talented team. Under what circumstances should managers be able to identify, say, a third of all their subordinates as meriting a Distinguished rating, or two-thirds of them as Superior?

The answer is, of course, if the results they achieve justify it. In any organization there will be pockets of excellence, typically produced by an extraordinary leader who assembles a team of genuinely remarkable subordinates, demands excellence and never settles for anything less than exceptional performance, routinely rids the team of any members who do not consistently perform to her high standards, and manifests all the competencies put forward in the leadership books. The results that her team of all-stars produce will be recognized by everyone in the organization as genuinely exceptional, and when she asks to be allowed to award more Distinguished and Superior ratings, let her do it.

TABLE 6-1

GROTEAPPROACH recommended distribution

Overall level of performance	Likely percentage of employees in each level
Distinguished	Up to 10%
Superior	About 20–30%
Fully Successful	About 60% or more
Needs Improvement	About 10–15%
Unsatisfactory	Less than 5%

But it's likely that she won't ask. Managers like this are also likely to be ones that hold their subordinates to tough and demanding standards, and she will probably find that the guidelines proposed in table 6-1 work well for her purposes. Earlier in the book, I observed that there seems to be an inverse correlation between business results and performance appraisal ratings: managers who turn in the worst results also seem to award the highest ratings. These are the managers whose feet need to be held to the fire, the ones who need a bit of spine-stiffening that a set of guidelines can help apply.

Allowing a set of ranges for each performance appraisal rating gives managers reasonable flexibility. Requiring that managers get formal authorization from the head of their business unit and HR before exceeding the guidelines makes good business sense. This approach will also take care of those unusual situations where a manager has a very small group of highly talented individuals for whom the standard guidelines simply aren't appropriate. The obvious example is the legal department of a small company or municipality where the three lawyers are all doing outstanding work.

There are other issues that are important to resolve for a forced distribution approach to performance appraisal ratings to work well. These include such concerns as who will police the system and what will happen if managers simply ignore the distribution requirement. These questions can't be answered through rules and guidelines. These can only be answered by building a culture of accountability, the issue we'll address in the final chapter.

7

Getting the Truth into Performance Management

ONE OF THE CHARACTERISTICS of almost every organization that employs a formal forced ranking process is that it also has a separate performance appraisal system. Performance appraisal is the important and well-established annual process that, done right, helps everyone on the team understand how his or her performance contributes to the achievement of the organization's mission. An effective performance appraisal system educates all members of the organization about the competencies that are critical to success for the company as a whole and in their individual jobs. It provides for the identification of their key job responsibilities and identifies the standards and measures that the boss will use to evaluate the quality of the subordinate's performance. It encourages setting important and meaningful goals and identifies the outcomes those goals will be expected to produce.

In fact, if a company does an outstanding job of performance appraisal—if its managers take their responsibilities seriously; if the procedure is used for both planning at the start of the year and assessment at the end of the year; if managers uniformly deliver accurate, tough-minded, and honest feedback; if performance appraisal ratings are used to make compensation, promotion, termination, and other personnel decisions; and if appraisees are as actively involved in the system as appraisers are—then the need for a forced ranking procedure is significantly reduced.

But few companies have truly effective performance appraisal systems, and even fewer use their systems to maximum advantage. In this chapter, we will discuss the components of an effective performance appraisal system and explain how the performance appraisal system and the forced ranking system should interact.

Performance Appraisal Versus Forced Ranking

One major difference between a performance appraisal system and a forced ranking system is that performance appraisal programs typically affect everyone in the company—nobody's immune to receiving an annual performance review—while forced ranking systems usually only examine people at the top of the organization. While it's critical for every member of the company to know what's expected of him and to set meaningful goals, the payoff for employing a separate procedure for assigning talent into A, B, and C pools is greatest with those who have the greatest impact on the organization's overall success. In other words, people earn the right to be involved in forced ranking by making their way to the top of the organizational hierarchy.

Another difference between the two systems is that performance appraisal largely focuses on the past. Forced ranking, on the other hand, focuses primarily on the future. The issue in performance appraisal is evaluating how well the person performed in the previous twelve months. The issue in forced ranking is the amount of stretch the person has over the next two or three years to lead the organization into the future.

In most companies that use a forced ranking procedure, the ranking sessions are conducted separately from the company's performance appraisal system. Performance appraisal data is an important source of information used in making the forced ranking determinations, but the focus is on comparing individuals against each other and projecting the contributions that the individual will be capable of making in the next few years. Forced ranking sessions are typically held at an entirely different time of year, unrelated to the performance appraisal schedule.

The Rater Reliability/Calibration Process

One of the most difficult issues in ensuring that ratings are fair and that there is a level playing field in performance assessment is controlling for the variations in expectations from one manager to another. We know from our school days that a B from Professor Jones was far harder to earn than an A from Professor Smith. And in organizations it's also true—what one manager considers exceptional work, another will judge as only routine. When performance appraisal time rolls around, the employees of the first boss will get higher ratings (and higher merit increases) than those of the second boss, even though their work might actually be inferior.

To overcome this very real problem that can have a debilitating impact on morale, a growing number of companies are instituting "rater reliability," or "cross-calibration," or "leveling" mechanisms as part of their performance appraisal systems. The purpose of this performance calibration procedure is to make sure that different appraisers apply similar standards in assessing the performance of their subordinates.

The procedure's operation is straightforward: managers prepare preliminary performance appraisals for all their direct reports, including their planned appraisal ratings. A group of managers, all whom supervise employees with similar job responsibilities, then meet for a calibration session. They post the names of each of their subordinates, together with the planned rating for the rest of the group to review. Session participants then discuss the proposed appraisal rating for each individual, talking about how each of them came to the conclusions about the appropriate rating for each person. They share information and make sure that they are using a common yardstick to evaluate performance. They make adjustments in proposed ratings, moving some up and some down, to ensure accuracy, consistency, and inter-rater reliability. When everyone has come to agreement on the appropriate performance appraisal ratings for all the individuals under review, the managers then prepare the final performance appraisals.

The advantages of incorporating a calibration procedure as part of an organization's overall performance appraisal system are clear:

- *The process ensures a level playing field.* This is the greatest benefit. Having raters come together to discuss openly the way they have evaluated the performance of their subordinates ensures that consistent standards of performance are applied to all individuals doing similar work.

- *Rating errors are reduced.* There are many common "rating errors" that can inadvertently creep into a performance appraisal, in spite of the evaluator's best efforts to be fair and consistent. These rating errors include positive or negative skew (one supervisor consistently evaluates her employees much higher or lower compared with how her colleagues rate their subordinates), recency effect (only the events of the last few week or months are considered), similar-to-me effect (the tendency of individuals to rate people who resemble themselves more highly than they rate others), halo/horns effect (a particularly good or bad aspect of the individual's performance colors the appraiser's judgment about performance in unrelated areas), leniency effect (the supervisor rates all employees as Superior regardless of their actual performance), and others. Rater reliability sessions help reduce these errors and make performance appraisal more accurate.

- *The probability that managers will take performance management responsibilities seriously is greatly increased.* If managers have to display and discuss their planned ratings with their peers before giving them to their subordinates, they take far more care to get them right.

- *Participating in a rater reliability procedure makes it easier for managers to deliver lower-than-expected performance appraisals.* Assume that a manager initially is considering giving a rating of Superior to Ellen. In the course of the calibration discussion, the manager realizes that, compared with people doing similar jobs but working for other managers, Ellen's performance actually falls into the Fully Successful range at best. The manager makes the appropriate adjustment and lowers Ellen's rating. When he later has the performance appraisal discussion with a disappointed Ellen, he is better able to explain to her why the rating is appropriate since he has already had a discussion about her performance with the managers of her peers.

- *Calibration increases defensibility if appraisal results are challenged.* The fact that not only was an employee's performance appraisal rating determined by his or her immediate supervisor, but the supervisor's judgment was confirmed in a calibration session where the proposed rating was discussed with the supervisors of employees in similar positions, reduces the chance that a third party will find that the rating was biased.

- *Calibration enhances appraisers' managerial skills.* Participating in a rater reliability session requires each participant to think carefully about how well each person has performed. They must come in with specific examples of job performance, both for their own direct reports and for the subordinates of other managers.

- *The calibration process provides the organization with useful data on the ability of managers to spot and champion talent.*

There are, however, some significant concerns and disadvantages to using a formal calibration procedure as part of a company's performance appraisal process:

- *Some managers may resist having to defend their performance appraisal judgments before their peers.* This drawback to calibration is most noticeable among weaker and less-skilled managers. There is likely to be a fairly high degree of anxiety among the session participants, particularly the first time they participate in a calibration session. However, if the organization is sincerely concerned about upgrading the skills of its management population, observing the quality of participation in a calibration session can provide valuable data on each person's management skills.

- *Employees may feel that their privacy rights are inappropriately compromised.* This is a legitimate concern. In the FAQ document about its process published by a large transportation company for all employees, the company responded to this question directly: "All the participants in the rater reliability meetings are members of (the company's) management team. No person will participate in a rater reliability meeting in which employees at a peer level are being reviewed. Even though the participants in the meeting may not be in your direct chain of command, most of them will be familiar with your job and your job performance. They will be able to ask questions of your immediate supervisor to make sure that he or she is applying appropriate standards in evaluating your performance and assigning your performance appraisal rating. They will also be able to provide additional insights which will help your supervisor come to the best decision about the performance appraisal rating to assign." In short, there is a legitimate need to know.

- *Glib appraisers may be able to exert excessive influence over the group's decision making.* This concern can be allayed by a skilled facilitator. The "glib appraisers" are usually known in advance of the meeting, and particular attention can be paid to their inputs to make sure that it is the performance of their subordinates and not the skill of their presentations that is influencing the decisions.

- *Managers may blame the procedure for forcing them to deliver less-than-stellar appraisals to subordinates.* Again, this is an issue that arises primarily with weak-willed managers who are excessively conflict-averse. While the organization may not be able to control what any given manager says to a subordinate, it can provide clear instructions about what senior management's expectations are and, if necessary, give them a recommended script to follow.

- *The process can be expensive and time-consuming.* Managers must receive some training before engaging in a cross-calibration session (even if it's just some reading to do in advance followed by a few minutes of instruction at the start of the session). Facilitators need to be present. And the sessions themselves take time.

The Operation of a Calibration Session

The first step in initiating a rater reliability or cross-calibration process in an organization is to clearly communicate what will happen and why. Stressing the importance of ensuring a level playing field is the primary—and most accurate—message that needs to be sent to everyone involved in the organization's performance appraisal process. Publishing an FAQ document at the time of performance appraisal makes sense, not only to make sure that all the questions are answered but, more important, to make sure that all the important questions have been raised.

Managers are typically asked to prepare the performance appraisals for their subordinates as they would without the existence of the new procedure. However, before reviewing the appraisal with their boss for approval (and certainly before reviewing it with the employee), the appraisers are scheduled to attend a calibration session.

Calibration sessions can work well with as few as two or three appraisers reviewing their results to as many as a dozen. Beyond this number, however, two problems arise. First, there will be too many employees to review to give appropriate attention to each of them. Second, there will be too many "calibrators" who don't have enough information on the people under review to make useful inputs. Depending on the size of the group to be reviewed, about two to three hours is a workable time frame. A group of four to six managers each reviewing four to six subordinates is ideal.

Session participants should be told to bring the draft performance appraisals they have written, along with any supporting information they feel they may need. Once everyone's assembled, the session facilitator reviews the ground rules and answers any questions about the process. Internal human resources specialists can be excellent facilitators for rater reliability sessions. Unlike in forced ranking sessions, where the nature of the discussions and the level of the participants make external facilitation advisable, an internal facilitator can easily handle the requirements of a calibration session. Internal HR professionals will also be able to answer questions participants have about the company's performance appraisal system or its linkages to compensation and other systems.

The facilitator's instructions to the group can be brief. Explain that once all the names have been posted, they will start by looking over all the names and proposed ratings. Each participant will explain the rationale for the proposed rating to the other participants. The role of the other participants is to ask questions and provide additional information and insights in order to make sure that everyone is applying similar standards in making performance appraisal judgments. Tell the group that the most effective way of discussing ratings is to offer and ask for actual examples of performance that are illustrative of particularly effective or ineffective performance in the area being assessed.

The ground rules for the session are straightforward:

- When an individual is under review, those participants in the session who are directly knowledgeable of that employee's performance will actively participate in the discussion, providing examples to confirm or question the performance appraisal rating recommended by the individual's manager.

- When an individual is under review, those participants in the session who are not directly knowledgeable of that employee's performance will remain engaged in the discussion, listening and asking questions to ensure that similar standards of performance are being applied by different managers.

- In determining the appropriateness of the specific performance appraisal rating to be assigned, participants will restrict themselves to discussing only the quality of the individual's performance during the appraisal period against the competencies, key job responsibilities, and other assessment items on the performance appraisal form. Other issues—such as long-term potential, unique skills, previous successes or failures, job criticality, and other factors that are not directly related to the specific quality of performance—will not be considered.

- When appropriate, participants will discuss their perceptions of the individual's unique strengths, needs for improvement, and suggestions for development. These factors, however, will not be considered in determining the appropriate performance appraisal rating.

- Confidentiality must be maintained by all participants. No disclosure of any comments made by oneself or others about individuals whose performance is reviewed in a performance calibration session is permitted.

Calibration Criteria

In most cases, the criteria used for the calibration sessions will simply be the various assessment items on the performance appraisal forms. The managers participating in a calibration session will have used the same performance appraisal form to make their tentative ratings of a group of people, all whom are doing either the identical job or ones that are reasonably comparable. In the course of the calibration discussion, their focus will be on making sure that the way assessor A evaluated her subordinates' performance is the same as the way assessors B, C, and D evaluated theirs.

But managers may be helped by providing some guidelines on how to tell whether they are in fact using the same yardstick—whether each of them is holding people to the same standard. Executives at a large West Coast food manufacturer have developed a set of criteria (see "Calibration Factors") that they provide to participants in calibration sessions to make sure that everyone is looking at performance through the same lens.

The third item on the company's list of calibration factors, collaboration, also demonstrates an effective way of minimizing the frequently raised concern that relative-assessment procedures, whether formal forced ranking sessions, forced distributions of performance appraisal ratings, or calibration sessions, will encourage an excessively competitive environment. If one of the factors people are evaluated on is whether they "respectfully collaborate with others" and put customer and organizational needs above their own agenda and goals, it's likely that the process will in fact build a genuinely collaborative organization.

Calibration Session Mechanics

To start the actual calibration process, I recommend that the facilitator give each supervisor who will be involved in the session a different-colored marker. Then ask the supervisors to write the name of each of the individuals for whom they have prepared a performance appraisal on a 4 × 6 sticky note, along with the performance appraisal rating (and the amount of salary increase recommended, if a merit increase is going to accompany the appraisal). Using different-colored markers

CALIBRATION FACTORS

1. Job complexity—What is the degree of job complexity relative to the jobs of others? For example:
   a. Market and business challenges
   b. Sheer scope of responsibility
   c. Resource constraints
   d. Number of critical functions/direct reports

2. Complexity of goals—What is the degree of complexity or difficulty for established goals relative to others? For example:
   a. Outreach or difficulty of goals
   b. Complexity of goals
   c. Number of goals

3. Collaboration—How collaborative is this individual relative to others? For example:
   a. Consistently and respectfully collaborates with others
   b. Collaborates proactively with others for the greater good of the organization even when particularly challenging
   c. Prioritizes customer and organizational needs above personal agenda and goals

4. Rare talent or expertise—Does the team member possess specific skill sets or talent that is rare or uniquely valuable to the organization relative to others?

5. Skill versatility—Does the team member possess a wide variety of skill sets beyond the current role uniquely valuable to the organization relative to others?

6. Talent development (managers only)—How successful is this individual in attracting, developing, and retaining talent for the organization relative to others?

will make it easy to identify each supervisor's subordinates once the names and ratings are posted on the flip charts. It's helpful to have several pieces of flip chart paper taped to the wall, each one labeled with one of the organization's rating labels on which the participants will place their sticky notes, similar to the procedure described in chapter 4 for forced ranking sessions.

When everyone has finished writing names and ratings, tell them to put their sticky notes on the appropriate flip charts to indicate the performance appraisal rating they feel is appropriate. They can put a sticky note either in the middle of the appropriate flip chart or close to the edge of the chart if the person's performance is either just barely into that rating area or just short of the next higher rating.

Using this technique provides an effective double-check mechanism. First, the performance appraisal rating is written on the sticky note, and then the sticky note is put on the appropriate flip chart for that rating. The facilitator should check to make sure that all the ratings on the flip charts correspond with the ratings written on the sticky notes. Next, check that the performance rating term and the increase recommended follow the organization's policies. Having supervisors write both pieces of information will confirm that there are no misunderstandings or inadvertent errors, like using an incorrect rating label (for example, writing "Satisfactory" when the official terminology for the middle rating label is "Competent") or recommending an out-of-range salary adjustment. Finally, this technique of using a different-colored marker for each participant helps the facilitator and the group as a whole identify immediately any supervisor whose overall performance appraisal ratings are significantly skewed in a positive or negative direction.

As soon as the group has completed posting all the sticky notes, the facilitator should point out to the group the variance (if there is any) between the number of names that are currently in each of the rating categories and, if there are recommended or required guidelines for the distribution of performance appraisal ratings, the number that need to be in each one in order to meet the targeted distribution. Tell the group that the most effective way to accomplish the task is to begin with the people at the extremes and move toward those in the center.

The facilitator might ask the supervisor of the individual with the highest rating to begin by explaining how he or she came up with that rating. The rater should describe to the group how he or she went about making the assessment, the criteria that were used, and any special circumstances taken into account. Invite the rest of the participants to help confirm or question the appropriateness of the rating. Then, once the appropriate rating for the first individual has been tentatively established, move to the bottom end of the ratings. Conduct the discussions for those individuals with Unsatisfactory or Needs Improvement ratings. Continue the discussions until every person under review has been discussed and assigned what appear to be the most appropriate ratings.

During this session it is likely (and healthy) that there will be a good deal of movement of sticky notes, as participants reconsider what the most appropriate rating for an individual is. Encourage this. Explain that nothing is final until it's final—they can always move a lowered rating back up again. And encourage the participants to move the sticky notes themselves. The facilitator shouldn't do it for them, since that way, they can't blame any mispostings on facilitator error.

Using a Calibration Session to Meet Distribution Guidelines

If the calibration process is being used not only to ensure a level playing field and that all supervisors are using similar standards and expectations in coming up with their performance appraisal ratings, but also to ensure that a group meets the organization's distribution guidelines for appraisal ratings, the second part of the calibration session starts. Once all the ratings of the people under review have been discussed and the group has settled on their recommended final ratings, point out any discrepancies between the number of ratings allowed by the guidelines for each category and the number of people currently in the category. If there is no variance, congratulate the group, remind them of the ground rule of confidentiality, and move to closure.

If there is a variance, point out to the group the changes that need to be made in order to meet the organization's distribution guideline for appraisal ratings. Unless there is an immediate suggestion on changes to be made to meet the target, ask the group what needs to be done in order to reach the target. This is a point in the meeting where the skilled facilitator can accomplish a lot through the use of silence. The participants know what they have to do; they just don't want to do it and are hoping that the facilitator will come to their rescue with a way out. Don't give it to them. Continue to explain to the group that the targeted distribution must be met. The clock is your friend. Fairly soon the discomfort of inaction will cause someone to recommend a change.

As changes are suggested in order to meet the distribution guideline, the facilitator must test to make sure that the changes recommended are genuinely based on performance and not on a weak manager's willingness to move someone to a lower rating just to get the meeting over. When the targeted distribution has been met, congratulate the group and move toward closure.

At the end, ask participants to discuss with each other their reactions to the final set of posted ratings. They should look for any ratings that surprised them or ones that, based on their necessarily limited knowledge of the individuals working for other raters, they feel might be either positively or negatively skewed. Raters should be asked whether they anticipate any significant disagreements or pushbacks when they announce the ratings and salary increases to their direct reports. The facilitator and the other raters can coach them on how to deal with these issues. In particular, the facilitator can suggest ways for a nervous appraiser to explain a lower-than-expected rating in ways other than, "I had you rated higher, but the other supervisors forced me to lower your rating."

In closing, remind the group of the need for confidentiality, and review the steps in the appraisal procedure that will happen next. Then, after the group has left, either make notes of the information and positions of all the sticky notes or grab your digital camera and take a picture of the flip charts for an exact record of the final results.

Distribution guidelines and calibration procedures are useful techniques for making an already-effective performance management process work better. But few organizations have performance management systems that provide clear direction to all employees at all levels about what the organization expects from them and how their contributions will be measured. Few have designed forms that system users find helpful in assessing performance and providing accurate feedback. Few have trained their managers how to do the difficult job of setting goals, communicating tough and demanding expectations, providing the coaching and support necessary for people to achieve those objectives, and delivering the straight-between-the-eyes feedback that is an indicator of an organization with integrity. And even fewer organizations have provided training for non-supervisory employees about how to get the most out of their company's performance management system. Finally, very few have addressed the most significant complaint I consistently hear from managers at senior levels—how to build a culture of accountability. These are the issues we will address for the rest of this chapter.

Building Performance Management Accountability

The consistent theme throughout this book has been the need to build accountability for performance management. Forced ranking, forced distributions of appraisal ratings, and calibration procedures are all aimed at one objective: getting the truth into performance management. If managers did their jobs of laying out clear expectations, setting tough and demanding standards of performance, communicating clearly and regularly with their subordinates on the quality of their performance, and accelerating the growth and development of their top performers while demanding that their poorest performers move up or out, all these procedures would be redundant or unnecessary. But managers don't consistently do these things, and organizations and senior executives must take direct action to build a culture of accountability.

While any individual in a leadership position can build a culture of accountability within his or her own work group, it is at the top of the organization that the efforts will have a companywide payoff. And the good news is, it's not that hard to do. For example, Dave O'Reilly, CEO of ChevronTexaco Corporation, in one of his regular "Chairman's Letter" e-mails to all employees, described his own performance management activities and encouraged all employees to ask their supervisors for feedback. O'Reilly wrote:

> During the past week, I have been conducting a midyear review of the PMPs [Performance Management Plans] of the top fifty or sixty leaders in the company. It is a good time of the year to review how we all are doing against our critical goals such as safety, production, profits, environmental performance, and personal diversity plans. I encourage each of you to do likewise—update your progress, sit down with your supervisor and ask for feedback on performance so far and identify priorities for the remainder of the year.[1]

Knowing that the top fifty or sixty leaders of one of the world's largest corporations each have PMPs and that the CEO reviews each one of them communicates clearly that managers down the line had better be doing the same. At ChevronTexaco, it's not "do as I say." It's "do as I do."

When he was CEO of pharmaceutical manufacturer Alcon Laboratories, Ed Schollmaier went even further. Every year he would write his own self-appraisal using the company's thirteen-page appraisal form and circulate it to his direct reports, with the expectation that they would share it further down the line. It was only in particularly good years that Schollmaier ever rated himself higher than GSP— Good Solid Performer, the middle position on Alcon's five-level rating scale. By writing and circulating his own self-appraisal, he made sure that there was no doubt among Alcon managers that the boss was serious about performance appraisal, and that he applied the same tough standards to himself that he expected them to apply to their subordinates.

At Hunt Oil Company, owner Ray Hunt and his VP of HR developed a performance appraisal procedure that was a model of simplicity: a requirement that each manager discuss thirteen open-ended questions about performance with each subordinate in March of each year. The only writing the system required was a memo that had to be sent by each manager to Hunt every year no later than March 31, saying either that the manager had conducted all his discussions, or that he hadn't with an explanation of the reason why. And the reason had better be good, the VP of HR explained, because on April 1 Ray Hunt picks up the phone and starts calling. "Why didn't you do what I asked you to do?" Hunt asks each manager who didn't complete the performance-discussion assignment. As the VP of HR explained, "You don't want to get that call from Ray Hunt."

Building Accountability Through Performance Reviews

If the company's procedures provide for a rater reliability or calibration procedure as discussed earlier in this chapter, that requirement will help ensure consistency among evaluators. Another critical requirement necessary to build accountability and ensure appraisal accuracy is to insist that senior managers review all performance appraisals before the supervisor who wrote them reviews them with his or her subordinates. One of the characteristics of organizations with strong result-focused cultures is the requirement that no manager may discuss a performance appraisal that has not been reviewed and approved by his or her boss.

The reviewer—the immediate supervisor of the manager who wrote the appraisal—has five important responsibilities:

- *Ensure timely completion of performance reviews.* The reviewer's most basic responsibility is to make sure that all subordinate managers in his or her work unit complete their performance appraisals and other performance management activities on time.

- *Ensure fair, thorough, and complete reviews.* While the people whose performance appraisals the executive will be reviewing don't work directly for him, he probably knows most of them reasonably well. Consider: Do the appraisals that their managers have written reflect your own feelings about how well they have done? Are all aspects of their performance covered? Are there any rating errors? Is it possible that any personal biases— positive or negative—are creeping in? If so, discuss these with the appraisal writer.

- *Ensure inter-rater reliability.* Are all managers applying the same standards to their people? Does one manager put more emphasis on competencies than another? Particularly if the organization is not using a calibration process, the reviewer's job is to make sure that individuals who perform at the same level will get the same performance appraisal rating, whether the appraisal is written by manager A, manager B, or manager C.

- *Make sure that tough-minded, demanding performance standards are set.* Are some managers tougher or more lenient than others? Unless there are compelling reasons to the contrary, the expectations of the toughest appraiser in the work group should set the standard for all managers charged with doing performance appraisals.

- *Coach appraisers for success.* Once the senior manager has reviewed and approved the written performance appraisals his managers have written, he should discuss their plans for conducting the appraisal discussions. It's likely that some of his subordinates may never have delivered a performance appraisal before. Senior managers can help them be successful by coaching them on their experience or engaging in a practice session.

A chorus of managerial groans usually greets the recommendation that in addition to writing performance appraisals on all their direct reports, they also be required to review all the appraisals that subordinate managers have written on their subordinates. But the job isn't that onerous. For the great majority of employees who are good solid performers, all the reviewing manager needs to do is glance through the intermediate sections of the appraisal and review closely only the final summary page, making sure that the appraiser has provided a complete and accurate analysis. Only those employees at the extremes of the performance curve need close scrutiny. In the case of poor performers, close scrutiny ensures that the appraisal writer is delivering a direct and unmistakable message about the need for immediate improvement. And in the case of top performers, the reviewing manager should check to make sure that they are getting the recognition they have earned. By kicking back for rework any appraisals that don't meet the standards of excellence they expect of their managers in the operational areas of their jobs, reviewers can let people know that they take performance management very seriously.

One strong benefit provided by asking senior managers to review and sign off on the appraisals written by their juniors is that senior managers will thereby be able to confirm or question their own feelings about where the talent in the organization lies. By paying particularly close attention to the appraisals written on those individuals who the manager sees as high potential, she can determine whether her opinion is shared by the individual's immediate supervisor. Another important benefit from senior management review will be an increase in the alignment between performance appraisal results and business results. Senior managers must demand that high overall performance appraisal ratings be justified by high business results. When a senior manager sends back all the reviews submitted to him for approval from the manager of a poorly performing unit because they don't reflect the relatively poor performance of that unit, the message that the organization takes both performance and performance management seriously will be reinforced. Carefully reviewing appraisals is the most important step mid-level managers through top executives can take to build accountability for performance management.

A particularly effective way to build accountability for performance management is to make the manager's performance in this area a subject of assessment on his or her performance appraisal. A large number of organizations have identified not only a set of core or cultural competencies that apply to everyone in the organization, but also a specific set of job-family competencies. For people in managerial/supervisory jobs, these competencies frequently include such items as command skills, developing and retaining talent, leadership, people management, team building, and other key attributes of success in a leadership position. If managers are appraised on how well they meet these responsibilities, and discover that a good chunk of their merit increase depends on demonstrating excellence, the amount of attention devoted to performance management will exponentially increase.

Salary increases for managers at PepsiCo, for example, are determined by an individual's success in two areas: business results and people results. Business results count for two-thirds of the increase; people results are worth a full one-third. Having one-third of your merit increase determined by your efforts and successes in people management unmistakably communicates that this is an area the company expects its managers to pay attention to.

At Baylor Health Care System, one of America's largest hospital systems, the performance appraisal process includes a separate "leadership supplement." In this one-page add-on to the company's standard appraisal document, eight competencies are listed, together with a paragraph describing what ideal performance in the area looks like. For the people management competency, ideal performance is described in this way:

> Regularly reviews performance and holds timely discussions. Hires the best people available and selects strong subordinates. Has a nose for talent. Understands how to make use of various individuals' strengths and interests. Is watchful for employees who appear to be having personal problems or concerns and encourages them to seek help. Holds employees accountable and takes corrective action when necessary. Rewards effort, hard work, and results. Works to promote high performers and eliminate non-contributors.[2]

Each Baylor manager and supervisor is appraised annually on how often he or she demonstrates ideal performance in meeting the company's expectations. Baylor uses a five-level frequency scale to assess performance, with 1 representing "sometimes" and 5 representing "always." If there's any confusion among Baylor managers about what the organization expects of them in meeting their people management responsibilities, all they need to do is read the words in their performance appraisal.

Using Process Evaluations to Build Accountability

One of the most effective ways to both highlight the importance of performance management and determine the quality of the organization's efforts in the area is to use some form of "process assessment."

A great advantage of Web-based performance appraisal systems is that they make process assessment extremely easy. In the GROTEAPPROACH system that my firm has developed, the final activity in the year-long performance management process is the completion of a survey focusing on how effective the performance management process was and how well it was executed. After the appraisal has been written, reviewed, and approved; discussed with the individual; and signed off on by everybody, the eleven-question process-evaluation questionnaire pops up on the computer screen of each reviewee. Some of the questions focus on how effectively the supervisor met his or her responsibilities for performance management: "Did your supervisor conduct a performance planning meeting with you at the start of the year?" and "Did you receive a midyear performance appraisal from your supervisor?" and "How would you describe your supervisor's participation in the performance management process?"

Other questions target the effectiveness of the process itself: "How long did the performance planning meeting last?" and "How useful was the performance appraisal form in helping you understand your strengths and improvement needs and succeed in your job for the future?" And some questions focus on whether the individual met his or her responsibilities for performance management: "Did you establish a development plan for the past year?" and "How successful were you in completing your development plan?"

Since GROTEAPPROACH is a computerized, Web-based system, the data generated by the process assessment produce an enormous database of information, the various elements of which can be compiled and analyzed in dozens of different ways to determine exactly where the organization is succeeding in its performance management efforts and where additional attention needs to be paid. The ease of doing process evaluation, together with the effortless ability to analyze all performance management data produced by the system to determine exactly how well the process is being used throughout the organization, by itself may justify the expense of bringing in a Web-based system.

In addition to a formal close-of-year process evaluation, organizations also find it useful to do quick informal surveys. The headquarters of a major oil company produces a Web-based "two-minute survey" and offers it on its intranet for use by HR managers in its operating companies. Only six questions long, the survey asks such questions as these: "Is it clear to you how your performance agreements and key job responsibilities support achievement of your team's business objectives?" and "Do you get useful feedback on your work performance and results?" Again, simply asking the question about the attention performance management gets is likely to raise the level of attention provided.

In addition to surveying participants' feelings about performance management activities, analyzing actual results produced by the system and communicating these results throughout the organization can get managers to pay more attention to meeting their performance management responsibilities and serve to get the truth into the process. For the research and development division of a large pharmaceutical company, I developed a list of areas for examination that the HR manager and I felt would go beyond just taking the temperature of program participants, to explore more fundamental issues. Among the questions we studied were these:

- Is there a significant difference between the ratings received by R&D professionals their first year on the job compared with the ratings that they receive in following years?

- Is there a consistent distribution of performance appraisal ratings at various job levels? In other words, for all people at salary level 23, what percentage are Fully Successful, what percentage are Superior? Is the percentage the same for level 24s, level 25s, and so on?

- What percentage of people received the same rating in year 2 as they did in year 1? What percentage got a higher rating (moved from Fully Successful to Superior)? What percentage got a lower rating (moved from Superior to Fully Successful)?

- Is the distribution of ratings for R&D professionals at various levels reasonably consistent with ratings for non-R&D professionals in other company divisions at the same levels? If there is a difference, are there data available to explain the cause?

- Is the face validity of the performance appraisal ratings distribution acceptable to top management? That is, if 60 percent of all exempts are rated as Fully Successful, 35 percent as Superior, and 5 percent as something else, does that seem appropriate? Are we overall being too tough, too lenient, or about right?

- Are there pockets of performance rating skew (positive or negative) within R&D as a whole?

Many companies regularly survey participants in their performance management process about the effectiveness of the system and where improvements are needed. In the survey done in 2004 by one of America's largest transportation companies, each employee was asked a question about how the person went about doing the self-appraisal their process required. While most of the respondents indicated that the basis for their self-assessment was "comparison to the competencies," 47 percent indicated that the basis of their self-assessment was "relative to peers."

Relative to Peers

"Relative to peers" has been the focus of this book. There are two distinct ways in which the quality of an individual's performance can be assessed. First, on an absolute basis, by assessing how well the individual performed against the goals and objectives and expectations that were established at the start of the year. Second, relative to peers.

While evaluating performance on an absolute comparison basis is fully accepted and widely practiced in organizations, companies and managers remain unnecessarily hesitant about using the equally legitimate, and frequently more informative, process of asking how well the person's performance compares relative to peers. Forced ranking is that relative comparison process which provides a separate and complementary lens through which human performance can be assessed. Forced ranking, along with the other techniques and procedures we have discussed throughout this book, is a valuable and legitimate way of answering the question, How am I doing?

Conventional performance appraisal has an important place in the talent management palette of any organization. So does forced ranking. Neither process by itself is complete; both have limitations. But together they can provide an accurate and well-rounded picture of the strengths and weaknesses of each member of the team.

Appendix A

Memos and Scripts
for Managers

IN THIS APPENDIX, I have included three documents that will be valuable references for any organization that is initiating a forced ranking procedure. They have resulted from my work in developing and implementing a major forced ranking system with several large organizations. Only the names of the companies and other identifying details have been changed to preserve their anonymity.

1. *CEO's memo to participants in the ranking process.* The memo was sent by the company's CEO to all employees who were to be assessed in the company's initial forced ranking process. The objective was to build understanding and acceptance of the new procedure.

2. *CEO's memo to executives who would serve as assessors in the company's forced ranking process.* The second memo, again changed only to blind the name of the company, was sent by the company's CEO to all company employees at the vice president level and above who would be involved in the forced ranking assessment meetings. The objective was to communicate the importance he placed on the procedure for building the company's future.

3. *Scripts*. These five scripts were written to help managers under-
    stand what they should say to announce the results of the
    forced ranking process to their subordinates who had been
    assessed.

MEMO 1

To: All Acme Employees in Salary Groups 14 and above
From: [name of CEO]
Date: February 19, 2002
Subject: Acme Leadership Assessment Program

Next month, we will initiate a new forced ranking procedure that is designed to help us better identify Acme talent. In this Leadership Assessment Program, Acme's senior managers will use a forced ranking process to identify:

- The top 20 percent of all Acme managers so that their career development can be accelerated

- The vital 70 percent—the great majority whose strong performance is essential to keep Acme competitive

- The bottom 10 percent whose talents and skills will be best used in other jobs or in other organizations

This program will benefit everyone who is involved. For those 90 percent of Acme managers who will end up being ranked in the top two groups, the ranking process will confirm the importance of their contributions. For those ranked in the top 20 percent, this program will highlight the talent they bring to Acme and accelerate their development. And for the 10 percent who are ranked in the bottom category, this process will allow the person to move to a job that better matches his or her skills, whether inside or outside the company.

The criteria to be used for this ranking procedure will be based on three of the most critical Acme values (execute with excellence, passion for results, and succeed with people) as well as the individual's ability to make tough decisions. In the forced ranking discussions, consideration will also be given to such important aspects as the individual's past performance, promotability, and intellectual strength.

The ranking decisions will be made by the vice presidents of the various Acme departments who are most familiar with the individuals under review. Each person who participates as a ranker will undergo several hours of training to ensure accuracy, fairness, and consistency. In addition, the most experienced HR managers who serve the various functions will sit in on the ranking sessions to provide additional input, as will members of the corporate HR staff. Finally, [name of vice president of human resources] and I will be active participants in every session.

We are taking every step to ensure the success and the fairness of this process. We have reviewed all of our plans with internal and external legal counsel and have engaged an experienced consultant to help us design the procedure and facilitate the meetings. We are requiring all meeting participants to attend a training program before they participate in a ranking session. We are using the key criteria from our Values in Action as the basis for our decisions. We will discuss the results with every person involved as soon as the ranking discussions are completed. And I personally will play an active role in every session.

Because the senior leadership of any organization has the greatest responsibility for achieving organizational results, we will be using the process this year with all individuals in salary groups 14 through banded, including my direct reports. In future years we may extend the program further, but we will start with those whose impact on our success is the greatest.

MEMO 2

To: All Vice Presidents
From: [name of CEO]
Date: February 19, 2002
Subject: Acme Leadership Assessment Program

We have just announced a new forced ranking procedure that will help us better identify Acme talent. In this Leadership Assessment Program, Acme's senior managers will use a forced ranking process to identify:

- The top 20 percent of all Acme managers so that their career development can be accelerated

- The vital 70 percent—the great majority whose strong performance is essential to keep Acme competitive

- The bottom 10 percent whose talents and skills will be best used in other jobs or in other organizations

As a vice president of Acme Services Company, you will be participating in one or more of the ranking sessions. A schedule of all sessions is attached.

The criteria to be used for this ranking procedure will be based on three of the most critical Acme values (execute with excellence, passion for results, and succeed with people) as well as the individual's ability to make tough decisions. In the forced ranking discussions, consideration will also be given to such important aspects as the individual's past performance, promotability, and intellectual strength.

Before you will be able to participate in any of the ranking sessions, you must complete the three-hour training program that is scheduled for [dates and times]. If you are unable to attend one of these two sessions, you will not be able to participate in any of the ranking sessions.

The training programs will be conducted by [name of consultant], a nationally recognized consultant who specializes in performance management. He will also serve as the facilitator for each of the ranking sessions.

It is critical to our success that we identify, reward, and retain our top talent. We must also make sure that none of our jobs is blocked by an individual who doesn't have the capability of making an outstanding contribution. The forced ranking process is admittedly difficult. However, the training you will receive, combined with the fairness, intelligence, and integrity you will bring to the ranking sessions, will make this process a significant success.

Scripts—What to Say to A, B, and C Players

It's easy to encourage managers to tell the truth in discussing performance. What's tricky is telling them exactly *how* to tell the truth—giving
them the actual words to say. It's particularly sticky in those difficult
cases where they have to tell an excellent performer just why she
didn't quite make the A-player category, or the B player that he's flirt-
ing with the bottom category, or the C player that her time with the
company is over.

This section contains five scripts I wrote for managers to use as
models in announcing the results of the ranking panel's decisions.
These scripts have been used by managers in actual organizations and
have been reviewed by employment lawyers to make sure that there
are no hidden traps.

While Acme Services Company, the real but disguised organization
referred to in these scripts, used a forced ranking procedure that
assigns individuals into three categories (top 20 percent, vital 70 percent, and bottom 10 percent), I discovered that I had to write scripts
for five different scenarios:

Script 1—A player

Script 2—high B player

Script 3—solid B player

Script 4—barely B player

Script 5—C player

While the scripts for the first four outcomes are probably appropriate for use by almost any organization, the script for the C Player
announces that the decision has been made to ask people in this category to leave the organization and, as part of that decision, to provide
them with a generous severance package and outplacement assistance. In this particular case, the company's decision had been to
allow any individual who received a C (bottom 10 percent) ranking
to challenge that ranking, reject the severance package, and be re-
reviewed by the same set of rankers three months later. If the person
had demonstrated in this period that he in fact was a solid B player or

better (in effect, demonstrating that either the original assessment had been wrong or that in a fairly short period of time he had been able to leapfrog over the performance level of people rated toward the low end of the B category), that new ranking would stand until the next iteration of the process.

A Performer—Pat

"Come in, Pat, sit down. I've got some good news for you.

As you know, we recently completed the Acme Leadership Assessment Program discussions. The outcome of those discussions is that you were evaluated as one of the top 20 percent of Acme leaders. Congratulations.

Before we talk further about what this will mean to you and your career here at Acme, are there any questions you'd like to ask me about the process?

Answer questions.

Let's talk about what's going to happen as a result of this decision and what some of your responsibilities are. To begin, your first responsibility is to maintain the confidentiality of the result. While the company is communicating openly about the fact that we are using a leadership assessment process and the way the program works, the actual evaluations of individuals are confidential. I expect you not to discuss your assessment with anyone who's not directly involved with the process.

The most important thing we need to talk about is your development plans. One of the reasons for inaugurating the Leadership Assessment Program is to accelerate the development of people like yourself, the ones whom we see as being the future leaders of the corporation. Let's begin by going over the impressions people shared about your development needs during the assessment discussion . . .

Review any discussion of the individual's development needs that took place during the ranking sessions. In particular, discuss which of the Acme criteria the individual was felt to be the strongest in and which the weakest.

As you think about your own strengths and weaknesses, Pat, do you feel that the group's assessment was on target, or are there other areas that you feel your development efforts should concentrate on?

Discuss individual's personal perceptions about his/her development needs. Say either:

A. As a result of your assessment in the top 20 percent group, one immediate action we have planned is [announce action—special *project assignment, job change, new responsibility added to job, request to serve as a mentor to another high-potential employee, assignment to a senior manager who will serve as a mentor, scheduling attendance at a special development program, etc.].*

B. While we have not created any immediate development plans for you, I need you to think about what you feel you need to do to accelerate your own development. When you think about your development needs, Pat, I want you to think much bigger than just attending some kind of training program. I want you to give some consideration to such things as special project assignments, possible job changes, or new responsibilities that might be added to your job. You might consider serving as a mentor to another high-potential employee, or working with a senior manager to acquire a broader view of the company, or anything else that might help you make a greater contribution to Acme. I'd like you to get back to me with your ideas for your development by [*date*].

Pat, I want you to know that everyone who was involved in your assessment in the Acme Leadership Assessment Program sees you having a very bright future with the company."

High B Performer—Chris

"Come in, Chris, sit down. I've got some good news for you.

As you know, we recently completed the Acme Leadership Assessment Program discussions. The outcome of those discussions is that you were not only evaluated as one of the vital 70 percent of Acme leaders, you were also ranked toward the top of this group. Congratulations.

Before we talk further about what this will mean to you and your career here at Acme, are there any questions you'd like to ask me about the process?

> Answer questions. In particular, discuss why the individual was not ranked in the top 20 percent category. If there is a specific deficiency that resulted in the individual's placement in the B-player category, discuss that deficiency and any obvious steps the person should immediately take to overcome it. If the ranking resulted from an overall competitive placement, explain that.

Let's talk about what's going to happen as a result of this assessment and what some of your responsibilities are. To begin, your first responsibility is to maintain the confidentiality of the result. While the company is communicating openly about the fact that we are using a leadership assessment process and the way the program works, the actual evaluations of individuals are confidential. I expect you not to discuss your assessment with anyone who's not directly involved with the process.

The most important thing we need to talk about is your development plans. One of the reasons for inaugurating the Leadership Assessment Program is to accelerate the development of people like yourself, the ones whom we see as being the future leaders of the corporation. Let's begin by going over the impressions people shared about your development needs during the assessment discussion . . .

> Review any discussion of the individual's development needs that took place during the ranking sessions. In particular, discuss which of the Acme criteria the individual was felt to be the strongest in and which the weakest.

As you think about your own strengths and weaknesses, Chris, do you feel that the group's assessment was on target, or are there other areas that you feel your development efforts should concentrate on?

Discuss individual's personal perceptions about his/her development needs. Say either:

A. As a result of your assessment in the top of the vital 70 percent group of Acme leaders, one immediate action we have planned is *[announce action—special project assignment, job change, new responsibility added to job, request to serve as a mentor to another high-potential employee, assignment to a senior manager who will serve as a mentor, scheduling attendance at a special development program, etc.].*

B. While we have not created any immediate development plans for you, I need you to think about what you feel you need to do to accelerate your own development. When you think about your development needs, Chris, I want you to think much bigger than just attending some kind of training program. I want you to give some consideration to such things as special project assignments, possible job changes, or new responsibilities that might be added to your job. You might consider serving as a mentor to another high-potential employee, or finding ways to acquire a broader view of the company, or anything else that might help you make a greater contribution to Acme. I'd like you to get back to me with your ideas for your development by *[date]*.

Chris, I want you to know that everyone who was involved in your assessment in the Acme Leadership Assessment Program sees you having a very bright future with the company."

Solid B Performer—Kerry

"Come in, Kerry, sit down. I've got some good news for you.

As you know, we recently completed the Acme Leadership Assessment Program discussions. The outcome of those discussions is that you were evaluated as one of the vital 70 percent of Acme leaders. Congratulations.

Before we talk further about what this will mean to you and your career here at Acme, are there any questions you'd like to ask me about the process?

> Answer questions. In particular, discuss why the individual was ranked in the vital 70 percent category. In particular, be sensitive to which of the four most common feelings the person is expressing (mad, sad, glad, or scared) and respond appropriately.
>
> If there is a specific deficiency that resulted in the individual's placement in the B-player category, discuss that deficiency and any obvious steps the person should immediately take to overcome it. If the ranking resulted from an overall competitive placement, explain that.

Let's talk about what's going to happen as a result of this assessment and what some of your responsibilities are. To begin, your first responsibility is to maintain the confidentiality of the result. While the company is communicating openly about the fact that we are using a leadership assessment process and the way the program works, the actual evaluations of individuals are confidential. I expect you not to discuss your assessment with anyone who's not directly involved with the process.

Let me explain what it means to be assessed as one of the vital 70 percent of Acme leaders. As I said at the start of the meeting, it's good news. It means that your contributions to the company are recognized and appreciated. It means that we see you having a solid future here.

The most important thing we need to talk about is your development plans. One of the reasons for inaugurating the Leadership Assessment Program is to accelerate the development of people like yourself, the ones whom we see as being the vital core of the corporation. Let's begin by going over the impressions people shared about your development needs during the assessment discussion . . .

Review any discussion of the individual's development needs that took place during the ranking sessions. In particular, discuss which of the Acme criteria the individual was felt to be the strongest in and which the weakest.

As you think about your own strengths and weaknesses, Kerry, do you feel that the group's assessment was on target, or are there other areas that you feel your development efforts should concentrate on?

Discuss individual's personal perceptions about his/her development needs.

While we will not be creating any specific development plans for you as a result of the Acme Leadership Assessment Program, I want you to think about what you feel you need to do to accelerate your own development. When you think about your development needs, Kerry, I want you to think much bigger than just attending some kind of training program. I want you to give some consideration to such things as special project assignments, new responsibilities that might be added to your job, or anything else that might help you make a greater contribution to Acme. I'd like you to get back to me with your ideas for your development by [*date*].

Kerry, I want you to know that everyone who was involved in your assessment in the Acme Leadership Assessment Program recognizes your contributions and sees you having a very solid future with the company."

Low B Performer—Tracy

"Come in, Tracy, sit down.

As you know, we recently completed the Acme Leadership Assessment Program discussions. The outcome of those discussions is that you were evaluated in the middle group, as one of the vital 70 percent of Acme leaders. While that in itself is good news, Tracy, quite frankly you were assessed toward the lower end of the middle group.

Before we talk further about what this will mean to you and your career here at Acme, are there any questions you'd like to ask me about the process?

> Answer questions. In particular, discuss why the individual was ranked in the lower end of the vital 70 percent category. Be sensitive to which of the four most common feelings the person is expressing (mad, sad, glad, or scared) and respond appropriately.
>
> If there is a specific deficiency that resulted in the individual's placement in the lower end of the B-player category, discuss that deficiency and any obvious steps the person should immediately take to overcome it. If the ranking resulted from an overall competitive placement, explain that.

Let's talk about what's going to happen as a result of this assessment and what some of your responsibilities are. To begin, your first responsibility is to maintain the confidentiality of the result. While the company is communicating openly about the fact that we are using a leadership assessment process and the way the program works, the actual evaluations of individuals are confidential. I expect you not to discuss your assessment with anyone who's not directly involved with the process.

Let me explain more specifically what your assessment means. It means that as we look at all Acme leaders, we see you as being among the great majority in terms of your talent and contribution and potential. It means your contributions to the company are recognized and appreciated. It means that we see you having the potential for a solid future here.

But Tracy, you need to get to work immediately to develop that potential. If we didn't think that you had the talent and capability to be a fully successful leader at Acme, you would have been ranked in the bottom 10 percent. You weren't. But quite frankly, it was a close call.

The most important thing that you need to think about is your development plans. The Acme Leadership Assessment Program is going to be an ongoing process in the company. You will need to demonstrate significant improvement in all of the Acme leadership criteria. I believe that next time you have the capability of being assessed as solidly in the middle of the vital 70 percent of Acme leaders . . . maybe even more. But right now, it's critical to your future that you demonstrate that's where you belong.

While we will not be creating any specific development plans for you as a result of the Acme Leadership Assessment Program, I want you to think about what you feel you need to do to accelerate your own development. When you think about your development needs, Tracy, I don't want you to think about attending some kind of training program. I want you to think about the ways in which you can better demonstrate the Acme leadership criteria and how you can make a greater contribution to the company. I'd like you to get back to me with your ideas for your development by [*date*].

Tracy, I want you to know that I believe that you have the capability to be a solid Acme leader in the future. I need you to prove me right."

C Performer—Jan

"Come in, Jan, sit down. I've got some bad news for you.

As you know, we recently completed the Acme Leadership Assessment Program discussions. The outcome of those discussions is that you were evaluated in the bottom 10 percent of Acme leaders.

As you know from the communications about the program that you received before we began *[and from your involvement as an assessor during the program]*, the purpose of the Acme Leadership Assessment Program is to identify the top 20 percent of all Acme leaders so that their development can be accelerated, the vital 70 percent, and the bottom 10 percent who will be asked to leave the company and find better opportunities for their careers in another company.

You were assessed carefully and thoughtfully against the Acme leadership criteria, and you have been assessed in the bottom 10 percent.

Before we talk further about where we go from here, are there any questions you'd like to ask me about the process?

> Answer questions. If there was a specific deficiency involving one of the Acme leadership criteria that resulted in the individual's being assessed in the lowest 10 percent, explain what that specific deficiency was. If the ranking resulted from an overall competitive placement, explain that. Don't argue or defend the assessment decision, other than saying:
>
> • The decision-making process was rigorous and fair.
>
> • You personally agree with the accuracy of assessment.
>
> If the individual asks about the possibility of appealing the decision or being given a "second chance," explain that you are prepared to talk about that separately. First, however, you want to review the plan of action that you believe will work out best for everyone.

Let's talk about what's going to happen as a result of this assessment. To begin, both of us have a responsibility to maintain the confidentiality of your assessment. While the company has communicated openly about the fact that we are using a leadership assessment process and the way the program works, the actual evaluations of individuals are confidential. I expect you not to discuss your assessment with anyone who's not directly involved with the process, and I will only be discussing your assessment with others on a formal and official basis.

Let me explain more specifically what your assessment means. It means that we will be asking you to leave the Acme Services Company and find a career opportunity with another organization.

We realize that this will be a difficult transition for you, and we want to do all that we can to make your departure as professional and dignified as we can.

We have prepared a separation package that I want to review with you.

> Review the details of the separation package. Discuss each element of the package and explain how it benefits the individual. Answer any questions. Discuss your belief that the package the company has put together is appropriate and generous, and that it is in the individual's best interest to accept it.
>
> Review the requirement that the individual must sign a release in order to be eligible to receive the package.
>
> Discuss the timing for accepting the package and leaving the company.

Jan, I believe that the assessment that was made is an accurate one and that your talents will be best used in another organization. I feel that the separation package the company has put together for you is very fair and that it is in your best interest to accept it.

You asked me if you have any recourse if you think that the assessment we have made is incorrect. Yes, you do have a recourse. If you sincerely believe that our assessment is inaccurate and you want to demonstrate that your performance against the four Acme leadership criteria is significantly better than that of the other Acme employees with whom you were compared, we will give you the opportunity to prove us wrong.

You will be allowed to reject the package I have just offered you. You will be given a maximum of ninety days to demonstrate that you genuinely excel in your performance against the four Acme leadership criteria of executing with excellence, demonstrating a passion for results, succeeding with people, and making tough decisions. At the end of that ninety-day period, the same people who made the original assessment will review you again against the same population of Acme leaders that you were compared against originally.

If this new assessment reveals that our original assessment was wrong and that you are solidly in the ranks of the vital 70 percent of all Acme leaders, that new assessment will stand. If, however, the new assessment is the same as the assessment that we have just made, you will be asked to immediately leave the company. In addition, the separation package we have just discussed will not be the same.

Review the revised separation package.

Jan, it is critically important that you understand what you will need to do if you choose to reject the separation package we are offering you. It is not a matter of getting better or improving your performance or solving a problem. You will need to demonstrate not only that you excel in the four Acme leadership criteria, but that your performance against these four criteria is significantly better than a large number of other Acme managers at your level.

If the individual decides to accept the package and leave Acme, thank the person for his service to the company and express your sincere conviction that he is making the right decision. Advise the individual that by law he has _____ days to change his mind. Advise the individual of any other legal or Acme Services Company policies or procedures that affect his departure.

If the individual says that he wants time to think things over, advise him of the time requirements for making a decision and any other policies or procedures.

Jan, I know that this is a very difficult situation for you. I want you to know that I personally believe that you have made a solid contribution to Acme, and that you will have a great deal of success wherever your career path takes you.

Appendix B

FAQs About the Forced Ranking System

THIS FAQ DOCUMENT WAS originally developed by the author as part of the development and implementation of a forced ranking system for a large consumer goods company, here also called Acme Services Company.

The document has been revised both to eliminate any references to the original organization and to make the questions and answers appropriate for any company that is implementing forced ranking. The term that Acme has chosen to use for its forced ranking process is *Leadership Assessment Program*.

This set of frequently asked questions is intended to provide a workable template for an organization to use in developing its own FAQ document for publication to the workforce. It will also be useful in considering the questions that are likely to arise in the course of developing and installing the system.

What is the Acme Leadership Assessment Process?

The Acme Leadership Assessment Process is a procedure in which each member of the senior leadership team of the Acme Services Company will be assessed against four criteria: execute with excellence, passion for results, succeed with people, and make tough decisions. Each individual being assessed will be assigned into one of three categories: the top 20 percent of all Acme leaders, the vital 70 percent, and the bottom 10 percent.

Why are we doing this?

In our very competitive industry, being good or being profitable isn't good enough. We must strive to be a high-performing, best-in-class organization. This starts with the leadership of the company. A disciplined, structured review process aggressively develops top leadership talent and in some cases deselects others. A process such as this is necessary to ensure that the leadership stays sharp, is of the highest caliber, does not become satisfied with mediocrity, and continues to move forward and grow the company.

Is this fair to do?

Yes. The leadership and employees of Acme have known for many years that *how* we get things done is as important as *what* is accomplished. It is entirely fair to hold the leadership responsible for a higher standard of performance not only in the delivery of operating results, but also in the demonstration of key leadership competencies. That's what we are doing. The criteria to be used in the Leadership Assessment Process are a reflection of our vision and values. There is nothing new here other than holding the leaders accountable for operating to those values, judging which executives do it the best, and determining which do it the worst. Thousands of people both inside and outside of the company rely on the leadership to lead successfully. It would be unfair to them not to hold our leaders accountable for the best leadership skills.

Is this something that will benefit Acme?

There is no question about it, yes. While this is a difficult process, the net result is that the development of our leadership will get special emphasis. We need to know that the individuals who are directing the business have all the tools and experiences necessary to deliver on their leadership responsibilities.

Another benefit is that the overall caliber of the leadership at Acme will rise. Some good performers of the past may not measure up to a raised bar of expectations, but they will be treated fairly and with dignity. But those individuals who are up to the challenge will in fact be given increased opportunities to lead and will reap the resulting rewards. Those who are not up to the challenge and competition will exit the organization. The ultimate result is that we will be a better-led, more successful enterprise.

Is this going to be done annually?

We expect to do another iteration of the process in about twelve months. At that point we will evaluate the timing of the Leadership Assessment Process and determine what the ongoing frequency should be.

How is the assessing being organized?

A number of assessment sessions will be conducted between May 8 and May 10. In the first one, our CEO will evaluate his staff. After that meeting, the project consultant, an external industry expert in performance management, will facilitate a meeting with our CEO and his immediate staff as they assess all employees at salary grade level 6 and above. On subsequent days, four additional facilitated assessment sessions will occur. They will be conducted by a panel of vice presidents serving as assessors. The four facilitated sessions are as follows:

- Sales and marketing

- Manufacturing

- Engineering, purchasing, and finance

- Human resources, information services, and legal

Who is doing the assessing?

The CEO and the senior vice president of human resources will be assessors for all assessment sessions. Senior vice presidents and divisional vice presidents will be assessors in the review sessions for their functions. Additionally, HR professionals who support the various divisions will be in attendance at sessions when their client groups are being assessed.

Are the assessors qualified to make these assessments?

Yes. Our consultant, a recognized industry expert in processes such as this, has trained all individuals participating in the assessment meetings. Each assessor has completed a review of study material and has engaged in significant discussions about the process.

Isn't this just a guise for a RIF?

No. First of all, this process looks at individuals, not at jobs. Secondly, individuals who leave the organization will be replaced, which will frequently result in advancement opportunities for people lower in the organization.

What will happen to me if I am assessed in the lowest 10 percent?

These individuals will be told of their status, as will all assessed employees. Obviously, this is bad news, but these individuals will be told truthfully that they do not have a leadership future at Acme and will be able to immediately consider changes in their career plans. They will be told that a separation package will be made available, as well as outplacement services should they opt to accept the initial separation package.

If any individual identified in the lowest 10 percent believes that the assessment is inaccurate, he or she will be given a period of time up to ninety days to demonstrate that their assessment was in fact inaccurate, after which their leadership capability will again be assessed against the four competencies. If, at the end of this period, they are still assessed as a lower 10 percent individual, they will be exited with a separation package only. Additional consideration offered earlier may not be available at this point.

What does this process mean to me and my development?

For the great majority of Acme leaders—the 90 percent—it will mean that a greater emphasis will be placed on their development. For those individuals who are part of the top 20 percent, it will mean very specific and rigorous development.

Will I be told where I came out in the process?

Yes. Beginning on May 13 and no later than by the end of June, there will be individual discussions between assessors and the people who were assessed.

Do other companies do this?

Yes. A large number of very well-managed companies, including GE, PepsiCo, Microsoft, Sun Microsystems, Intel, and many others, utilize management processes such as this.

Will the people who are exiting the organization now through the early retirement program be considered as part of the lower 10 percent?

No. Individuals in salary grade level 14 and above who indicated a decision to retire as part of the early retirement program will not be part of the population being assessed, regardless of the timing of their retirement.

Some departments have routinely been aggressive in weeding out poor performers. Won't those departments be disadvantaged by beginning this process now?

No. Such departments have typically used Acme's performance management system and other tools quite effectively, and this should continue. But the Leadership Assessment Process is not focused on individuals who are considered to be "performance problems." Almost universally, the individuals who are being assessed are rated good or above.

This process specifically measures Acme leaders against four key leadership criteria and forces the assessors to identify the best. In this process the lower 10 percent of the individuals are just that—relatively weaker leaders. They may be adequate in other organizations, but as we raise the standard for leadership at Acme, they do not meet that standard here.

What if my department has more than 10 percent lower-rated individuals? What if we end up with less?

First, the assessment is not done on a department basis. In each assessment session, a good-sized grouping of executives, as described earlier, is being discussed. That said, there will be 10 percent of individuals identified from each of the sessions. Assessors could identify more.

*What if my department has more than 20 percent top performers?
What if we end up with less?*

Again, the assessment process is not done on a department basis. That said, there will not be more than 20 percent top performers identified in any session, as we want to identify the best of the best. This permits a targeting of somewhat limited development time and resources to the best leaders.

Will the lower 10 percent be let go on one particular date? If so, what if we don't have a backup?

An exit strategy for each person identified in the lower 10 percent will be established on an individual basis. In all instances the dignity and respect for the individual will be maintained. Not having a ready backup is not an adequate reason to maintain a weak leader in a leadership role.

What if I am recognized as a top 20 percent one year and not the next? Will my development be affected?

Yes.

Are managers going to be held accountable for ensuring that development plans for the top 20 percent are actually formulated and executed?

Yes. Senior management will be directly monitoring the progress of top 20 percent individuals. Additionally, managers of top 20 percent individuals are also assessed in the Leadership Assessment Process. One of the four criteria on which they are judged is "succeeding with people," which directly speaks to their efforts in the development of people.

Shouldn't all employees have been put on notice that this would be done, so that they could concentrate on demonstrating the behaviors that are all of a sudden so important?

Acme expects every employee at every level to demonstrate excellence from the day he or she is hired. All employees were specifically informed of our mission, vision, and values at the time that they were hired. These statements have been an ongoing part of our business and a part of all of our performance management systems and activities.

Employees have regularly been told that the way in which they meet their objectives is as important as what is achieved. All employees have been told that they are responsible for how they get work done. It is perfectly acceptable to hold leadership accountable to demonstrate leadership excellence at a higher level than the company would expect of anyone else. In fact, one could argue that any leader who was not exhibiting the values and now is seeking a reprieve in order to exhibit them was withholding what they knew to be the highest level of effort and leadership, and should be removed from the organization.

Don't you run the risk that some of the individuals who are being assessed will be assessed by people who don't know them, particularly for some individuals from small departments that provide services across the company?

Assessors will be asked to directly assess the people whom they know the best. Usually, that equates to the people who report to them in their respective divisions, and those in related areas. In the assessment sessions, when one assessor is discussing an employee, the other assessors will be expected to ask probing questions, pressing for clear examples and generally ensuring that the rigor of the process is applied consistently.

If an individual is simply not very well known (or possibly unknown to the panel of assessors), will this person automatically be placed in the bottom 10 percent?

An individual who is simply not known, even by their department vice president, will default to the vital 70 percent. Under no circumstances would such an individual, as described in this question, be placed in the top or bottom grouping.

However, it should be pointed out that it is highly unlikely that this could occur, what with the composition of the assessor groups, the preparation leading up to the assessment session, the oversight by HR, and the professional facilitation.

Is it fair to compare people at salary level 16 (from whom presumably greater leadership is expected) against people at salary level 14 (from whom presumably a somewhat lower level of leadership is expected)?

This is a very good question. It is not so much a matter that "greater leadership" is expected from one job versus another, but rather the

degree to which a person exhibits the leadership that his or her position calls for. For example, a person who holds a salary grade level 14
and absolutely nails the leadership expectations associated with their
role will fare much better than a person at a salary grade level 16 who
does not, even though the person at salary grade level 16 is in a position of greater responsibility. In this respect, it is fair and equitable to
compare individuals based on observable behaviors irrespective of
their salary grade level.

*If we are going to do this every year, is it really fair to assess the people
who replaced last year's bottom 10 percent? Won't they be too new?
Wouldn't it be better to do this every other year?*

Generally speaking, a newly appointed individual will default to
the vital 70 percent, to allow the individual time to exhibit their
leadership. In our Leadership Assessment Program next year, the
assessors may choose to leave a person in the middle grouping, or
they may feel that adequate time has elapsed that permits them
to make a valid assessment and place the individual in a different
category. Generally, if an individual has been in a position less than
six months, we will consider that time as too short to make an
assessment.

What role will EEO considerations play in the assessment?

The final composition in each session of the three groupings (top
20 percent, middle 70 percent, lower 10 percent) will be based exclusively on the leadership criteria used. There will be no quota based on
age, sex, race, or any other criteria than leadership. The rigor of treat-
ing all individuals fairly, observing them through the same lens and
measuring them against the same yardstick, will be consciously and
strictly observed.

*Ford did this and had to stop because of employee backlash. Is
that true?*

Ford attempted to use a review process somewhat similar to ours as
part of its overall performance management process covering over
eighteen thousand employees, which we are not doing. The Leadership
Assessment Process is independent from our performance appraisal

process. Acme is taking very careful and deliberate action to ensure that fairness and rigorous review criteria are being adhered to.

Isn't this illegal?

No. There is nothing illegal about evaluating how well people perform against the company's expectations that they display Acme's four leadership competencies. In addition, the entire Leadership Assessment Process has been reviewed by both our internal and outside legal counsel.

The evaluation of people's performance against Acme's leadership competencies is just the subjective opinion of the assessors. This seems unfair.

The Acme Leadership Assessment Process has been specifically designed to remove subjective opinion. Every one of the assessors has been specifically trained. Assessors will only discuss people whose performance they are directly familiar with. In addition, assessors who do not have direct, firsthand knowledge of the individual under review are instructed to make sure that other assessors provide examples of actual performance and not just unsupported opinion.

Finally, it is far more fair for the performance and potential of individuals to be discussed by senior management out in the open, in a controlled and structured environment, against specifically defined criteria, than in any other less rigorous and less objective way.

If I am told by my assessor that I came out on the lower end of the 70 percent group, will I be at risk for being placed in the bottom group when the assessment process occurs next year?

You will certainly be at risk if you don't do anything about the feedback you received and wait until next year's assessment. Openness and candor are one of the pluses of this program. If your manager tells you that you ended up in the middle 70 percent group, but that the discussion was such that you were clearly identified as being on the borderline of being placed in the lowest 10 percent group, you have some serious decisions to make. You can work with your manager to execute better against the leadership criteria and develop yourself, or you can ask yourself the question, "Is Acme the right place for me?"

Isn't this an example of Acme not caring about the people who work here?

Absolutely not. Having the right leadership that can execute in the best possible way to successfully move the company forward is one of the best ways Acme can show that it cares for its people. There are thousands of employees at Acme, and countless thousands who directly and indirectly depend on Acme and the effectiveness of its leadership. By using this process, Acme will have a higher-caliber leadership. This is evidence that Acme cares about its long-term health and future and its people.

Appendix C

Forced Ranking and the Law

HAVE YOU BEEN READING the headlines in the past few years? Take a look:

"Ranking Systems Gain Popularity but Have Many Staffers Riled"[1]

"P&G Executive, in Federal Suit, Claims Firm Discriminates Against Older Workers"[2]

"Forced Ranking Stirs Fierce Debate: Benefits of Identifying Best Workers Often Offset by Low Morale, Discrimination Claims"[3]

"Employee Lawsuits Brew at Capital One"[4]

"Companies Turn to Grades, and Employees Go to Court"[5]

"Age Discrimination at Sprint? AARP Lawyers Join Lawsuit"[6]

To judge by the headlines, using a forced ranking system is a one-way ticket to a discrimination lawsuit. But while the headlines concentrate on the lawsuits filed, they don't tell the rest of the story: many of these lawsuits, like the one filed against Microsoft, are thrown out of court. Peter M. Browne, a high-ranking African American employee, claimed that Microsoft's evaluation, promotion, and compensation practices had a disproportionately negative effect on African American and older employees. He claimed that managers, including himself, were forced to rate very small groups of employees without objective criteria and ended up favoring those individuals with whom

they socialized—typically, white males. The U.S. District Court for
the Western District of Washington granted Microsoft's motion for
summary judgment in May 2001, finding that "Mr. Browne fail[ed]
to come forward with evidence sufficient to show that members of a
protected class have been disproportionately selected for employment
and promotion at Microsoft."[7] Other lawsuits have been settled for
amounts that turn out to be relatively nominal compared with the
payoffs to organizations from developing and retaining a highly talented workforce.

"Lawsuits stemming from companies' use of forced ranking certainly have attracted a great deal of media attention over the past few
years," observes Jordan Cowman, partner in Akin Gump's employment law practice and U.S. employers' deputy delegate to the United
Nations' International Labor Organization. "But the real story is not
how many lawsuits the forced ranking procedure provokes, but how
few lawsuits actually are filed compared with the large number of
companies [that] routinely use a relative comparison process in
various parts of their performance management and compensation
procedures."[8]

"Forced ranking a large number of employees will not necessarily
lead to litigation," assert the attorney-authors of an article on forced
ranking published by the Association of Corporate Counsel.[9] "Sun
Microsystems includes 43,000 employees in its forced distribution
ranking program and has not been the target of a class-based discrimination suit. Sun gives employees early notification of low ratings and
provides one-on-one coaching to help the bottom 10 percent improve
their performance. Sun's experience suggests that, through strong management, a company can overcome or at least minimize the problems
associated with ranking a large number of employees."

Using a forced ranking system may in fact increase the legal defensibility of personnel actions. Critics of forced ranking systems generally
point to the same problems that arise out of any performance evaluation procedure—namely, that the rankings are based on subjective
factors, reflect the biases of individual managers, and may not take
into account the particular talents or weaknesses of an individual,
especially if that individual is a member of a particularly strong or
weak unit. Clearly, the lawsuits filed against Microsoft, Ford, and
Conoco demonstrate the downside of implementing ranking systems,

acknowledge Christine A. Amalfe and Heather Adelman of the Gibbons law firm:

> However, these lawsuits and the criticisms leveled against ranking systems should not dissuade companies from engaging in effective performance evaluation procedures. Companies should engage in an evaluative process that encourages managers to provide honest feedback to employees. Written performance evaluations used in tandem with a ranking system and diversity program can actually assist companies in defending against discrimination and harassment lawsuits. If done properly, the procedures should provide companies with written documentation justifying any legitimate and non-discriminatory employment decision subsequently made. Indeed, it is so much more difficult to defend an employment decision when there is not evidence justifying it or where the employee did not receive negative feedback prior to the adverse employment action.[10]

Attorney Marty Denis argues that using a forced ranking system as the mechanism for determining layoffs will actually have the effect of strengthening the employer's defensibility:

> Being ranked at the bottom of one's department ought to be a good business reason for selecting an employee for layoff. After all, ranking systems can be a good human resource tool for selecting employees for a layoff. Ranking employees has several merits. The same criteria are used. A current appraisal is used, no so-called "old" performance appraisals. Old performance appraisals may tend to be too praiseworthy. With the normal performance evaluation process, supervisors may hesitate to upset the "apple cart" by being candid about performance deficiencies of subordinate employees. Equally important, a ranking system allows the employees to be compared on paper vis-à-vis their performance. That provides contemporaneous documentation of the employer's decision.[11]

The Legalities of Forced Ranking

To begin: There is nothing inherently illegal in using a forced ranking system. That exact statement or a close variation on it appeared in almost a dozen articles and legal opinions I read written by attorneys representing both plaintiffs and defendants about the approach. But using a forced ranking system may indeed subject a company to being the target of a discrimination lawsuit (as may virtually any other personnel action an employer takes). Over the last few years, Microsoft, Ford, Goodyear, Conoco, Capital One, Sprint, and several other large organizations have been sued by employees alleging that the company's forced ranking process resulted in illegal discrimination. Interestingly, no set pattern has arisen as to the type of discrimination alleged. The Ford, Conoco, Goodyear, and Sprint plaintiffs charge age discrimination. Microsoft and Ford employees claimed bias on the basis of race and gender; in the Ford case, against white males. The Conoco suit included claims of citizenship discrimination. An employer, therefore, must be conscious of many potential issues when implementing or applying such a plan.[12]

Disparate Treatment and Disparate Impact

The legal arguments used by plaintiffs include both the disparate treatment and disparate impact theories of discrimination. Under a *disparate treatment* theory, plaintiffs claim that a company used a ranking system to discriminate against their class or the particular plaintiffs individually. In the recent Ford case, for example, the Amended Complaint included allegations that Ford's strong push for affirmative action caused managers to rate white males at the lower end of the spectrum, resulting in the white males receiving lower bonuses. In this situation, therefore, it is not the existence of the ranking system, but the unfair or discriminatory application of the system that is the reason for the litigation.

In disparate treatment cases, the employee must prove there was a discriminatory motive for the employer's action. If the employee establishes a *prima facie* case of apparent discrimination, the employer must articulate a legitimate business reason for the action taken (e.g., the employee received a low ranking), and the employee must prove the stated business reason is simply a pretext used to mask the true discriminatory intention. Disparate treatment claims necessarily involve allegations of *intentional discrimination* against employees because of their race, age, national origin, or other protected category, and intent is the deciding issue.

When employers assert low rankings as their legitimate business reason for terminating employees, employees often argue that the ranking system is merely a pretext for discriminatory action. Some plaintiffs have argued, for example, that the ranking systems were implemented to rank older workers lowest, thereby masking the employer's discriminatory objectives. While this is the theory, employees find it difficult to prove that such an action was in fact a mere pretext.

The success of plaintiffs suing their prior employers under a disparate treatment theory has been mixed. In 1993, plaintiffs in Alabama sued their employer, claiming the ranking system led to discriminatory terminations.[13] In that case, the court dismissed the claim because the employees did not present sufficient evidence of a discriminatory intent. The court found the ranking policy was applied across the board, to all employees regardless of age. Although the ranking system was subjective, the court said that an employer may rely on subjective criteria, as long as those criteria do not result in discrimination.

In contrast, there are decisions sustaining jury verdicts in favor of employees who claimed discrimination from forced rankings. In those cases, the courts have typically found enough evidence to support the jury verdicts.[14] Whether plaintiffs will be successful under a disparate treatment theory, therefore, will depend upon the facts of each individual case.

Disparate Impact

Under a *disparate impact* theory of discrimination, plaintiffs claim that the ranking system had a negative impact on members of a certain protected group. Unlike the disparate treatment analysis, this theory does not require evidence of intentional discrimination. Instead, plaintiffs must prove that a specific policy or practice (e.g., ranking employees) causes a significant adverse impact upon a protected group.

Disparate impact claims are, by definition, class claims. "Such claims concern a challenge to a policy or practice which, while applied neutrally, has the unintended effect of disproportionately harming or disadvantaging a protected group. Discriminatory intent is not an issue in such claims. As such, the basic question is purely statistical: did the neutrally applied employment practice have a disparate impact on the protected group?"[15]

In disparate impact claims, plaintiffs must use statistics to prove the existence of a negative impact. If the plaintiffs succeed in establishing adverse impact, the employer must show that the procedure under challenge is job related for the position in question and consistent with business necessity. Even if the employer successfully clears that hurdle, the plaintiffs may still prevail by establishing that there is an alternative employment practice with a lesser adverse impact that the employer refuses to adopt. The disparate impact theory, therefore, will put into issue at some point the very idea of using a forced ranking system. In the Ford case, for example, the plaintiffs claimed that the ranking system had a harmful effect on whites, males, and older workers, and that the system served no significant business need.

Forced Ranking and Age Discrimination

While lawsuits alleging discrimination may be filed based on a number of different factors as mentioned above—race, gender, national origin—it appears that the primary focus of lawsuits alleging that a forced ranking process resulted in illegal discrimination will spring from complaints of age discrimination.

The Age Discrimination in Employment Act (ADEA) of 1967 protects individuals who are forty years of age or older from employment discrimination based on age. The ADEA's protections apply to both employees and job applicants. Under the ADEA, it is unlawful to discriminate against a person because of his or her age with respect to any term, condition, or privilege of employment, including hiring, firing, promotion, layoff, compensation, benefits, job assignments, and training.

It is also unlawful to retaliate against an individual for opposing employment practices that discriminate based on age or for filing an age discrimination charge, testifying, or participating in any way in an investigation, proceeding, or litigation under the ADEA.

The ADEA applies to employers with twenty or more employees, including state and local governments. It also applies to employment agencies and labor organizations, as well as to the federal government.[16] As explained by the American Bar Association, "The ADEA (29 U.S.C. Sections 621-634) prohibits discrimination in employment based on age. For purposes of this statute, age is defined as at least forty years of age or older. Thus, it would not be a violation of the ADEA for an employer to refuse to hire an individual because that person was twenty-five years old. However, some state laws that prohibit age discrimination have a broader definition of the protected class; for example, Oregon prohibits age discrimination against any individual eighteen years of age or older."[17]

Thirteen years after the passage of the ADEA, the act was amended to clarify some areas through the passage of the Older Workers Benefit Protection Act (OWBPA) of 1990. The OWBPA amended the ADEA to specifically prohibit employers from denying benefits to older employees. Congress recognized that the cost of providing certain benefits to older workers is greater than the cost of providing those same benefits to younger workers, and that those greater costs would create a disincentive to hire older workers. Therefore, in limited circumstances, an employer may be permitted to reduce benefits based on age, as long as the cost of providing the reduced benefits to older workers is the same as the cost of providing benefits to younger workers.[18] Among other things, the OWBPA provided that employees could waive their rights under the act, provided that certain conditions were met. According to the Equal Employment Opportunity Commission (EEOC):

An employer may ask an employee to waive his/her rights or claims under the ADEA either in the settlement of an ADEA administrative or court claim or in connection with an exit incentive program or other employment termination program. However, the ADEA, as amended by the OWBPA, sets out specific minimum standards that must be met in order for a waiver to be considered knowing and voluntary and, therefore, valid. Among other requirements, a valid ADEA waiver must:

- be in writing and be understandable;

- specifically refer to ADEA rights or claims;

- not waive rights or claims that may arise in the future;

- be in exchange for valuable consideration;

- advise the individual in writing to consult an attorney before signing the waiver; and

- provide the individual at least 21 days to consider the agreement [45 days if it is for a group of individuals] and at least seven days to revoke the agreement after signing it.

If an employer requests an ADEA waiver in connection with an exit incentive program or other employment termination program, the minimum requirements for a valid waiver are more extensive.[19]

Complaints of age discrimination, after growing for several years, declined in 2004. Since 1992, the percentage of age-related claims filed with the EEOC has ranged from a low of 18.3 percent of all claims to a high of 23.6 percent in 2002. In 2003, age discrimination complaints accounted for 23.5 percent of the 81,293 charges filed. (Race-based claims accounted for 38.5 percent, and claims of sex discrimination constituted 30 percent of all claims.)[20] EEOC complaints by older workers saw the biggest drop of all types of complaints in 2004. At about 17,800, filings were down nearly 7 percent from 2003.[21]

The risk of exposure to age-related lawsuits stemming from forced ranking processes was highlighted in a study by attorneys Camille Olson and Gregory Davis published by the Society for Human Resource Management in its SHRM legal report:

> In an organization or work group that has a history of giving inflated reviews, we have seen that it is primarily long-tenured, older employees who have been given average reviews in the past, who receive the lower rankings. These employees typically feel that they were "forced" by the system into lower rankings and believe that they are being pushed out of the company. These are the employees who file lawsuits, both individually and on a class-wide basis. And given the typical age demographic of those who receive the low rankings, companies that adopt a forced ranking system are most vulnerable to claims of age discrimination.[22]

Age Discrimination Charges at Capital One and Sprint

Two of the most prominent recent discrimination cases involved charges of age discrimination based on a company's use of a forced ranking system. In December 2002, a group of older workers sued credit card services company Capital One, claiming that their terminations had resulted from a job performance rating system "unfairly implemented by younger managers." AARP attorneys joined the case on the side of the plaintiffs in March 2003.

In support of their claims that the forced ranking system encouraged managers to rank older workers lower, lead plaintiff Thomas

Feltman pointed to Capital One's "youth culture," which, he claimed, resulted in only younger workers being identified as high-potential employees. AARP and the plaintiffs noted further that the company's marketing approach emphasized the youth of the firm's workplace, that its annual reports and public statements stressed that "the future of the company is in its young MBAs," and that the company's recruitment materials boasted of the fact that its workers' average age is 26–29.[23]

In commenting on the case, AARP took specific aim at forced ranking systems, asserting devious motives and hypocritical public pronouncements on the part of organizations that, like Capital One, are forced by adverse business conditions to reduce headcount: "Older workers are especially vulnerable to reductions-in-force and corporate reorganizations. Although employers are astute enough not to declare that they intend to get rid of older workers, they have developed numerous subtler ways to accomplish the same feat. One such strategy is to rank employees' performance so that the older workers get unwarranted low ratings rendering them ripe for termination."[24]

On June 10, 2003, the case was settled when Chief Justice Robert E. Payne of the U.S. District Court for the Eastern District of Virginia approved a settlement that resolved all claims asserted by the plaintiffs. While both parties agreed to keep the terms of the settlement confidential, the disappointed comments of lead plaintiff Feltman and the AARP attorneys suggest that the settlement had been in the company's favor.

Kansas City–based Sprint was forced to make major layoffs between October 2001 and March 2003 following the collapse of the telecommunications industry, eliminating more than twenty thousand jobs. Now a company of sixty-five thousand employees, as many as sixty-eight hundred of those let go were workers older than forty and subject to the protection of the ADEA and the OWBPA. Sprint, the lawsuit asserts, used a forced ranking system to make the difficult who stays/who goes decisions.

In March 2003 a lawsuit was filed against the company by lead plaintiff Shirley Williams and 119 other former Sprint employees alleging that Sprint engaged in a "pattern and practice of age discrimination" in lowering performance ratings and moving over-forty workers into positions targeted for layoffs, according to the *Kansas*

City Star.[25] The AARP lawyers hopped aboard the case in July 2004. A second lawsuit was filed in March 2005.

Sprint not only denied any "policy or practice" that targeted older workers, but contends that AARP didn't do its homework before piling on. "Sprint agrees with the AARP that older workers are essential to the well-being of companies across the country and applauds the AARP in its tireless advocacy on behalf of older citizens," the company said in a prepared release. But company spokeswoman Jennifer Bosshardt pointed out, "In fact, during the period of time in question, the median and average age of the Sprint employee base increased, and the percentage of employees over 40 also increased. This is not the trend that would result if Sprint were purging its older workforce as the plaintiffs allege."[26]

In July 2004 U.S. District Judge John Lungstrum granted provisional certification of the collective action, in effect granting a class action status to the lawsuit. As of this writing, discovery is expected to continue through May 2005 with the case coming to trial, unless settled earlier, in 2006. Curiously, Sprint was named number 11 on DiversityInc's "Top 50 Companies for Diversity" in 2004 and has been named by *Fortune* magazine as one of America's "Best Companies for Minorities."

Courts Are Reluctant to Intervene in Employment Decisions

Laura Fisher and her colleagues, in writing for the Association of Corporate Counsel about ways in which employers can avoid foundering on legal shoals, point out that courts are reluctant to impose their judgment for that of an employer.

> When employers offer an employee's ranking as the reason for an employment action, such as the denial of a merit increase or a termination, employees often claim that the ranking system is a pretext for discriminatory action. But employees have had difficulty attacking ranking decisions. As a general rule, an employer will prevail if it can show that an employee's low ranking was justified by substandard performance. The employer need not show that its assessment of an employee's performance was accurate, only that the person(s) making the ranking decision honestly believe the assessment. Furthermore, a plaintiff cannot

prove pretext simply by disagreeing with the process or the outcome, because courts generally refuse to substitute their business judgment for that of the employer.[27]

Attorney Rita Risser, author of the book *Stay Out of Court: The Manager's Guide to Preventing Employee Lawsuits,* invites questions on her Web site, FairMeasures.com. In one Q&A exchange, she got right to the heart of the issue in her blunt response to a manager's question:

Is a review illegal because it contains a manager's opinions?

I recently gave an annual appraisal to one of my employees. In his written response, he states that he disagrees with the review and because my comments are based on my opinion of him, they should be excluded from his review. He states that if they are not removed that he will sue me and my firm. Does he really have any legal ground to stand on?

Rita Risser's response:

No. Of course your comments are based on your opinion. That's what you are hired to do—the company trusts your opinion as a manager, and you are expected to hold employees to your standards. If they don't like it, tough.

Now if your opinion is based on some bias or prejudice, obviously the person could have grounds for a discrimination lawsuit. But if your opinion is based on your observations of his work performance, there [are] no grounds for suit. If your opinion is based on "facts" that you know to be untrue, the review might be grounds for a claim of defamation. But if it's just a straightforward disagreement between employee and manager, you win.[28]

Attorney William R. Hopkins points out that various lower-court opinions have acknowledged the need to preserve an employer's independence in setting its own standards in rendering those judgments deemed necessary to operate its business—the mark of free enterprise. This deference to employers has been given through application of the *business judgment rule.* This rule, Hopkins writes, has been stated in many ways: "The trier of fact is not at liberty to review the soundness or reasonableness of an employer's business judgment."[29] "Furthermore, as we have stated repeatedly, we do not assume the role of a 'super personnel department,' assessing the merits or even the rationality of employers' nondiscriminatory business decisions." [30]

The Exxon Cases

Two cases involving legal challenges to forced ranking from Exxon demonstrate the fact that when the process is carefully designed and well used, companies can be reasonably confident in being upheld if the decisions they make based on forced ranking data are challenged.

Roper v. Exxon Corp.

The first of these cases involved a member of the oil giant's legal staff. In *Roper v. Exxon Corp.*, the court granted summary judgment for Exxon in an age discrimination case because the reasons for discharge—low performance evidenced by a performance appraisal system and the employee's bad attitude—were found not to be pretextual. The plaintiff, a litigation attorney, filed an age discrimination case against Exxon alleging that his department's appraisal process was discriminatory. The Exxon legal department annually evaluated and ranked its employees on a multifaceted process that involved input from the attorney, supervisors, and clients. This resulted in a ranking based upon one's relative contribution and performance among the other attorneys in that rank group (i.e., a group consisting of lawyers with similar job classifications and responsibilities within the law department). Each attorney was then given a rank group percentile (RG%), with 99 RG% being the relatively best-performing attorney and 0 RG% being the relatively worst-performing attorney.

Exxon also adopted a Continuous Performance Improvement (CPI) guideline, in which employees at the bottom 10 RG% were advised of their position and received special management attention. If the employees' relative performance did not show sustained improvement, they were subject to reassignment, declassification, or separation from the company. The plaintiff was in the 10 RG% the last three years of his employment. In accordance with the CPI guidelines, plaintiff was advised of his ranking and that he would be terminated.

The court noted that during the three ranking years, there was no distinguishable correlation between age and rank. For each year, there were several individuals of age fifty-five or older who were above the 10 RG% cutoff. The court also noted Exxon's careful documentation of the plaintiff's consistently low performance and negative attitude, and held that these factors established significant reasons and justification, without regard for his age, for terminating his employment.[31]

Coleman v. Exxon Corp.

The next case highlights various safeguards used by the company to ensure an accurate and defensible process. In this case involving a race and gender discrimination claim, the court granted summary judgment for Exxon, and held that Exxon's ranking process was facially neutral, noted that it contained protections against discrimination, and concluded that plaintiffs failed to show that Exxon's reliance on the system was pretextual.

In this case, a number of supervisory employees had alleged that the ranking system that Exxon used to determine wages allowed racial and/or gender biases of the rankers to run unchecked. The supervisors' job performance was evaluated in two ways. First, each supervisor received a personal evaluation from his or her immediate manager. The evaluation was a standardized form listing various performance criteria in which the employee was rated "better" than, "similar to," or "below" most. The form also provided room for the manager's comments. Second, all supervisors were competitively ranked against each other. The rankings were performed by the employees' immediate managers, with review and supervision of the process from human resources and senior management. As a result, a rank list was produced and divided into five quintiles, the first quintile being the highest. A supervisor's quintile placement was a significant factor in determining salary. Although only the quintile ranking impacted salary, the supervisors were given individual rankings from a high of 99 to a low of 1.

In concluding that the ranking process was not discriminatory, the court relied upon various safeguards of the company's ranking process. First, the human resources manager held a "kickoff meeting" for all managers that included a discussion of the procedures and objectives of the process, provided for questions and answers, stressed the seriousness of the process and the need to be fair and open, and stressed the company's commitment to diversity. Second, each manager assembled performance evaluation information on the supervisors who reported to them. Third, each manager selected those supervisors they would rank. The managers were not required to use any particularized criteria in this ranking, but they were encouraged to consider the performance dimensions of leadership, communication, safety/health, job knowledge, and people development. Fourth, the individual rank lists were calculated according to a computer algorithm. Fifth, all managers met to determine the rankings. Sixth, the human resources staff ran "skewing data" on the rank list, revealing the average ranking for each subgroup of employees being evaluated (by department and by job type) and for minorities and women. Seventh, the managers met again to consider the skewing data and to provide their opinions of that year's ranking process. Finally, members of senior management met to finalize the rank list.[32]

Ensuring Legal Defensibility

The steps that Exxon took, detailed in the previous paragraph, helped the company prevail against a suit alleging illegal discrimination. For the balance of this appendix, we will explore several specific actions companies should consider taking in order to make sure that two outcomes result: first, a reduction in the likelihood of legal challenge. Even though they may not like the decision that their employer has made, and even when that decision impacts them in a strongly negative way, employees are much less likely to call a lawyer when they feel that they have been treated fairly. Second, if a lawsuit is filed, to reduce the chances that the plaintiffs will prevail or increase the odds that an acceptable settlement can be quickly reached. These are the do's and don'ts for building legal defensibility.

Of course, these suggestions—like making sure that phrases like *getting rid of ancient deadwood* or the need to hire *young up-and-comers* never appear in any corporate documents—are not specifically related to forced ranking or even to performance management. They are simply good business practices. But reviewing your business practices, particularly before beginning a relative comparison or forced ranking process, will generate increased legal defensibility and fewer sleepless nights.

Earlier, in chapter 3, I provided a large number of step-by-step recommendations that, if followed, will result in the development of a system that not only meets the tests of legal acceptability but also helps ensure the achievement of corporate goals for talent management. For now, however, we will concentrate specifically on those items that relate directly to the legal aspects of forced ranking.

Before Implementing a Forced Ranking System

The most important step to take before instituting a forced ranking system that has the potential to have a significant impact on a large segment of the organization or the company as a whole is to review your plans with both internal and external counsel. This involvement of counsel from the very start can help avoid inadvertent errors that might otherwise slip through. Both inside and outside attorneys are important and have complementary roles to play. First, your inside counsel should know the company and its culture to have a finger on the pulse and be sensitive to any areas where significant problems or resistance may occur. Inside counsel may also be aware of specific situations that need to be explored before implementing a firm-wide procedure.

Your outside counsel should bring a solid depth of knowledge about the forced ranking procedure itself, preferably having had experience guiding other clients through the process of creating a successful system. Using both inside and outside counsel ensures both breadth and depth of experience: your inside attorney knows the company well—its history, its sensitivities, its culture. Your outside counsel knows the intricacies of employment law and will be valuable in suggesting ways that a relative comparison process can be tailored to meet your organization's specific needs and desired outcomes.

Your attorneys will undoubtedly suggest the next obvious step in the early stage of designing a forced ranking system: examine your actual state of readiness. This involves such obvious but necessary activities as updating your policies and handbooks to make sure first, that there's nothing in them that could be used as fodder if they have to be provided as part of a discovery process; and second, that they don't make any statements that contradict the intention of using a relative comparison process. For example, if the employee handbook makes reference to the fact that, at your organization, promotions and other discretionary benefits are provided to those who have "demonstrated loyalty over a long period of time," your intention of creating a forced ranking system directly contradicts that statement, since now these discretionary benefits will be provided to those who have earned them, not to those who simply have stayed around the longest.

Being sensitive to the language used in other documents, too, is important, including such apparently mundane items as e-mails and memos written by senior managers, reports and white papers provided by external consultants, training outlines and evaluations from diversity programs, and other such ephemera. Is it censorship? Yes, it's censorship, but it's self-censorship. It's better to expunge it now than to have to explain something indelicate when you're called to the witness stand.

Conducting a thorough review of past performance appraisals is critically important, particularly if your intent is to use your forced ranking system to identify top talent who will be targeted for promotions and more challenging assignments and those at the other end of the curve who may be reassigned, downgraded, or asked to leave.

It's almost impossible to find a record of performance appraisal results that exactly mirrors the outcomes of a well-conducted forced ranking process, with those at the top of the ranking curve having significantly higher appraisal ratings than the rest of the population and vice versa. In fact, if that were the case, there might not be a need for forced ranking at all. In reviewing performance appraisals, look particularly for any examples of known marginal employees who have a history of fully successful appraisal ratings. These are the individuals who, if they do end up at the bottom of your ranking process, will need the most counseling and consideration when you announce the results or take actions based on the outcome.

While you are checking the records of past performance appraisals, it is also wise to check whether members of a protected class have received on an overall basis ratings that are significantly higher or lower than the population as a whole. If the appraisal results for older employees have been higher than those of less experienced employees, there could be trouble ahead if the ranking exercise demonstrates that these ratings scores have been inflated. Of course, routinely checking companywide performance appraisal results is a wise thing to do regardless of whether you decide to create a forced ranking process, since it may alert you to areas where potential problems currently lie. For example, if you have an organizational unit that is known for both a marginal quality of performance and a large number of members of a protected class, and your appraisal checkup reveals that people in this unit actually get higher performance appraisal ratings than people in better-performing units, it's wise to have a conversation with the manager of that unit (or that manager's boss) to ask what's going on.

One way to reduce your legal exposure when developing a forced ranking system is to consider introducing it gradually, starting at the top. Laura Fisher and her colleagues make a valid observation about the legal benefits of a slow-rolled introduction:

> Your company should introduce forced ranking gradually, beginning at the top of the organization. After a year or two, the system can then be introduced to the lower ranks. This gradual approach serves two purposes. First, it mitigates the implementation and administration problems of ranking hundreds or thousands of diverse employees overnight. Second and perhaps more important, forced ranking has a strongly negative connotation among U.S. employees, who generally assume that the goal of the system is to eliminate employees. Gradual introduction of forced ranking allows an appropriate time for cultural acceptance.[33]

Of course, if the intent of introducing a forced ranking process is to jump-start a cultural change and build a climate of high performance and accountability rapidly, a slow-rolled start may not be appropriate. But in cases like these, making sure that the process applies to those at the top helps assuage the concerns of those at the bottom. In one organization I worked with to develop a forced ranking system, the first person to exit the organization following the conclusion of the ranking sessions was the company's chief financial officer. It was easier for the rest of the organization to swallow the other cuts in lower-level staffers that followed when they saw that the first person to leave was a direct report to the CEO.

Telling and Training

Consider the extent to which the organization is willing to publicize the fact that it is using (or is about to begin using) a forced ranking system. Opinions vary—in some companies, the existence of the procedure itself, let alone the results generated by the process, is considered company-confidential information. Other companies adopt a posture of full disclosure. While in chapter 3 I discussed the pros and cons of announcing the use of a forced ranking system, when it comes to reducing the potential of legal problems, a company is probably better off being open about the existence of the system and the method of its operation, if for no other reason than it's difficult to keep such a process secret very long. Adopting a posture of reasonable (if not full) disclosure allows the organization to craft the messages about the purpose and function of the system so that they focus on talent management and retaining/rewarding the company's highest-performing individuals, rather than letting the rumor mill control the process and position it as a draconian rank-and-yank exercise.

Finally, another safeguard against legal problems is the training of all who participate in ranking sessions. Providing specific training will lower the likelihood of a ranker refusing to follow the agreed-upon procedures or making some boneheaded remark during the ranking sessions. Another benefit of training as it specifically relates to increasing legal defensibility is that training participants will help to ensure that the mechanisms of the process as designed are the mechanisms that are actually used. Not only will the rankers be more qualified to make their assessments, but the procedures followed in session A will closely replicate those followed in B and C and D. This consistency will demonstrate that individuals were all evaluated on a level playing field.

During the Ranking Sessions

The obvious recommendation to avoid legal problems is to guard against inappropriate comments during the ranking sessions. Although a dim-witted comment about an employee's age or sex or race uttered in the middle of a spirited discussion of that individual's proper placement is likely to be disregarded (if not immediately censured) by the rest of the group with no record made, it could turn out that one of the participants in the ranking session later is called upon to testify about what happened in the course of the ranking discussions. If the person testifying is asked about whether certain statements were made in the course of the discussion, it may turn what was a minor slip into a major liability. For this reason, it's critical to have a skilled facilitator monitor the sessions and immediately admonish any inappropriate remarks. This is particularly true when these casual remarks come from the mouths of senior executives. While courts are reluctant to put much weight on casual remarks, the fact that they are spoken and go unchallenged communicates to others in the room that the core attitudes of the company's top dogs are tinged with race- or sex- or ageism.

Another action that will increase legal defensibility is simply to make sure that any criteria that have been decided on for use in the ranking sessions are actually used by the rankers in making their decisions. Make sure that managers understand the criteria that are being used to assign people into the A, B, and C groups (or whatever ranking scheme your organization has settled on) and stick with them. In his article on avoiding litigation when making layoff and termination decisions, Marty Denis states this recommendation strongly:

> If you adopt criteria in selecting employees for layoff—or, for that matter, hire, promotion, and performance raises—make sure that your managers are given the criteria and use those criteria. You may not be able to devise a fail-safe system that ensures that, but if you want to avoid having your managers (or former managers) testify that they were never given such criteria, then, at a minimum, you might consider asking your supervisors and managers to sign-off on a checklist confirming their receipt of and application of those criteria. There is nothing like a former manager's signature on a document, particularly one that is dated, that can serve as a persuasive deterrent to that manager, when later deposed or at trial, denying knowledge of the actions in question. This may be formalistic. The checklist may involve more paperwork. But memories fade. At least the signed checklist will give you some persuasive confirmation that may be useful down the road.[34]

Applying the criteria objectively during the ranking sessions is important in heading off legal problems. Almost invariably, the criteria used by organizations to make a relative assessment of the talent pool of the organization are not amenable to strict quantitative analysis. For example, GE's four-E criteria (the *edge* to make tough yes/no decisions, high *energy* level, the ability to *energize* others around common goals, and the ability to consistently *execute* and deliver on promises) can't be reduced to a numerical formula. And yet, they certainly can be described in a highly objective manner, with raters providing clear and concrete examples of the behavior of the individual under consideration as it relates to the criterion under review.

Objectivity is not a function of quantifiability. The truth is that being objective means to be uninfluenced by emotions or personal prejudices, as an objective critic would be. To be objective is to be *fair*, to base one's judgments on observable phenomena and to present them factually. This is what constitutes an objective appraisal, and counting widgets has nothing to do with it. It is this kind of objectivity that we must demand of all appraisers and rankers, and when we get it, we meet the test of being objective.

Consider Allowing Additional Input

Some organizations consider allowing employees to submit a brief summary of their achievements and accomplishments as one of the sources of data provided to the rankers in advance of the ranking session. This procedure, while not common, might be useful to allay employees' fears about whether they will get a fair hearing, particularly in the first year of the company's using the approach. Whether or not the rankers pay much attention to what may turn out to be self-serving and one-sided presentations, the fact that employees were allowed and encouraged to provide input to the process will certainly not hurt if the process is later challenged.

Other companies have taken this idea one step further and have allowed rankees to submit peer evaluations of their performance for use by rankers, similar to the data that might emerge from a 360-degree feedback exercise. But while this might seem like an effective way of getting a rounded picture of the individual under review, it's likely that an "I'll scrub your back, you scrub mine" mentality will develop and lead to glowing but distorted reports on the individuals under review, adding little of real value to the process. It's unlikely that any individual would invite peer feedback to be submitted unless she was sure that only her finest attributes would be reported.

More important, these peers will not be involved in making the important talent management decisions that result from a forced ranking process, like promotions and bonus allocations and assignment to executive development programs. Their input, while perhaps of minor importance, should not mitigate the responsibilities senior managers have to evaluate and assess the talent pool of the organization.

Finally, these peer assessments, even when honestly done, just don't contribute much in the way of accurate data. In a major research project published several years ago in *Psychological Bulletin*, Frank Landy and James Farr conducted a study of all research that had been conducted over a thirty-year period on one specific aspect of the entire performance management process—the performance rating. They studied every aspect of performance ratings: the effect of different rating formats, the influence of varying rater and ratee characteristics. The Landy and Farr report repudiated one universally accepted piece of folk wisdom: that peers are tougher than bosses in evaluating performance. Three different studies reported that "supervisors were less lenient in their ratings than were the peers of the ratee." Two other studies also found that supervisors were more consistent in their ratings than were peers: there was "more interrater agreement with supervisory ratings than with peer ratings."[35]

Rankers and Ranking Groups

It's wise to make sure that the population comprising a group of individuals to be ranked is reasonably comparable. While it's impossible to limit ranking pools exclusively to people who all hold the identical job, it is problematic to force-rank a pool of people that consists of a manager, her direct reports (some of whom supervise others in the group), the group's individual contributors, and the secretaries and administrative assistants who support the rest of the team. Fisher, Lindner, and Davis highlight the difficulties here:

> Managers in a business unit may be asked to rank a work group of diverse employees at various levels in the company, such as from clerical employees to managers. When this situation occurs, the managers may base their rankings less on performance and more on some other less-defined and possibly biased criteria. In a forced distribution ranking system, a manager might give a clerical employee a low rating even though the employee satisfied performance expectations, because the manager considers a first-line supervisor who also performed satisfactorily more valuable to the work group and wants to reward him or her with a higher rating. When you rank apples against oranges, you invite a legal challenge based on perceived unfairness.[36]

Another unbreakable rule for avoiding legal problems is to make sure that rankers are only involved in actively ranking people of whom they have direct knowledge and experience. In a ranking session in which a large pool of individuals is being reviewed by a large number of reviewers, the participants are likely to be the individual's immediate supervisor, who has extensive knowledge of the individual; a few others who are well acquainted with the quality of his performance and potential; some who have a passing familiarity; and perhaps one or two who don't know the individual at all. In this case, those with the most knowledge should do the most talking, but that doesn't mean that the rest can walk out and catch a smoke. While they cannot directly comment on the talent or qualifications of the candidate, they can make sure that those who do know her well are sticking to the criteria and challenge their colleagues for evidence and examples behind their opinions.

Another way to guard against future legal problems is to provide guidance to rankers on note taking. In some organizations, participants in ranking sessions are directly instructed not to take any notes at all, with the recording of the deliberations left to the members of the HR staff present and, if there is one, the outside facilitator. While this does eliminate the possibility of an imprudent margin note being introduced as evidence of a discriminatory mind-set, it also works against the benefit of using a forced ranking procedure in making sure that the organization's talent is visible and remembered by the organization's senior leaders. If managers can't take notes about people who are discussed during a ranking session, they won't be able to refer to those notes later when they are looking outside their immediate pool of subordinates to fill an important job slot. Since members of any company's ranking pool are likely to be reasonably bright and sensitive to the legal issues regarding documentation, the best course may be to sensitize rankers about the importance of keeping appropriate notes and then rely on their maturity and good judgment to do so.

Analyzing the Results

Once the ranking sessions have been completed, one of the first things to do is to review the results and determine whether they indicate that members of a protected class are ranked significantly lower than the general population under review. But it is likely that with all of the ways in which the data generated by a forced ranking procedure involving a large number of sessions and rankers and rankees can be assembled and reviewed, it will be impossible to cut and slice the data in some fashion that can prove that some protected class came out lower than the rest of the population. What should the organization do?

Attorney Rita Risser, moderator of the Q&A section offered on FairMeasures.com, her law firm's Web site, was presented with this question in its bluntest form:

Our layoff list has a high percentage of minorities. Is that illegal?

What should a company do when a forced ranking procedure, honestly and objectively done, reveals that the blacks or women or disabled employees just aren't as talented as the white ones? Should they do what some college professors do and award As to all the blacks just to keep them from squawking? Or engage in a little race-norming to boost the scores of low-rated performers who are members of a disadvantaged class?

Rita Risser replies:

Keeping less qualified minority employees and laying off white employees instead is illegal race discrimination. That's the textbook answer. Many Human Resource managers believe that minority employees are more likely to sue than white employees, and will keep them on to avoid suit. This is wrong, both morally and factually. Today, white employees are just as likely to sue for race discrimination, and they are finding a sympathetic ear in the courts.

Whether you lay off the white employees or the minority employees, you may get sued. But if you lay off the less qualified employees, no matter what their race, you will win.[37]

Kim Moore, employment law counsel with international law firm Strasburger, points out another reason for leaving the results just as they come out: "I personally would not recommend tinkering with the ranking/distribution after it occurred. If it was done fairly and under justifiable criteria, then manipulation would seem to make that suspect and give rise to further legal issues in the form of reverse discrimination lawsuits. It may well be, however, that the top performer was also from that same protected group and thus the lawsuit is not very strong."[38]

In addition to looking at group results, it's also important to analyze any significant discrepancies between the results of the ranking process for those individuals who came out at the bottom and their past performance appraisal ratings, particularly for those who are members of a protected class. It is quite likely that there will be those on the bottom of the forced ranking distribution who, for years, have been lulled into complacency by inflated performance appraisal ratings. Now the forced ranking process is about to tell them that although the company's official word has always been that they have met whatever expectations they have been assigned, compared with their peers they're at the bottom of the heap. Olson and Davis explain the challenge this situation presents: "It is very important to analyze each and every situation in which an employee drops from an average-level rating to a lower rating. As these are the situations that are likely to be challenged legally, senior managers and HR personnel should review the rating decline with the employee's manager/supervisor before it is finalized and ensure that there is proper documentation to support the rating change."[39]

In companies where the results of the forced ranking process are not considered company confidential and the outcomes are discussed with individuals, it's appropriate to talk directly with the individual and explain the reason for the differences whenever there is a significant divergence between an individual's history of high or "meets expectations" performance appraisal ratings and a justified low ranking in the forced ranking procedure. It is entirely reasonable that people can receive fully acceptable performance appraisal ratings and low salary increases when the compensation decisions are made using a forced ranking process. "Equally important, employees who receive average performance ratings for satisfying performance expectations will feel more secure about their employment and thus less demoralized by the forced ranking process, even if they receive less pay as a result of a low ranking when compared to their peers. Under such a system, average-rated, but low-ranked employees may be less likely to file discrimination complaints," the authors of the Association of Corporate Counsel article assert.[40]

One final suggestion regarding analyzing the data to see if there is any disparate impact on protected groups: this analysis is best done with the assistance of legal counsel to protect the confidentiality of the data and the analysis. In fact, in the initial discussions with both inside and external legal counsel, the company's executives should discuss the steps necessary to bring all analyses and decisions resulting from the procedure within attorney-client privilege and protected from disclosure if litigation ensues.

Offering Severance

In those organizations that use their forced ranking procedure to remove those who are ranked at the bottom, it is common to offer what is often a fairly generous severance package, combined with a release that releases the company from legal liability. This approach is attractive for two reasons. First, it may in fact reduce your exposure to legal problems. As Laura Fisher and her coauthors explain, "You can also offer severance to employees who lose their employment as a result of low ranking in exchange for a release, as Sun Microsystems and GE do under their systems. And although you might be sued for age discrimination and/or for class-wide discrimination, the juris-diction in which your company is sued may not recognize ADEA disparate impact claims, and under the right circumstances, you may be able to defeat class treatment, thus limiting your company's actual potential liability."[41]

The other reason is more mundane—it's just the right thing to do. When a forced ranking system reveals that, compared with her peers and coworkers, Mary is a low contributor with little ability to grow and stretch, but has a history of—to put it bluntly—being misled by supervisors who didn't have the courage to tell the truth in her perfor-mance evaluations, the company bears some of the responsibility. Had she been told years before that senior managers felt she wasn't up to snuff, she could have made a decision either to improve and prove them wrong or to cut her losses and start afresh with another firm. But having been seduced by management into a false "I'm OK, you're OK" belief, she now finds herself not only unemployed but also less employable than she otherwise might have been. The company is not blameless in this situation. A generous severance package, including not only salary and benefit continuation but the services of a first-rate outplacement firm, will not only make things easier for the indi-viduals who leave but cast the organization in a good light by her colleagues who stay.

A final note on reducing exposure to legal challenges once the forced ranking process has been completed: keep all the documents.

You've got nothing to hide, so don't hide (or destroy) them. If ever you are faced with having to justify your system in front of a jury, you don't want the additional burden of explaining why you destroyed the documents that related to it.

Keeping Things Legal

Earlier in this appendix I discussed a lawsuit against Exxon Corp. that was brought by a group of supervisors who were unhappy about the results of its forced ranking system. To conclude this chapter, it would be worthwhile to review the specific safeguards employed by Exxon to ensure the successful defensibility of its procedure:

1. The human resources manager held a kickoff meeting for all managers that included a discussion of the procedures and objectives of the process, provided for questions and answers, stressed the seriousness of the process and the need to be fair and open, and stressed the company's commitment to diversity.

2. Each manager assembled performance evaluation information on the supervisors [the population that was being ranked] who reported to them.

3. Each manager selected those supervisors they would rank. In doing the ranking, the managers were not required to use any particularized criteria in this ranking, but they were encouraged to consider the performance dimensions of leadership, communication, safety/health, job knowledge, and people development. These are certainly criteria that not only are capable of being objectively described with factual and observable examples but also are factors that are important to success in a leadership position.

4. The individual rank lists were calculated according to a computer algorithm. While the specific algorithm is not available, simply testing the data resulting from a ranking procedure using various data-sorting methods can point out any results that seem to be out of kilter with the overall pattern.

5. All managers met to determine the rankings.

6. The human resources staff ran skewing data on the rank list, revealing the average ranking for each subgroup of employees being evaluated (by department and by job type) and for minorities and women.

7. The managers met again to consider the skewing data and to provide their opinions of that year's ranking process.

8. Members of senior management met to finalize the rank list.

The Exxon procedure is a virtual model of excellence not only in ensuring legal defensibility but in doing an important job right. Its procedure was arduous and, I'm sure, the subject of many complaints from those involved in it: "Why do we have to go through so many steps?" "Isn't there an easier way?" And in spite of doing things right, the company still got sued.

But Exxon won. And while defending its action undoubtedly was expensive, what the company also got besides a courtroom victory was a rigorous, data-based, and accurate assessment of its supervisory talent—as accurate as fallible humans with imperfect tools could develop. Is the game worth the candle? In this case, I certainly believe it to be.

Notes

Preface

1. GE 2000 annual report to shareholders.

2. Peter F. Drucker, *Management: Tasks, Responsibilities, Practices* (New York: Harper & Row, 1973), xv.

Chapter 1

1. James Brian Quinn, Philip Anderson, and Sydney Finkelstein, "Managing Professional Intellect: Making the Most of the Best," *Harvard Business Review*, March–April 1996.

2. Larry Bossidy and Ram Charan, *Execution* (New York: Crown Business, 2002), 95.

3. Iman Anabtawi and Lynn A. Stout, "An Inside Job," *New York Times*, March 27, 2005, 11.

4. Geoffrey Colvin, "Value Driven," *Fortune*, August 13, 2001.

5. Geoffrey Colvin, "Think You Can Bobsled? Ha!" *Fortune*, March 18, 2002.

6. Scott Cohen, PhD, national director for talent management, Watson Wyatt Worldwide, personal conversation with author, May 6, 2004.

7. Byron Woollen, "Forced Ranking: The Controversy Continues," white paper, Worklab Consulting LLC.

8. Beth Axelrod, Helen Handfield-Jones, and Ed Michaels, "A New Game Plan for C Players," *Harvard Business Review*, January 2002, 83.

9. Camille A. Olson and Gregory M. Davis, "Pros and Cons of Forced Ranking and Other Relative Performance Ranking Systems," SHRM (Society for Human Resource Management) Legal Report, March 2003 (citing Hay Group working paper, Achieving Outstanding Performance Through a "Culture of Dialogue," Hay Group, 2002).

10. Michelle Quinn, *Mercury News*, http://www.siliconvalley.com.

11. Holman W. Jenkins Jr., "How to Execute 10%, Nicely," *Wall Street Journal*, July 18, 2001, Editorial page.

12. Steven E. Scullen et al., "Forced Distribution Rating Systems and the Improvement of Workforce Potential: A Baseline Simulation," *Personnel Psychology* 58 (2005): 3.

13. Ibid., 1.

14. Ibid., 17.

15. Ibid.

16. Ibid., 24.

17. Ibid., 27.

18. Ibid., 28.

19. Ibid.

20. Ibid.

21. Ibid., 3.

22. Ibid., 19.

23. Ibid., 24.

24. Andy Meisler, "Dead Man's Curve," *Workforce Management*, July 2003.

25. Mark Lowery, "Forcing the Performance Ranking Issue," *Human Resource Executive*, December 22, 2003.

26. John Greenwald, "Rank and Fire," *Time*, October 12, 2001.

27. Olson and Davis, "Pros and Cons of Forced Ranking."

28. Matthew Boyle, "Performance Reviews: Perilous Curves Ahead," *Fortune*, May 28, 2001.

29. Workforce.com online survey, results as of July 14, 2003.

30. Jim Kochanski, Colette Alderson, and Aaron Sorenson, "The 'State of Performance Management' Study," *Perspectives* 12, October 6, 2004, <pp?>.

Chapter 2

1. Camille A. Olson and Gregory M. Davis, "Pros and Cons of Forced Ranking and Other Relative Performance Ranking Systems," SHRM Legal Report, March 2003.

2. Gerry Ledford and Matt Lucy, "The Rewards of Work: The Employment Deal in a Changing Economy," *Perspectives* 11, September 30, 2003.

3. Olson and Davis, "Pros and Cons of Forced Ranking."

4. Robert E. Kelley, *How to Be a Star at Work: Nine Breakthrough Strategies You Need to Succeed* (New York: Times Business Books, 1998), xvii.

5. Winsborough Limited, "Selecting for Productivity," quoting Adrian Furnham, *Personality at Work* (London: Routledge, 1992).

6. Robert Kelley and Janet Caplan, "How Bell Labs Creates Star Performers," *Harvard Business Review*, July–August 1993, 129.

7. Dr. John Sullivan, "Hiring Advice: Calculate the Value of Talent," white paper, Yoh Company Technology Staffing, http://www.yoh.com/hiringadvice-full.cfm?CD=120.

8. Linkage, Inc., "Forced Ranking: Friend or Foe?" White paper, Linkage Center for Organizational Research, August 2001.

9. Christian M. Ellis, G. Barrow Moore, and Anne M. Saunier, "Forced Ranking: Not So Fast," *Perspectives—Insights for Today's Business Leaders* 11, no. 2, April 1, 2004.

10. Lisa Weber, quoted in Janet Wiscombe, "Can Pay for Performance Really Work?" *Workforce Management*, August 2001.

11. Andrall E. Pearson, "Muscle-Build the Organization," *Harvard Business Review*, July–August 1987.

12. Olson and Davis, "Pros and Cons of Forced Ranking."

13. Definition excerpted from *The American Heritage Dictionary of the English Language*, 3rd ed. (Boston: Houghton Mifflin Company, 2002).

14. Richard Goodale, March 28, 1998, http://www.learning-org.com.

15. Byron Woollen, "Forced Ranking: The Controversy Continues," white paper, Worklab Consulting LLC.

16. Susan Gebelein, quoted in Kris Frieswick, "Truth and Consequences," *CFO Asia*, July–August 2001.

17. Del Jones, "More Firms Cut Workers Ranked at Bottom to Make Way for Talent," *USA Today*, May 30, 2001.

18. Ibid.

19. Edward E. Lawler III, "The Folly of Forced Ranking," *Strategy and Business*, Third Quarter 2002.

20. Malcolm Gladwell, "The Talent Myth," *New Yorker*, July 22, 2002, 29.

21. Ibid.

22. Ibid.

23. Andy Meisler, "Dead Man's Curve," *Workforce Management*, July 2003.

24. Grote quotation from Meisler, "Dead Man's Curve," 49.

25. Steven E. Scullen et al., "Forced Distribution Rating Systems and the Improvement of Workforce Potential: A Baseline Simulation," *Personnel Psychology* 58 (2005).

26. Charles Murray, *Human Accomplishment: The Pursuit of Excellence in the Arts and Sciences, 800 B.C. to 1950* (New York: HarperCollins, 2003).

27. Steve Constantine, quoted in Mark Lowery, "Forcing the Performance Ranking Issue," *Human Resource Executive*, October 16, 2003.

28. Dr. John Sullivan, "Is Your Human Resources Department Unwittingly a 'Socialist' Institution?" *Workforce Management*, http://www.workforce.com/archive/article/23/91/05.php.

29. Ibid.

30. Lawler, "The Folly of Forced Ranking."

31. Linkage, Inc., "Forced Ranking."

Chapter 3

1. Lisa D. Sprenkle, "Forced Ranking: A Good Thing for Business?" Workforce.com, http://www.workforce.com/archive/feature/23/09/95/2#2.

2. Camille A. Olson and Gregory M. Davis, "Pros and Cons of Forced Ranking and Other Relative Performance Ranking Systems," SHRM Legal Report, March 2003.

3. Details of GE's process drawn primarily from Jack Welch, *Jack: Straight from the Gut* (New York: Warner Business Books, 2001).

4. Details of Sun Microsystems procedure drawn from John Greenwald, "Rank and Fire," *Time*, October 12, 2001, and Del Jones, "More Firms Cut Workers Ranked at Bottom to Make Way for Talent," *USA Today*, May 30, 2001.

5. Information on GE's changes in the forced ranking system from the *Wall Street Journal*, July 11, 2001.

6. Andrall E. Pearson, "Muscle-Build the Organization," *Harvard Business Review*, July–August 1987.

7. Ibid.

8. Alan Goldstein, "EDS Drops Staffers After Assessing Jobs," *Dallas Morning News*, July 10, 2001.

9. Robert J. Herbold, "Inside Microsoft: Balancing Creativity and Discipline," *Harvard Business Review*, January 2002.

10. Ibid.

11. Janet Wiscombe, "Can Pay for Performance Really Work?" *Workforce Management*, August 2001, 28–34.

12. Deb Capolarello, interview with editor Todd Raphael, *Workforce Management*, December 2002.

13. Discussion of rank ordering provided by "Installing Pay-for-Performance Plans in Your Organization," Course 77, Economic Research Institute, http://www.eridlc.com/courses/course77/text/text_main16.htm.

14. Heath Row, "Is Management for Me? That Is the Question," *Fast Company*, February–March 1998.

15. Values statement posted on http://www.intecap.com/Overview/Values.html.

16. Anne Fisher, "Ask Annie," *Fortune*, December 2, 2002.

17. Peter F. Drucker, "How to Make People Decisions," *Harvard Business Review*, July–August 1985.

18. Christian M. Ellis, G. Barrow Moore, and Anne M. Saunier, "Forced Ranking: Not So Fast," *Perspectives* 11, no. 2, April 1, 2004.

19. Welch, *Jack: Straight from the Gut*, 161.

20. Olson and Davis, "Pros and Cons of Forced Ranking."

21. Laura C. Fisher, Laura A. Lindner, and Gregory M. Davis, "Forced Ranking of Employees: Assessing the Legal Risks," *ACCA Docket* 21, no. 3 (March 2003): 60–76.

22. Michael O'Malley, "Forced Ranking: Proceed Only with Great Caution," *WorldatWork Journal*, First Quarter 2003.

23. Memorandum from outside counsel to client corporation regarding mechanics of planned forced ranking system.

24. Ellis, Moore, and Saunier, "Forced Ranking."

25. Data on Sun process from John Greenwald, "Rank and Fire."

26. Fisher, Lindner, and Davis, "Forced Ranking of Employees," 60–76.

27. O'Malley, "Forced Ranking."

28. Byron Woollen, "Forced Ranking: The Controversy Continues," white paper, Worklab Consulting LLC.

29. ICI Paints information reported by Woollen, "Forced Ranking."

30. The fact that the relative standing of performers will vary according to the caliber of others has been noted by Judy Olian, "The Force in Performance Reviews," Penn State Smeal: News Page, October 2002, http://www.smeal.psu.edu/news/releases/oct02/force.html.

31. Olson and Davis, "Pros and Cons of Forced Ranking."

Chapter 4

1. Excerpted from *The American Heritage Dictionary of the English Language*, 3rd ed., (Boston: Houghton Mifflin Company, 2002).

2. Andrall E. Pearson, "Muscle-Build the Organization," *Harvard Business Review*, July–August 1987.

3. Robert Kelley and Janet Caplan, "How Bell Labs Creates Star Performers," *Harvard Business Review*, July–August 1993, 138.

4. Melvin Sorcher and James Brant, "Are You Picking the Right Leaders?" *Harvard Business Review*, February 2002.

5. Barbara Pachter, "Bosses Behaving Badly," *Harvard Business Review*, June 2002.

Chapter 6

1. Peter F. Drucker, "What Makes an Effective Executive?" *Harvard Business Review*, June 2004, 58–63.

2. Camille A. Olson and Gregory M. Davis, "Pros and Cons of Forced Ranking and Other Relative Performance Ranking Systems," SHRM Legal Report, March 2003.

3. Alfie Kohn, *Punished by Rewards* (Boston: Houghton Mifflin, 1999), 93.

4. Edward E. Lawler III, *Treat People Right* (San Francisco: Jossey-Bass, 2003), 192–193.

5. The GROTEAPPROACH Web-based, performance management-system is available at http://www.groteapproach.com.

Chapter 7

1. David J. O'Reilly, "Chairman's Letter" e-mail to Chevron employees, July 31, 2001.

2. Baylor Health Care System, Dallas, TX, performance appraisal form, Leadership Supplement.

Appendix C

1. *Wall Street Journal*, May 15, 2001.

2. *Wall Street Journal*, August 2, 2001.

3. *Detroit News*, April 29, 2001.

4. *Global News*, April 2002.

5. *New York Times*, March 19, 2001.

6. Linda Bean, "Age Discrimination at Sprint? AARP Lawyers Join Lawsuit," DiversityInc, August 12, 2004, http://www.diversityinc.com/members/7817.cfm.

7. Christine A. Amalfe and Heather Adelman, "Forced Rankings: The Latest Target of Plaintiff's Employment Lawyers," April 1, 2004, http://www.gibbonslaw.com/publications/articlesuser2.cfm?pubid=790.

8. Personal correspondence with author, February, 2005.

9. Laura C. Fisher, Laura A. Lindner, and Gregory M. Davis, "Forced Ranking of Employees: Assessing the Legal Risks," *ACCA Docket* 21, no. 3 (March 2003): 60–76.

10. Amalfe and Adelman, "Forced Rankings."

11. Marty Denis, "Termination of Employment, Layoffs, and an Ageist Corporate Culture: A Risky Mix," *HR Advisor*, March/April 2002.

12. Information on forced ranking litigation and the legal aspects of disparate treatment and disparate impact based on "Forced Ranking Performance Evaluations at Center of Pending Discrimination Litigation," source unknown.

13. *Bibby v. Drummond Co.*, 818 F. Supp. 325 (N.D. Ala. 1993).

14. *Godar v. Petrolite Corp.*, 982 F.3d 525 (Table), 1992 WL 389228 (8th Cir. 1992); *Finch v. Hercules, Inc.*, 941 F. Supp. 1395 (D. Del. 1996)

15. Bernard R. Siskin, PhD, "Using Statistical Analysis in Reduction-in-Force ADEA Litigation, American Bar Association, http://www.bna.com/bnabooks/ababna/eeo/99/eeo32.pdf.

16. Summary of the ADEA provided by the Equal Employment Opportunity Commission, http://www.eeoc.gov/types/age.html.

17. American Bar Association, http://www.abanet.org/publiced/practical/workplace_agediscrimination.html.

18. Summary of the OWBPA provided by the Equal Employment Opportunity Commission, http://www.eeoc.gov/types/age.html.

19. See http://www.eeoc.gov/types/age.html.

20. Bean, "Age Discrimination at Sprint?"

21. Krysten Crawford, "EEOC Complaints Down, Fines Up," CNN/Money, February 15, 2005, http://money.cnn.com/2005/02/15/news/economy/eeoc/.

22. Camille A. Olson and Gregory M. Davis, "Pros and Cons of Forced Ranking and Other Relative Performance Ranking Systems," SHRM Legal Report, March 2003.

23. Summary of Capital One litigation and quotes from AARP, "Age Discrimination," http://www.aarp.org/research/litigation/show_case?case_id=662.

24. AARP, "Age Discrimination."

25. Diane Stafford, "Judge Allows Collective Case Against Sprint," *Kansas City Star*, July 3, 2004.

26. Jennifer Bosshardt quote and details of the Sprint litigation from Stafford, "Judge Allows Collective Case Against Sprint."

27. Fisher, Lindner, and Davis, "Forced Ranking of Employees," 60–76.

28. Rita Risser, "Ask a Lawyer," FairMeasures.com, http://www.fairmeasures.com/asklawyer/archive/fall97/ask146.html.

29. William R. Hopkins, "Rethinking the Business Judgment Rule in Discrimination Cases," http://www.expertlaw.com/library/attyarticles/business_judgment.html; *Dept. of Correction v. Gibson*, 308 N.C. 131, at 140, 301 S.E.2d 78 at 82, 84 (1983).

30. *Mesnick v. General Elec. Co.*, 950 F.2d 816, 825 (1st Cir. 1991).

31. *Roper v. Exxon Corp.*, 27F. Supp. 2d 679 (1998 ED LA). Source of case summary unknown.

32. *Coleman v. Exxon Chem. Corp.*, 162 F. Supp. 2d 593 (2001 SD TX). Source of case summary unknown.

33. Fisher, Lindner, and Davis, "Forced Ranking of Employees," 60–76.

34. Denis, "Termination of Employment, Layoffs," 46–47.

35. Frank J. Landy and James L. Farr, "Performance Rating," *Psychological Bulletin* 87, no. 1, reprinted in *The Performance Appraisal Sourcebook* (Amherst, MA: Human Resource Development Press, 1995): 134.

36. Fisher, Lindner, and Davis, "Forced Ranking of Employees," 60–76.

37. Rita Risser, FairMeasures.com, April 28, 2002, http://www.fairmeasures.com/asklawyer/questions/ask289.html.

38. Personal correspondence with author, August 2, 2004.

39. Olson and Davis, "Pros and Cons of Forced Ranking."

40. Fisher, Lindner, and Davis, "Forced Ranking of Employees," 60–76

41. Ibid.

Further Reading

Books

Bossidy, Larry, and Ram Charan. *Execution*. New York: Crown Business, 2002.

Buckingham, Marcus, and Curt Coffman. *First, Break All the Rules*. New York: Simon & Schuster, 1999.

Cronin, Doreen. *Click, Clack, Moo: Cows That Type*. New York: Simon & Schuster, 2000.

Drucker, Peter F. *Management: Tasks, Responsibilities, Practices*. New York: Harper & Row, 1973.

Giuliani, Rudolph W. *Leadership*. New York: Hyperion, 2002.

Kelley, Robert E. *How to Be a Star at Work: Nine Breakthrough Strategies You Need to Succeed* (New York: Times Business Books, 1998).

Kohn, Alfie. *Punished by Rewards*. Boston: Houghton Mifflin, 1999.

Lawler, Edward E. III. *Rewarding Excellence: Pay Strategies for the New Economy*. San Francisco: Jossey-Bass, 2003.

———. *Treat People Right*. San Francisco: Jossey-Bass, 2003.

Lawler, Edward E. III, Susan Albert Mohrman, and Gerald E. Ledford. *Creating High Performance Organizations: Practices and Results of Employee Involvement and Total Quality Management in Fortune 1000 Companies*. San Francisco: Jossey-Bass, 1995.

Longenecker, Clinton O., and Jack L. Simonetti. *Getting Results*. San Francisco: Jossey-Bass, 2001.

Michaels, Ed, Helen Handfield-Jones, and Beth Axelrod. *The War for Talent*. Boston: Harvard Business School Press, 2001.

Murray, Charles. *Human Accomplishment*. New York: HarperCollins, 2003.

Welch, Jack. *Jack: Straight from the Gut*. New York: Warner Business Books, 2001.

Articles

Abelson, Reed. "Companies Turn to Grades, and Employees Go to Court." *New York Times*, March 19, 2001.

Anabtawi, Iman, and Lynn A. Stout. "An Inside Job." *New York Times*, March 27, 2005.

Axelrod, Beth, Helen Handfield-Jones, and Ed Michaels. "A New Game Plan for C Players." *Harvard Business Review*, January 2002.

Bates, Steve. "Forced Ranking." *HR Magazine*, June 2003, 62–68.

Bennis, Warren. "Where Leaders Come From." *Fortune*, September 19, 1994, 242.

Boyle, Matthew. "Performance Reviews: Perilous Curves Ahead." *Fortune*, May 28, 2001.

Charan, Ram. "Ending the CEO Succession Crisis." *Harvard Business Review*, February 2005, 72.

Charan, Ram, and Geoffrey Colvin. "Why CEOs Fail." *Fortune*, June 21, 1999, 70.

Collins, Jim. "Good to Great." *Fast Company*, October 2001, 100.

Colvin, Geoffrey. "We Can't All Be Above Average." *Fortune*, August 13, 2001, 144–148.

Dalton, Maxine A. "Using 360-Degree Feedback Successfully." *Leadership in Action* 18, no. 1 (1998).

DeLong, Thomas J., and Vineeta Vijayaraghavan. "Let's Hear It for B Players." *Harvard Business Review*, June 2003.

Denis, Marty. "Termination of Employment, Layoffs, and an Ageist Corporate Culture: A Risky Mix." *HR Advisor*, March/April 2002.

Drucker, Peter F. "How to Make People Decisions." *Harvard Business Review*, July–August 1985.

———. "What Makes an Effective Executive?" *Harvard Business Review*, June 2004.

Ellis, Christian M., G. Barrow Moore, and Anne M. Saunier. "Forced Ranking: Not So Fast." *Perspectives—Insights for Today's Business Leaders* 11, no. 2, April 1, 2004.

Fisher, Anne. "Do I Fire the Bottom 10% Just Because Jack Did?" *Fortune*, September 9, 2002.

Gary, Loren. "The Controversial Practice of Forced Ranking." *Harvard Management Update,* October 2001.

Gladwell, Malcolm. "The Talent Myth." *New Yorker*, July 22, 2002.

Greenwald, John. "Rank and Fire." *Time*, June 11, 2001.

Goode, Erica. "Among the Inept, Researchers Discover, Ignorance Is Bliss." *New York Times,* January 18, 2000.

Grote, Dick, "Forced Ranking." *Executive Excellence*, July 2003.

———. "Forced Ranking: Behind the Scenes." *Across the Board*, November/December 2002.

Groysberg, Boris, Ashish Nanda, and Nitin Nohria. "The Risky Business of Hiring Stars." *Harvard Business Review*, May 2004.

Herbold, Robert J. "Inside Microsoft: Balancing Creativity and Discipline." *Harvard Business Review*, January 2002.

HR Focus. "Forced Rankings: Tough Love or Overkill?" February 2002.

———. "Kinder, Gentler Reviews: A Forced Ranking Backlash?" April 2002.

Hymowitz, Carol. "In the Lead: Ranking Systems Gain Popularity But Have Many Staffers Riled." *Wall Street Journal*, May 15, 2001.

———. "Readers Tell Tales of Success and Failure Using Rating Systems." *Wall Street Journal*, May 29, 2001.

Institute of Management and Administration. "Forced Rankings: Today's Performance Reviews Are Taking a More Serious Tone," *IOMA's Pay for Performance Report*, October 2001.

Jenkins, H. W. Jr. "How to Execute 10%, Nicely." *Wall Street Journal*, July 18, 2001.

Kelley, Robert, and Janet Caplan. "How Bell Labs Creates Star Performers." *Harvard Business Review*, July–August 1993.

Kirkpatrick, David. "Dell and Rollins: The $21 Billion Buddy Act." Interview with Michael Dell and Kevin Rollins. *Fortune*, April 19, 2004.

Kochanski, Jim, Colette Alderson, and Aaron Sorenson. "The 'State of Performance Management' Study." *Perspectives* 12, October 6, 2004.

Lawler, Edward E. III. "The Folly of Forced Ranking." *Strategy and Business*, Third Quarter 2002.

Ledford, Gerry, and Matt Lucy. "The Rewards of Work: The Employment Deal in a Changing Economy." *Perspectives* 11, September 30, 2003.

Levinson, Meredith. "How to Find, Fix, or Fire Your Poor Performers," *CIO Magazine*, November 1, 2003.

Longnecker, B. M. "Rank and Yank: The Problems with Forced Ranking." *Workforce Management*, July 2003.

Lowery, Mark. "Forcing the Performance Ranking Issue." *Human Resource Executive*, December 22, 2003.

Ludeman, Kate, and Eddie Erlandson. "Coaching the Alpha Male." *Harvard Business Review*, May 2004.

McBriarty, M. A. "Performance Appraisal: Some Unintended Consequences," *Public Personnel Management* 17 (Winter 1988), 421–434.

McLaughlin, Michael. "Four Ways to Lose Your Best People." *Workforce Management*, December 4, 2001.

Meisler, Andy. "Dead Man's Curve." *Workforce Management*, July 2003.

———. "The Ethics of Forced Ranking." *Workforce Management*, July 2003, 49.

———. "Grading on the Curve." *Workforce Management*, July 2003.

Nobile, Robert J. Esq. "Your Compensation Analysis. Can It Be Protected Against Discovery?" *HR Advisor*, March/April 2002, 31.

O'Malley, Michael. "Forced Ranking: Proceed Only with Great Caution." *WorldatWork Journal*, First Quarter 2003.

Paulos, John Allen. "An Excess of Excellence." *Wall Street Journal*, October 27, 2000.

Pearson, Andrall E. "Muscle-Build the Organization." *Harvard Business Review*, July–August 1987.

Personnel Today. "Making the Grade." April 2, 2002, 21–22.

Quinn, James Brian, Philip Anderson, and Sydney Finkelstein. "Managing Professional Intellect: Making the Most of the Best." *Harvard Business Review*, March–April 1996.

Satterfield, Terry. "From Performance Management to Performance Leadership." *WorldatWork Journal*, First Quarter, 2003.

Sorcher, Melvin, and James Brant. "Are You Picking the Right Leaders?" *Harvard Business Review*, February 2002.

Sprenkle, Lisa D. "Forced Ranking: A Good Thing for Business?" *Workforce Management*, July, 2003.

Stoskopf, Gregory A. "Taking Performance Management to the Next Level." *Workspan*, February 2002.

Wiscombe, Janet. "Can Pay for Performance Really Work?" *Workforce Management*, August 2001.

Research Studies and White Papers

Davis, Patty, and Bob Rogers. "Managing the 'C' Performer: An Alternative to Forced Ranking." White paper, Development Dimensions International.

Fisher, Laura C., Laura A. Lindner, and Gregory M. Davis. "Forced Ranking of Employees: Assessing the Legal Risks." *ACCA Docket* 21, no. 3 (March 2003): 60–76.

Kruger, Justin, and David Dunning. "Unskilled and Unaware of It: How Difficulties in Recognizing One's Own Incompetence Lead to Inflated Self-Assessments." *Journal of Personality and Social Psychology* 77, no. 6 (December 1999): 1121–1134.

Linkage, Inc. "Forced Ranking: Friend or Foe?" White paper, Linkage Center for Organizational Research, Burlington, MA, August 2001.

Olson, Camille A., and Gregory M. Davis. "Pros and Cons of Forced Ranking and Other Relative Performance Ranking Systems." SHRM (Society for Human Resource Management) Legal Report, March 2003.

Scullen, Steven E., Paul K. Bergey, and Linda Aiman-Smith. "Forced Distribution Rating Systems and the Improvement of Workforce Potential: A Baseline Simulation." *Personnel Psychology* 58 (2005): 1–32.

Woollen, Byron. "Forced Ranking: The Controversy Continues." White paper, Worklab Consulting LLC, New York City.

Internet Resources

AARP. "Age Discrimination." http://www.aarp.org/research/litigation/show_case?case_id=662.

Amalfe, Christine A., and Heather Adelman. "Forced Rankings: The Latest Target of Plaintiff's Employment Lawyers." April 1, 2004. http://www.gibbonslaw.com/publications/articlesuser2.cfm?pubid=790.

Armour, Stephanie. "Job Reviews Take On Added Significance in Down Times." *USA Today*, July 22, 2003. http://www.usatoday.com/money/workplace/2003-07-22-reviews_x.htm.

Bernthal, Paul, Roger Sumlin, Patty Davis, and Bob Rogers. "Performance Management Practices Survey Report." Development Dimensions International (DDI). http://www.ddiworld.com/ pdf/CPGN43.pdf.

Clark, Kim. "Judgment Day." *US News*, January 13, 2003. http://www.usnews.com/usnews/biztech/articles/030113/13performance.htm.

Hopkins, William R. "Rethinking the Business Judgment Rule in Discrimination Cases." http://www.expertlaw.com/library/attyarticles/business_judgment.html.

Osborne, Tom, and Laurie A. McCann. "Forced Ranking and Age-Related Employment Discrimination." *Human Rights Magazine.* American Bar Association. http://www.abanet.org/irr/hr/spring04/ forced.html.

Risser, Rita. "Ask a Lawyer." FairMeasures.com. http://www.fairmeasures.com/asklawyer/archive/fall97/ask146.html.

Sullivan, Dr. John. "Hiring Advice: Calculate the Value of Talent." White paper, Yoh Company Technology Staffing. http://www.yoh.com/hiringadvicefull.cfm?CD=120.

———. "Is Your Human Resources Department Unwittingly a 'Socialist' Institution?" *Workforce Management.* http://www.workforce.com/archive/article/23/91/05.php.

Young, Mary B. "Coming Clean to High-Performers: Should You Tell Them of Their Potential?" *Workforce Management.* http://www.workforce.com/archive/feature/22/28/74/index.php.

Index

About the Author

Dick Grote is Chairman and CEO of Grote Consulting Corporation in Dallas, Texas. He is the developer of the GROTEAPPROACH Web-based performance management system, and the author of the books *Discipline Without Punishment* and *The Complete Guide to Performance Appraisal*. Both books were major book club selections and have been translated into Chinese and Arabic. His most recent book is *The Performance Appraisal Question and Answer Book*.

Paramount Pictures bought the movie rights to *Discipline Without Punishment* and produced the award-winning video series *Respect and Responsibility*, with Dick as host.

Dick Grote's articles and essays have appeared in the *Harvard Business Review, Wall Street Journal, Across the Board*, and more than two dozen other business and general-interest magazines and journals, including *Cosmopolitan*. For five years he was a commentator on life in the workplace for National Public Radio's *Morning Edition* program. For more than twenty years he was adjunct professor of management at the University of Dallas Graduate School.

In college Dick was a member of Colgate University's retired undefeated *GE College Bowl* team. At 63 he still competes regularly in 5K and 10K races (occasionally bringing home a third-place trophy).